# Security and Microservice Architecture on AWS

*Architecting and Implementing
a Secured, Scalable Solution*

*Gaurav Raje*

Beijing · Boston · Farnham · Sebastopol · Tokyo

**Security and Microservice Architecture on AWS**

by Gaurav Raje

Published by O'Reilly Media, Inc., 1005 Gravenstein Highway North, Sebastopol, CA 95472.

O'Reilly books may be purchased for educational, business, or sales promotional use. Online editions are also available for most titles (*http://oreilly.com*). For more information, contact our corporate/institutional sales department: 800-998-9938 or corporate@oreilly.com.

| | |
|---|---|
| **Acquisitions Editor:** Jennifer Pollock | **Indexer:** Potomac Indexing, LLC |
| **Development Editor:** Corbin Collins | **Interior Designer:** David Futato |
| **Production Editor:** Caitlin Ghegan | **Cover Designer:** Karen Montgomery |
| **Copyeditor:** nSight, Inc. | **Illustrator:** Kate Dullea |
| **Proofreader:** Shannon Turlington | |

September 2021:     First Edition

**Revision History for the First Edition**
2021-09-07:    First Release

See *http://oreilly.com/catalog/errata.csp?isbn=9781098101466* for release details.

978-1-098-10146-6

[LSI]

# Table of Contents

# Table of Contents

# Preface

There is no denying that security is important and the lack of it can cause significant destruction of value in otherwise growing organizations. To that extent, embedding security into the fabric of an organization's culture is important. However, the culture of security should not be a culture of no. In my professional opinion, security professionals have gained a notorious reputation in many businesses as being the point of friction in value-adding activities. Security professionals should help developers in adding value and not getting in the way of value-adding activities.

I came across microservice architecture a few years ago, and after studying and implementing microservices in various organizations, I realized you could leverage some of the principles to aid in securing your application.

## Goals of This Book

This book assumes that you already have a basic knowledge of Amazon Web Services (AWS), microservice architecture, and security, and you would like to figure out how you can make all three of these work with one another in order to unlock the synergistic value of your application.

Through this book, I hope to spread the knowledge of how security professionals and developers can work together to increase the value of enterprise applications. This book tries its best to come up with innovative solutions to security problems where security can be implemented through efficient design and simple solutions, and by leveraging the tools that AWS provides us.

I hate bad security implementation as much as any developer. As a result, throughout this book, I will try my best to impress upon you the importance of security through simplicity and stop you from implementing any security control that creates friction for the developers or managers within your company.

My goal is, through this book and all activities that I perform from now on, to spread as much of my knowledge as possible. However, I understand that income disparity and social inequality affect a lot of people. For what it's worth, I have decided to donate all the royalties from this book to Girls Who Code, a fantastic nonprofit that aims at narrowing the gender gap in the IT industry. I think of my work as volunteering for this fantastic organization. However, they are the true champions of this work and deserve all the praise they can get.

## Who Should Use This Book

Maybe you have implemented a microservice system on AWS, and you suddenly realized that you need to secure your system. Or maybe you work in an industry where security is an important consideration; you would like to create a new greenfield application, and you have just discovered microservices. Or you joined a company that uses microservices, and you are curious to figure out if they follow the best practices in terms of security. Or you are just someone who is interested in learning the various types of cloud design patterns and trying to find out more information on the tools that AWS provides you with their cloud offering. No matter which of these readers you are, I am confident that you will learn something new from this book.

## Conventions Used in This Book

The following typographical conventions are used in this book:

*Italic*

> Indicates new terms, URLs, email addresses, filenames, and file extensions.

`Constant width`

> Used for program listings, as well as within paragraphs to refer to program elements such as variable or function names, databases, data types, environment variables, statements, and keywords.

`Constant width italic`

> Shows text that should be replaced with user-supplied values or by values determined by context.

> This element signifies a tip or suggestion.

> This element signifies a general note.

This element indicates a warning or caution.

# Using Code Examples

Supplemental material (code examples, exercises, etc.) is available for download at *https://github.com/chimbs86/Security-And-Microservices-On-AWS*.

If you have a technical question or a problem using the code examples, please send email to *bookquestions@oreilly.com*.

This book is here to help you get your job done. In general, if example code is offered with this book, you may use it in your programs and documentation. You do not need to contact us for permission unless you're reproducing a significant portion of the code. For example, writing a program that uses several chunks of code from this book does not require permission. Selling or distributing examples from O'Reilly books does require permission. Answering a question by citing this book and quoting example code does not require permission. Incorporating a significant amount of example code from this book into your product's documentation does require permission.

We appreciate, but do not generally require, attribution. An attribution usually includes the title, author, publisher, and ISBN. For example: "*Security and Microservice Architecture* by Gaurav Raje (O'Reilly). Copyright 2021 Gaurav Raje, 978-1-098-10146-6."

If you feel your use of code examples falls outside fair use or the permission given above, feel free to contact us at *permissions@oreilly.com*.

# O'Reilly Online Learning

 For more than 40 years, *O'Reilly Media* has provided technology and business training, knowledge, and insight to help companies succeed.

Our unique network of experts and innovators share their knowledge and expertise through books, articles, and our online learning platform. O'Reilly's online learning platform gives you on-demand access to live training courses, in-depth learning paths, interactive coding environments, and a vast collection of text and video from O'Reilly and 200+ other publishers. For more information, visit *http://oreilly.com*.

# How to Contact Us

Please address comments and questions concerning this book to the publisher:

O'Reilly Media, Inc.
1005 Gravenstein Highway North
Sebastopol, CA 95472
800-998-9938 (in the United States or Canada)
707-829-0515 (international or local)
707-829-0104 (fax)

We have a web page for this book, where we list errata, examples, and any additional information. You can access this page at *https://oreil.ly/SMAonAWS*.

To comment or ask technical questions about this book, send email to *bookquestions@oreilly.com*.

For more information about our books, courses, conferences, and news, see our website at http://www.oreilly.com.

Find us on Facebook: http://facebook.com/oreilly

Follow us on Twitter: http://twitter.com/oreillymedia

Watch us on YouTube: http://www.youtube.com/oreillymedia

# Acknowledgments

I would like to thank my parents, Varsha and Ravindra Raje, for constantly believing in me, even though my school grades left much to be desired. It was their constant belief and their support that gave me the courage and dedication to constantly move forward in life. I would also like to thank Elizabeth Walker for the constant motivation and all the support that she gave me during the process.

Next, I would like to thank the entire O'Reilly Media team for their help. Writing a book is always a team effort; in my case, O'Reilly Media made it feel like we were on one team at each step of the process. More specifically, Jennifer Pollock, Corbin Collins, Shira Evans, Rita Fernando, Jill Leonard, Caitlin Ghegan, Carol Keller, Shannon Turlington, and possibly a lot more who worked behind the scenes to push this book through the production process.

A great aspect of writing a book is the opportunity I was given to connect with some of the leading experts in the industry who helped me in making sure that the quality of the book is not compromised. The countless debates I had during the process helped me in shaping my own opinions and views and helping me learn so many new things. To that end, I would like to thank Lee Atchison, John Culkin, and Jason Katzer for their attention to detail. I would also like to thank Aileen Nielsen, a fellow O'Reilly Media author, for being an invaluable mentor throughout the process and guiding me whenever I felt lost.

It is impossible for anyone to write a book without having a set of friends who voluntarily devote their time to helping shape the final product. So, thank you to Julian Khandros, Ulises Melendez, and Rohit Salecha, who have spent their time reading the manuscripts and helping me drive change.

I have used numerous online resources, read a lot of books, and watched a lot of videos for free in order to compile all of what I think is worth passing along. My only motivation toward writing this book has been to spread knowledge. I hope this book will assist you in your quest for knowledge, and hopefully, you can pay it forward. To that end, I will promise to donate each and every penny that I make out of this book to charitable causes (whether it is the royalties or future salary increases). I think of this as volunteer work that I would like to do for the computing community. If this book speaks to you or adds value to your life in any way, I would like to appeal to you to do the same and donate to great nonprofits. I would like to thank you, the reader, in advance for your charity.

# Introduction to Cloud Microservices

Cloud computing and microservices have become a dominant theme (*https://oreil.ly/ tPh02*) in the software architecture world. Microservices have added complexity to an era in which security attacks are far too common, and they have raised the importance of security practitioners in every organization.

This is a story (that I heard for the first time on YouTube (*https://oreil.ly/nsNzy*)) that may sound familiar to many of you. A fast-paced company is building a microservices-based application and you are on the security team. It is possible that you have stakeholders, such as a CEO or a product manager, who want your product to be launched in time to gain market share. The developers in your company are doing their best to meet deadlines and ship code faster. You are brought in at the end of the process, and your mandate is to make sure that the final product is secure. This should immediately raise red flags to you. If the product is developed independently of you (the security team), you will be the only ones standing in the way of a product that adds value to the company. In my experience, in many dysfunctional firms, security professionals have been viewed as naysayers by development teams, product managers, and other stakeholders at organizations.

The problem with superficial security initiatives is that they interfere with value-adding activities. Bad security initiatives are notorious for causing frustration among developers. This is usually due to bad design and poor implementations, both prevalent in the industry. Hence, security policies are, at times, associated with "corporate bureaucracy" and have led, in my experience, to some unpleasant conversations in meeting rooms. This has compelled many developers to sneak around security measures to develop faster. More importantly, since a lot of security initiatives were framed before the era of cloud computing or microservices, they fail to incorporate some of the benefits that new software designs and technologies provide you.

Clearly, there has to be a better way. In this chapter, I aim to show you how incorporating security in the architectural phase of microservice design and then using some of the tools that AWS provides can help in creating systems that are simple, secure, and quick to develop at the same time. I start by talking about some desirable traits in secure systems that are correlated with better security outcomes. I then explain how microservices can help you create systems that have these desirable traits. And finally, I go into how AWS can help you in designing these microservices and scaling them to build a secure system.

# Basics of Cloud Information Security

Before I go into the fundamentals of cloud security, let's define some basic information security terms since many of them are used interchangeably, sometimes causing confusion:

*Vulnerability*
 A vulnerability is any deficiency in the system that makes our system less secure. A vulnerability could be anything in the software that could be exploited. This may also be due to the fact that your system uses an older version of the operating system or a library that could be exploited.

*Threat*
 Just because a vulnerability exists, that doesn't mean someone will exploit it. Indeed, hidden vulnerabilities can continue to exist in every application, sometimes for years, as in the Heartbleed bug (*https://heartbleed.com*). But the moment the vulnerability becomes exploitable, it can be deemed a *potential threat*. If this vulnerability is exploited, the threat is said to have been *realized*. For example, losing your house key is a vulnerability. A hypothetical thief finding this key is a potential threat. A thief *actually* finding it is the realization of this threat. A realized threat has a financial, reputational, or operational impact on your organization.

*Malicious actor/threat actor/threat agent*
 The *threat actor* (or *threat agent*) is anyone that takes advantage of a vulnerability to cause the threat.

*Responsibility*
 In the context of security, the *responsibility* parameter dictates who is responsible for ensuring that a potential threat never becomes reality. This responsibility can be assumed by an employee or automated system or may be offloaded to a third-party product or a service provider. For instance, in the case of banks (branches), the responsibility of preventing physical theft is assumed by the security firms.

*Risk*

> *Risk* is the metric that tries to evaluate the probability of a threat being realized that would result in a loss of some kind. This loss may be financial, reputational, or operational. An application's *aggregate risk* is the probability-weighted sum of all the threats that it might face. The ultimate goal of any secure design is to reduce the aggregate risk.

*Control/countermeasure*

> A *control* or *countermeasure* is any activity that may result in lowering the aggregate risk (or the negative impact of the potential threat specified by a risk). Controls are usually directed at specific threats and have well-defined scopes. Controls may also be *indirect* where certain activities indirectly reduce the aggregate risk of the organization (for example, when cybersecurity awareness and training are promoted within the organization, incidents tend to decline).

## Risk and Security Controls

The process of security design includes identifying the controls that can be implemented to reduce the aggregate risk in an organization. For example, organizations where network systems run without firewalls have a higher aggregate risk than those with well-configured firewalls, which is why firewalls are recommended by most security professionals. More specifically, security professionals may add firewalls as a countermeasure against the threat of unauthorized network access. In this case, they identified a potential threat and preemptively implemented a countermeasure to reduce the probability or impact of the threat (and thus, by definition, reduce the risk of the application). This process is known as *threat modeling*.

 Many security firms have extensively studied and prepared frameworks for identifying common threat scenarios. One example of a great framework is the Lockheed Martin cyber kill chain (*https://oreil.ly/paGb6*), which identifies what the adversaries must complete to achieve their objective.

Security controls are said to be *blunt* if they unilaterally block all requests without trying to understand their context or specifics (for example, a fence around a house that blocks everyone from crossing over regardless of whether they own the house or not). Controls are said to be *precise* or *sharp* if they identify and block specific (potentially unauthorized) requests (for example, a lock on a door that allows those with a key to open it, thus not barring legitimate users, but blocking anyone without access to a key). As a rule of thumb, blunt controls are generally strong and easy to implement. However, they may also cause friction among legitimate users and may prevent employees from doing their jobs. On the other hand, sharp controls can take a significant amount of time to tune properly, even though they are effective. Depending on the application, both of these types of controls may be required to prevent different types of attacks. In Chapter 2, I will talk about authorization and authentication controls which are extremely sharp and can provide granular protection against potential threats to the organization. In Chapter 5, I will discuss network security, which acts as a powerful but blunt instrument.

Some controls may not be targeted specifically at potential threats and yet can reduce the aggregate risk of the application. As an example, implementing proper monitoring and alerting may result in quick action by the security team. Organizations may choose to implement strong monitoring systems, called *detective controls*, to dissuade malicious actors from attacking such systems, thus reducing aggregate risk.

 You can think of controls as levers that security professionals can pull in any organization to adjust the security posture and the aggregate risk of any application.

## Organizational Security Policy

It might be tempting to take on every potential threat and implement strong controls against every vulnerability. As with all aspects of software engineering, however, there are trade-offs to this idea.

Many organizations adopt a piecemeal approach toward security controls instead of a holistic one. Very often I find myself in the following situation:

1. A security professional identifies a very specific vulnerability.

2. The organization identifies a control or marketplace product that addresses that vulnerability.

3. The vulnerability may be addressed by the solution from Step 2, but a wider set of vulnerabilities may continue to exist. Such a control may provide a solution without considering the broader implication of the change on the overall application.

4. Either the control may be too precise, and hence over time additional controls may be required, or the solution may be too broad and hence may get in the way of legitimate activities that developers may perform.

Since *point solutions* (solutions that have a narrow, specific goal) often have side effects, such as developer friction, it is almost impossible to quantify the true cost of a security control compared to the potential impact of the risk. A number of factors can limit organizations' ability to mitigate individual vulnerabilities, such as costs, timelines, and revenue targets.

A *security policy* is an abstract plan that lays out broader the vision for identifying and implementing security controls. Security policies define the role security and controls play in an organization. The purpose of a security policy is to quantify and compare the cost of a potential incident against the cost of implementing a countermeasure. The cost can either be a monetary cost or a cost to the operational efficiency of the organization (something that gets in the way of value-adding activities). The security policy provides the security team with a high-level vision that helps them choose the right controls for the job and decide whether the controls in place are acceptable or need to be sharpened in order to be effective.

If security controls are the levers that can be used to adjust the potential risk of an application, a security policy guides how much each of these levers needs to be pulled to find the sweet spot that is acceptable to senior management. A security policy should be high level and should identify a broad range of threats that you want to protect against. This will allow its implementers to innovate and come up with a broader set of tools that fit well into your organization.

While designing a security policy, it is important to think about the three types of threats: possible, plausible, and probable. A lot of threats are possible. A significantly smaller subset of these threats are plausible. And an even smaller subset of threats are probable. For companies where the impact of security incidents is not significant, it may not be prudent to set up controls against every possible threat, but it may certainly be a good idea to set up controls against all the probable ones. On the other hand, a company operating in a sensitive industry may not be able to afford to ignore some possible threats, even if they are not plausible or probable.

This book's main goal is to help organizations frame and implement controls based on a well-framed security policy. To determine the effectiveness of controls within organizations, several metrics can be utilized, such as the Center for Internet Security Benchmarks (*https://oreil.ly/bHtUN*).

## Security Incidents and the CIA Triad

A security incident is said to occur when a potential threat is realized—in other words, a vulnerability has been exploited (possibly by a malicious actor).

Any security incident can compromise one of three different parameters: confidentiality, integrity, and availability. Together, these are called the *CIA triad (https:// oreil.ly/EZQ2r)* of information security:

*Confidentiality*

A security incident where data or information is exposed or leaked to anyone not authorized access to this information is said to affect the confidentiality of the system. Examples of such incidents include sensitive data leaks, password leaks, and so on.

*Integrity*

A security incident where an unauthorized change is perpetuated into the system, resulting in an undesired state, is said to affect the integrity of the system. Examples of such incidents include data tampering, viruses, ransomware, and so forth.

*Availability*

A security incident where a malicious actor overwhelms the system to prevent it from performing its usual tasks is said to affect the availability of the system. Examples of such an incident include brute force (*https://oreil.ly/txG5C*) attacks, denial of service (DoS) (*https://oreil.ly/GKTy2*) attacks, and more.

Any security incident or attack may have a negative impact on one or more of these parameters. As security professionals, our job is to quantify the impact of such a risk and compare that to the cost of the countermeasures that may have to be put in place to prevent it from happening.

## AWS Shared Responsibility Model

I have already talked about responsibility in the context of security—it is critical as a security professional to identify who is responsible for protecting against specific threats to applications hosted on AWS. This is where the AWS Shared Responsibility Model (SRM) (*https://oreil.ly/QmVTq*) comes into the picture. Understanding the SRM helps you identify potential threats and vulnerabilities for which you need to provide countermeasures instead of relying on AWS to automatically do so.

One simple way of understanding the responsibility split between AWS and the customer is to understand that AWS is responsible for *security of the cloud*. This means AWS is responsible for protecting the infrastructure supporting all the services provided by AWS. This includes physical security of the machines that run the application from theft. AWS assumes the responsibility of making sure that your application runs in a virtualized environment that is logically separated from other clients.

On the other hand, the customer is responsible for security of the application in the cloud. Applying regular security patches on software and implementing proper access control, encryption, and authentication requirements are all part of the responsibilities that AWS expects customers to bear.

More importantly, customers are also expected to have the right configurations in place to enable secure computing practices, in line with their security policy.

An exception to the above rule of thumb is the case of managed AWS services, where AWS assumes a larger responsibility than simply protecting the physical cloud infrastructure. I will elaborate more on that later in the chapter.

If you work in an environment that requires regulatory compliance and has frequent compliance audits, AWS compiles all of its compliance-related documentation under AWS Artifact (*https:// aws.amazon.com/artifact*). Documentation available on AWS Artifact includes compliance reports and regulatory attestation for managed AWS services. Through AWS Artifact, you can convince auditors of the regulatory compliance of managed AWS services and in effect, your software application.

# Cloud Architecture and Security

Designing secure systems involves looking at software applications by taking a high-level *systems view*. Architects generally aim for the forest instead of trees and frame abstract design principles, while leaving the implementation for the developers. A secure architecture design acts as an enabler for better security controls. You can boost the security posture of your application by following some fundamental security principles when designing the application. You can learn a great deal about the principles of security architecture in the book *Enterprise Security Architecture* by Nicholas Sherwood (CRC Press).

Although the principles of information security architecture predate microservices and cloud systems, researchers have discovered ways to leverage the benefits of cloud-based microservice systems to reduce the aggregate risk of your application. I review some of these architectural patterns in this section. These patterns are not mutually exclusive. With their help, I will lay the case for why cloud-based microservices reduce the risk to your applications.

## Security Through Modularity

Most modern-day applications are complex. A systems approach to software development considers a software application to be made up of smaller, easier-to-manage modules. A *modular* application is one that can be broken down into smaller pieces that can be worked on independently. A modular application is easier to patch and hence easier to eliminate vulnerabilities from. Modularization is the key benefit that microservices provide.

From the point of view of security professionals, it is easy to frame a security policy for modular applications since such a policy can be more flexible and can better fit the contours of your application.

## Security Through Simplicity

Simple systems are easier to secure than complex ones. Complexity of software can be destabilizing if you cannot manage it well. Vulnerabilities in small, isolated applications are easier to spot and patch than are those of larger complex projects. If you want a building metaphor, small buildings with limited entrances are easier to secure than complicated mazes. Thus, if your applications are small, you can eliminate vulnerabilities before they become threats, and thus reduce the risk to your applications.

A large modular application composed of smaller, simpler modules ends up being easier to manage and secure. Thus, a guiding principle while designing secure applications is to make them as simple as possible. Any deviation from simplicity should be evaluated, not just in terms of manageability but also for security since it is inherently harder to secure complicated applications.

 In my experience, the terms *complex* and *complicated* are used interchangeably to describe software architectures. In reality, though, they are not the same. A software architecture is *complex* if it is made up of a vast number of smaller but simpler applications. Complexity is a necessary consequence of scale. *Complicated* software is software that may be monolithic and may involve large components that may not be easy to understand or secure. Complicated software may require specialized skill to maintain. Organizations should avoid making their applications complicated.

## Security Through Fully Managed AWS Services

I mentioned the AWS SRM, where I talked about how AWS is responsible for the "security of the cloud." AWS managed services are a way to offload additional responsibility onto AWS.

In a managed service, AWS assumes a larger share of the responsibility of running a specific piece of infrastructure for the user. In the case of running MySQL, AWS offers the AWS Relational Database Service (RDS), which offers multiple MySQL options to end users. On AWS RDS, AWS assumes the responsibility of running and patching the database engine as well as the underlying operating system. AWS keeps the underlying operating system current and eliminates any vulnerabilities that may exist on it.

Just because you use an AWS managed service does not automatically mean that you have zero security responsibilities. You may still be responsible for controlling access to the services and configuring firewalls and other basic security measures. Any time you use a managed service, it is important to figure out how much of the security responsibility is assumed by AWS and how much is still on you as the customer.

With managed AWS services, you can reduce the responsibility of your security team and scale your organization without losing focus. If you replace an existing component of your infrastructure with an AWS managed service, you can trust that AWS will provide you with the right countermeasures to reduce your application's risk.

The use of managed services may reduce the burden of meeting compliance requirements as well, since most managed services are compliant with most regulatory requirements (HIPAA, HITRUST, GDPR, SOC, NIST, ISO, PCI, and FedRAMP). Throughout the book, I will recommend the use of a fleet of managed AWS services that help in increasing the security.

## Blast Radius, Isolation, and the Locked Rooms Analogy

Let me take you back to the process of threat modeling. In this process, you identify vulnerabilities in the application and then start thinking of potential threat actors who could exploit these. You build hypothetical scenarios where you assume that the malicious actor has indeed exploited this vulnerability and has caused unauthorized issues to your application, affecting any of the CIA metrics that you have been tracking.

The parts of your application that the hypothetical threat actor in your threat-modeling scenario may have influence over is called the *blast radius* (also known as *attack surface*) of your application.

In a well-architected system, you want to keep this blast radius at a minimum. That way, even if a threat actor is able to gain unauthorized access, the rest of the application is able to function. From an architectural standpoint, it is possible to achieve this goal of reducing blast radiuses by using the concept of *isolation*. You can think of a large modular application as a series of locked rooms in a building. The fact that one of the rooms was breached by an unauthorized person does not mean the other rooms will be as well. You can have a modular application in which individual modules are isolated from one another and require strong authentication. The threat actor can then be isolated to only the module they were able to breach, while keeping the rest of the application secure and functional.

# Defense-in-Depth and Security

Have you ever wondered why all airplanes still have ashtrays (*https://oreil.ly/VpXY3*) even though smoking has been banned in all commercial flights for decades? In the briefing before takeoff, you are reminded that tampering with the smoke detector in the lavatory is a criminal offense. There is also a sign in there reminding you of this law, but right below that sign, you'll find an ashtray. In 2009, a flight was grounded (*https://oreil.ly/cDU4s*) for not having an ashtray.

The Federal Aviation Authority (FAA) explains that even though smoking is banned, some people still manage to sneak in cigarettes and smoke on flights. After smoking, passengers may throw cigarette butts in trash receptacles, which may be a fire hazard. Security-wise, this is a threat that increases the risk of an aircraft catching fire. Having an ashtray ensures that if people do somehow manage to bring cigarettes on the flight, they have a place to stub them safely. Ashtrays are the controls that reduce the risk of fire.

You might be wondering, seeing how dangerous smoking is on a flight, why aren't greater security controls added at airports to ensure that passengers cannot bring cigarettes on board planes? Why require a costly installation of redundant ashtrays in every flight, all around the world?

The answer is in a security concept called *defense-in-depth*. In secure systems, multi-layered, at times redundant, or even obsolete controls have been shown to be more effective than a single point-based solution. Having multiple controls dispersed at different layers rather than one perfectly reliable control is shown to result in a lower risk for the application. In designing each control, you assume that an upstream control failed at stopping an intruder. This ensures that there is no single point of failure. In the case of airlines, you assume that the airport security failed at catching the cigarettes, and hence the ashtray is used to further reduce the risk of fire.

In secure systems, you are often required to independently assess the efficacy of each of your controls. Many times, the presence of multiple controls may seem redundant, but with defense-in-depth, you can justify their presence and use. Throughout this book, I will recommend the introduction of multiple controls. As an example, in Chapter 5 I will recommend controls that work at the network layer, whereas in Chapter 7, I will discuss encryption in transit that primarily operates at the transport layer.

If you look around, you can see examples of defense-in-depth everywhere, in many different aspects of life. Buildings with sprinklers still have fire extinguishers. Buildings with strong security at the entrances still have locks on the doors of individual office spaces. Overlapping security controls are what protect us from the failure of individual controls, and embracing such a reality is what helps in the evolution of a secure-thinking strategy.

## Security Through Perimeter Protection

I start this section by admitting that I am a cynic of this approach. In this approach, organizations create a strong firewall against any requests that come from the public internet. This firewall is known as a *perimeter*, which is secured to protect your application against external threats. Remote employees are then provided with virtual private network (VPN) solutions to have a similar experience as their in-person counterparts. In the context of security, *trust* refers to accessing systems with little or no verification of who someone is or why they need this access. In this architecture, users or services within a *trust boundary* (generally within the organization's data center or VPN) are trusted, and hence do not go through an additional layer of authentication. Here, the belief is that most attackers are external to the organization, and trusted users are assumed to have only the best intentions. Hence, controls in this architecture are directed mainly toward external threats. Many security professionals say that such an architecture tries to *defend the castle* against external attacks. Many regulators still require the presence of such a perimeter protection and hence, if you work in a heavily regulated industry, you may not have a choice around perimeter protection.

## Security Through Zero Trust Architecture

In recent years, it has become apparent that both external *and* internal attackers pose serious threats to organizations. The notion that robustly securing the perimeter is enough to achieve security is outdated. A *zero trust architecture* is therefore employed in many modern organizations. A zero trust architecture assumes that threats to your application are omnipresent (internal and external to the organization). Thus, you cannot trust internal services and must implement controls, assuming there are malicious actors working well within your trust boundaries. In other words, this model assumes that the attackers are already inside your castle walls and, instead of protecting your castle, you must think of individually protecting all your resources. Many recent high-profile incidents have indeed been caused by trusted insiders or malicious actors posing as insiders, as seen in the 2019 Capital One breach. Hence, a zero trust architecture is preferred.

Chapter 8 will introduce you to some of the tools that AWS offers, which will help you implement zero trust architecture in your organization while reducing friction with your development team.

 I'm not the only one in favor of a zero trust architecture. On May 12, 2021, US president Joe Biden signed an executive order (*https:// oreil.ly/Oojeg*) that aims at improving the US information security architecture. As part of this order, the federal government has been tasked, among other things, to "develop a plan to implement zero trust architecture."

# A Brief Introduction to Software Architecture

Although you may already be aware of the basics of microservices and their advantages, I want to spend a little time providing a refresher on the basics of microservice design. Application architecture usually takes a systems approach toward software design. The majority of enterprise software consists of smaller parts that are put together to create the desired system.

## Tier-Based Architecture

Consider a typical ecommerce website application. Assume this application supports four end-user actions:

- A user can buy an item.
- A user can return an item.
- A user can check their balance.
- A user can check the available supply of inventory.

The goal of a *tiered* (layered) architecture is to have presentation (user interface), application management, and data management functions separated from one another. This style of architecture has been the de facto standard for most applications, primarily because of its simplicity, familiarity, and low cost. Figure 1-1 shows a typical tiered application.

The layered architecture style, while having many advantages, also has some distinct disadvantages. One of these is the lack of agility and scalability, which has led to the discovery of other architectural styles. Authors Neal Ford and Mark Richards, in their book *Fundamentals of Software Architecture* (O'Reilly) (*https://oreil.ly/Mthy0*), discuss in detail all the pitfalls of such a design.

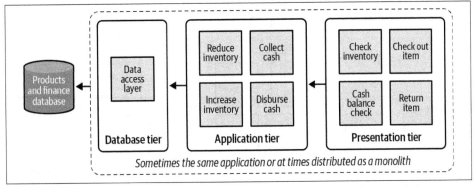

*Figure 1-1. In a layered approach, the application logic can be divided into different layers, depending on the tier the application runs in.*

## Domain-Driven Design

A contrast to the traditional tier-based approach is *domain-driven design* (DDD). In DDD, it is assumed that every software program relates to some activity or interest of its user or the business function. An architect can divide the application in a way that aligns with its business and functional units by associating application logic to its functional domain (and at times, more granularly into subdomains).

For example, if you were to group the services from Figure 1-1 based on their domains (and subdomains), you would see three functional domains that exist:

*Inventory or product domain*
    This domain deals with all services related to managing products. It includes keeping track of the inventory of products, prices, and descriptions.

*Customer domain*
    This domain is responsible for accepting customer's requests, such as checking out of the application or returning any items.

*Finance domain*
    This is responsible for charging the customer and keeping track of balances and all other money movement.

If you are to partition the services from Figure 1-1 into functional domains, it might look something like Figure 1-2.

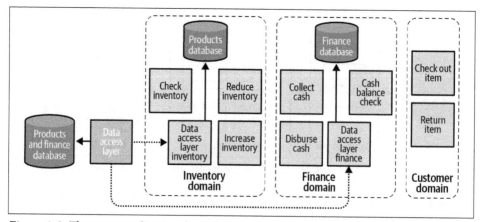

*Figure 1-2. The same application from Figure 1-1, with the same modular components, can be segregated in a different way using DDD. DDD preserves the business domains while dividing applications.*

In a domain-driven approach, services that satisfy a common business domain are more likely to have a strong relationship with one another and, therefore, make sense to be grouped together. Additionally, DDD makes it easier to manage larger business projects by aligning the software architecture with the business requirements more closely. Such groups are generally called *bounded contexts* where services within a bounded context share a close relationship with one another, while any interaction with any external entity can be thought of as a formally defined contract. Conversely, all services within bounded contexts should only have loose relationships with any service that is outside their bounded contexts.

Within a bounded context, applications are designed for interoperability. They speak the same proverbial language. In an ideal world, a bounded context and a subdomain should have the same constituent services. In practice, however, especially when legacy software systems are involved, there may be some differences.

## Coupling and Cohesion

In their book *Fundamentals of Software Architecture* (O'Reilly), Mark Richards and Neal Ford introduced me to two fundamental metrics that could be used to measure the quality of our DDD:

*Coupling*

Coupling is the measure of interdependence between bounded contexts. It identifies how closely services from one context relate to services from another context. Coupling may occur as a result of contexts sharing business logic or knowledge of internal processes. Loose coupling often correlates with stable development. From a security perspective, contexts that are loosely coupled can continue to operate without outages when a security incident threatens one of them. Furthermore, it is possible to deploy countermeasures quickly in such systems. A good DDD model should aim at reducing coupling across contexts.

*Cohesion*
Cohesion is a measure of how related the services are within a bounded context. High cohesion is associated with several desirable software characteristics, including robustness, reliability, reusability, understandability, and most important, security. Revisiting Figure 1-1, applying this metric to the presentation tier's services (which deal with products, customers, and finance), we find little cohesion because the services within this tier belong to multiple functional domains. In contrast, when services with common domains are grouped together, as in Figure 1-2, cohesion increases.

# Microservices

So what makes any architecture a *microservice architecture*? Unlike a monolithic application, a *microservice-based application* is made up of a large number of lightweight services, which are:

*Independently deployed*
You can upgrade, patch, or remove individual services without affecting the rest of the application.

*Independently scalable*
You can scale up or down individual services if there is additional load on individual parts of the application without affecting the rest of the application.

*Loosely coupled*
Degradation or changes to individual services should not affect the rest of the application.

*Domain-driven*
Services are modularized and grouped into contexts according to the business domains they belong to.

*Responsible for one single business task*
Microservices are supposed to follow the single-responsibility principle (SRP).

A key step in defining a microservice architecture is figuring out how big an individual microservice has to be. What differentiates a microservice from a regular application, though, is that a microservice is required to follow the SRP.

The SRP proposes that every microservice encapsulates a single part of an application's functionality. This ensures that each microservice is lean, lightweight, deployment agnostic, and simple to understand.

If you search for online literature on microservices, you often find them generally compared (*https://oreil.ly/49YGT*) to LEGO' bricks. A microservice architect views any large application as consisting of several microservices that are patched together, similar to a LEGO construction. Within these applications, individual microservices are expected to follow the SRP. These individual services are also supposed to be autonomous and should have limited or no dependence on other services.

 Throughout the book, I will be referencing the SRP quite frequently. It is the single most important principle to remember while designing microservice architectures.

In "Cloud Architecture and Security" on page 7, I promised you that cloud microservice architectures will help in realizing the secure design patterns I mentioned in the section. With the help of the formal definition of microservices, I am sure you can see why:

*Security through modularity*
Since by definition microservice applications are made up of small modular services, it is possible to easily implement security controls.

*Security through simplicity*
Since each modular microservice is small and follows the SRP, it is much easier to achieve the goal of simplicity in a microservice architecture.

*Security through isolation*
Since microservices follow DDD, it is easier to create an isolated environment to run individual microservices.

*Security through zero trust architecture*
By better using the AWS SRM, and by using the granular controls that microservice architectures afford, it is possible to easily implement a zero trust architecture.

To sum up, microservices are atomic and discrete business functions, each with one function. Microservice developers should be free to choose the tool that provides them with the best return while designing their specific microservice to perform the single task that it is supposed to perform. As an architect who is responsible for integrating these individual microservices into a bigger, cohesive application, the most important thing you should care about is the business function of the microservice. Everything else is background noise and should not drive policy decisions.

# Implementation of Microservices on AWS

There is no rule regarding how a microservice should be actually implemented. Nevertheless, it is important to modularize the application and loosely couple these modules so that these services can be swapped out, upgraded, replaced, or scaled on their own.

Over the last few years, due to various reasons, there has been a consolidation in the industry where many organizations have decided to adopt one of two ways:

*Container-based approach*
> In this approach, the microservices are encapsulated into lightweight, autonomous containers (such as Docker containers (*https://oreil.ly/0bEb4*)), which are shipped to run on top of a container engine such as Docker engine (*https://oreil.ly/YhriQ*). As long as there is a Docker engine that can run these containers, developers can use whichever tool, language, or runtime they want to write these services in. Each physical server (called a *node*) runs the Docker engine, and multiple containers can be deployed on them.

*FaaS-based approach*
> In this approach, the business function is run directly on a Function as a Service (FaaS) platform. Instead of packaging your application in a container, you write your business function in a standardized way so it can run directly on a cloud platform, which hands over the responsibility of running it securely to the cloud provider.

Both options have advantages and limitations from a security and scalability perspective. There is a lot of online literature on both approaches and their trade-offs. (One great article I read on container-based microservices was in a blog from Severless (*https://oreil.ly/Z4UdQ*).) Throughout this book, I will focus on ways to increase security around both of these approaches by leveraging the tools that AWS provides us with.

## Container-Based Microservice Architecture

Going back to the SRP, since everything else outside the business function of the microservice is background noise, wouldn't it be great if we could package the business function and all its dependencies into a dedicated, sandboxed virtual environment and deploy it everywhere? This is the container approach to microservices.

In this approach, all the business logic, along with any dependencies, is packaged into a lightweight, portable, deployable *container*. This container contains the business function that the microservice is supposed to perform, along with the exact instructions that are needed to run this application code anywhere, on any environment that supports running such a container. The same container (along with its application logic) is tested across different development environments and deployed to your application environment. This container can be scaled up, upgraded, or swapped out depending on the needs of the application. Docker has proven to be a popular container technology in the industry, so for the purpose of this book, I will be using Docker for my examples.

Your entire application is now a mesh of such containers providing the business functionality that is needed to run the application. When implementing a container-based approach, the architect typically creates a document (called a *spec*), which specifies which containers should run in production, creating the blueprint of your entire application. As long as all the services defined in the spec are available, the application is deemed to be healthy.

Figure 1-3 shows such an application where containerized microservices are deployed to provide a unified product offering.

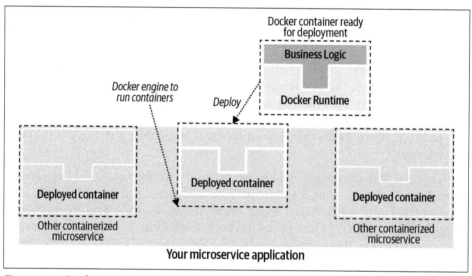

*Figure 1-3. Docker containers can be shipped and deployed to compose and create a unified product offering made entirely of modularized and containerized microservices.*

From a security perspective, you rely on Docker to isolate and containerize the business logic. Multiple containers may run on the same physical server, and therefore you rely heavily on the Docker engine's ability to isolate each container from interfering with code running on another container. Any vulnerability that enables services from one container to interfere with the host operating system or another container is called a *breakout vulnerability*. So, in technical terms, you rely on Docker to assume the responsibility of preventing breakouts. This means it is critical to ensure that you run the latest versions of both the Docker container as well as the engine that runs these containers.

These containers are typically stored in a container *registry*, a specialized storage system for Docker containers. On AWS, these containers can then be securely stored inside Amazon Elastic Container Registry (ECR).

 For a detailed overview of Docker, I recommend the book *Docker: Up and Running* (*https://oreil.ly/YlTUV*) by Sean Kane and Karl Matthias (O'Reilly).

## A Very Brief Introduction to Kubernetes

Although each Docker container is a *unit-of-deployment*, in most production environments, you want to bind them together to work as a cohesive unit. Container orchestrators such as Kubernetes (*https://kubernetes.io*) are what enable you to run multiple Docker container-based microservices. You can instruct a Kubernetes cluster to run a certain number of instances of each of the Docker containers, and Kubernetes can run them for you.

Setting up a Kubernetes cluster is the sole topic of many other books and hence I will not go into the details. But I will give you the gist of what a Kubernetes cluster does for you. If you're more interested in the setup process, I recommend *Kubernetes in Action* by Marko Luksa (Manning Publications). The official documentation (*https:// oreil.ly/sccOl*) for Kubernetes also has some great material that can help you run your clusters. Kubernetes, as you may know, is an orchestrator that you can use to run any number of services at any time. If you provide Kubernetes with a spec of the number of instances of each service you want to keep running, it will spin up new containers based on the configuration you define in the spec.

The most basic microservice unit in a Kubernetes cluster is called a *pod*. A pod is a group of one or more containers, with shared storage and network resources. A *node* is a worker machine in Kubernetes and may be either a virtual or a physical machine. Kubernetes runs your microservices by placing containers into pods to run on nodes. As you can imagine, you can scale individual microservices by adding new pods to your cluster. Pods virtualize the runtime of your microservice. Pods run on underlying hardware that can be scaled by adding new nodes to the cluster. The part of the Kubernetes cluster that administers and facilitates the orchestration of the pods is called the *control plane*. Figure 1-4 illustrates this setup.

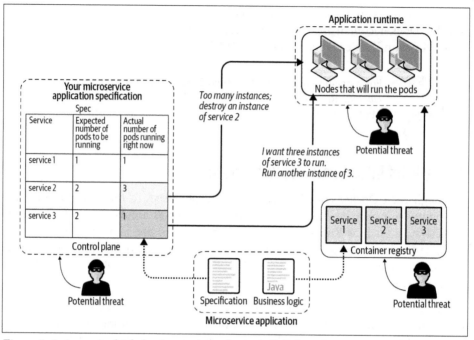

*Figure 1-4. A concise high-level overview of a typical Kubernetes setup.*

To sum up, in a Kubernetes setup, the main goal is to run the application logic, which is then containerized and stored in a container registry. Based on the specifications you provide to this cluster, containers execute this business logic on the nodes. Malicious actors could target either the control plane, the container storage, or the application runtime environment (nodes) in order to cause unwanted issues in the application.

 I think of the specification as the *recipe* that I provide to my Kubernetes cluster. Based on this recipe, Kubernetes makes a list of all the services (containers) that it needs to run, fetches all the containers from the container registry, and runs these services on my nodes for me. Thus, it spins up an entire microservice application based simply on my spec. You can configure where these microservices, which are specified in your spec, run by configuring the nodes in your cluster.

AWS provides you with two managed options to run your Kubernetes cluster:

- AWS Elastic Kubernetes Service (Amazon EKS)
- AWS Elastic Kubernetes Service, Fargate Mode (Amazon EKS Fargate)

Since AWS assumes the responsibility of running, scaling, and deploying your functions onto AWS Lambda, you do not need a separate orchestrator.

So how do you decide how to run your microservices? Because security is the concern, I have created a handy flowchart that you can follow to make such a decision, shown in Figure 1-5.

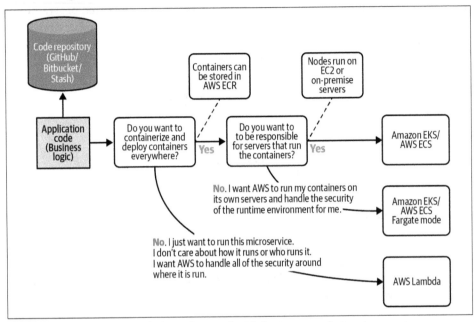

*Figure 1-5. A flowchart to help architects decide how to run their microservices.*

The next section goes into the details of these implementation methods.

AWS Elastic Container Service (AWS ECS) is also an option if you want to orchestrate containers on AWS. Although ECS differs slightly from EKS in its offering, there is a fairly large overlap between EKS and ECS from a security point of view. Hence, to avoid repetition, I will focus my attention on Amazon EKS and AWS Lambda. If you're interested in an in-depth overview of ECS, apart from the AWS documentation (*https://oreil.ly/DMliv*), *Docker on Amazon Web Services* by Justin Menga (Packt Publishing) goes into the details.

## Function as a Service: FaaS Using AWS Lambda

FaaS is a different way of approaching microservices. AWS realized that the business logic is the core feature of any microservice. As a consequence, AWS provides an environment where users can run this logic without having to use containerization or packaging. Simply plug your business function, written in a supported programming language, into the cloud environment to run directly. AWS Lambda provides this runtime capability. Figure 1-6 shows a microservice application where AWS Lambdas are deployed to provide a unified product offering.

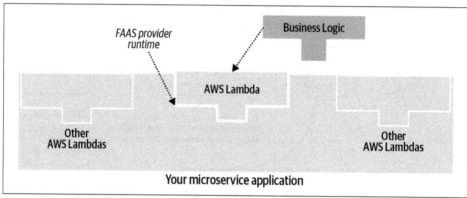

*Figure 1-6. Functions providing business logic can be deployed to AWS Lambda to run together to provide a unified product offering.*

The great part of AWS Lambda is that AWS assumes the responsibility of running the function, thus taking away some of the security responsibilities from you as part of the SRM. In this setup, you do not have to worry about container security, running nodes, or securing any of the orchestration setup.

# Overview of Cloud Microservice Implementation

From a security perspective, there are many places where security professionals can anticipate security incidents in a microservice environment. A typical microservice is illustrated in Figure 1-7. This section briefly covers what each of these layers means and how an attacker could exploit your application at each of these layers to gain unauthorized control:

*Business logic*

Also, sometimes called *function* or *application* logic, this is the application code that runs the core business function that your microservice aims to address. This code is very specific to the domain and should stick to the SRP. It may also be written in the user's choice of programming language. Since this code is domain

---

specific, it is possible for malicious actors to hijack this code to perform unauthorized activities.

*Runtime environment (container environment)*

The container environment should contain the language runtime environment that is required to run the application logic from component 1. This is the environment where the application logic runs in a sandboxed environment, thus isolating the runtime and containing the blast radius of the microservice (up to an extent). However, as with any application runtime, keeping the container version current and patching older vulnerabilities in the containers and their runtime is important to ensure securing your application.

*Container runtime (container engine)*

This is the software that is capable of running containers from component two. Since microservices running in containers run in an isolated, sandboxed environment, it is important to make sure that security vulnerabilities in the virtualization layer of container runtime do not affect the host operating system or other containers running on the same machine. This isolation is the responsibility of the container runtime. Such breakout vulnerabilities (*https://oreil.ly/Oom5c*) may be identified from time to time and patched immediately by Docker. So it is important to continuously update the container runtime to ensure that you are running the latest Docker engine.

*Virtual machine*

This is the virtual machine (VM) where you will be running the container engine. Each VM may contain multiple containers running containers; you can host multiple microservices on each VM. Since a VM is similar to any other operating system, attackers may be able to exploit OS-level vulnerabilities, especially with VMs not running the latest version of the operating system.

*Physical hardware*

This is the most basic layer within the microservice infrastructure and refers to the physical hardware that may be providing the computational power necessary to run the microservices. Like any other physical item, these servers may be vulnerable to theft, vandalism, or hacking using flash drives (*https://oreil.ly/8mPU0*) or other physical devices.

*Container storage*

It is common to store prebuilt containers as part of the development process in dedicated storage systems. If prebuilt containers are not stored securely, an attacker may be able to tamper with built images by injecting malicious code into them or swapping out images and replacing them with malicious code.

*Container orchestration*

An *orchestrator* makes decisions on how many instances of a particular service need to be kept running to achieve application health. Orchestration allows you to build application services that span multiple containers, schedule containers across a cluster, scale those containers, and manage their health over time. An orchestrator is responsible for making sure that services are kept running or restarted whenever they go down. It can also make decisions regarding scaling up or scaling down services to match traffic.

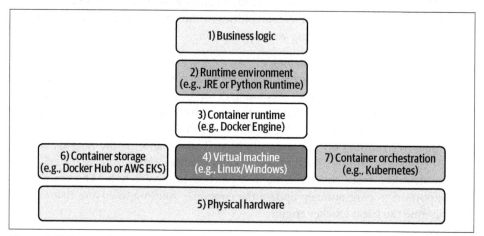

*Figure 1-7. Layered representation of a microservice running in a cloud environment.*

The next sections go over the various microservice runtime options and, from a security perspective, discuss your responsibilities as opposed to the responsibilities assumed by AWS. I start off with the option that assigns you with the most amount of responsibility within the three choices and then end with the option where AWS assumes most of the responsibility.

## Amazon EKS

Control planes play a crucial role in a Kubernetes setup, since they constantly control application availability by ensuring that the runtime services act according to the spec. Given its importance, AWS provides users with a fully managed control plane in the form of Amazon EKS. Amazon EKS is a managed service that allows you to set up the Kubernetes control plane on AWS. By doing so, AWS assumes the responsibility of the infrastructure that runs the control plane that runs your cluster as part of the SRM. Having said that, you are still responsible for configuring and securing the settings that make this control plane secure.

Figure 1-8 illustrates the setup using Amazon EKS. AWS ensures that the risk of a malicious actor taking over your control plane is mitigated as part of the SRM. However, in Amazon EKS you are still responsible for running the nodes, so the risk of a malicious actor taking over your nodes still remains.

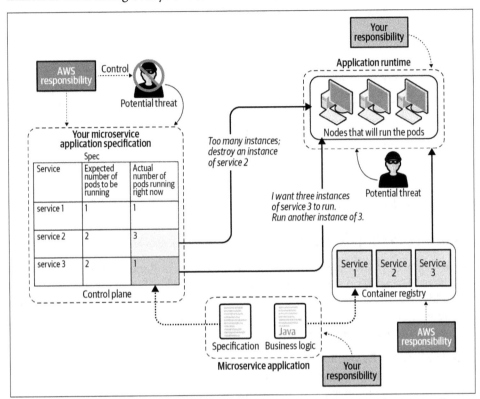

*Figure 1-8. Amazon EKS is a fully managed Kubernetes control plane that can orchestrate the microservices you run on servers you have to manage.*

Figure 1-9 shows the split in responsibilities and how EKS leverages the AWS SRM to relieve you of some of the security responsibilities of running containers by comparing it with the model described in Figure 1-7.

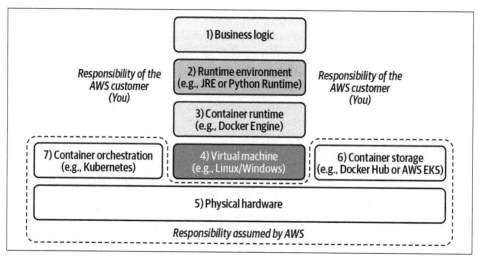

*Figure 1-9. Container orchestration, container storage, and the security of the physical hardware can be assumed by AWS in this model.*

## Amazon EKS Fargate Mode

A shortcoming of the regular EKS mode, as described in the previous section, is that you have to bear the responsibility of running the nodes. For many administrators, this adds an extra set of responsibility that is, at times, unnecessary. If the only aspect of microservice architecture you care about is the single business function it provides, you may want to delegate the responsibility of running nodes to AWS.

This is where the Fargate mode comes into the picture. In Fargate mode, you can create the Docker containers you want to run in production, configure EKS to create a cluster of these containers, and then hand over these containers to AWS to run on their servers. In this way, AWS takes care of securing the servers, the operating systems on them (keeping the OS up to date), and maintaining network and physical security of the hardware that supports these servers—while you focus on the microservices themselves instead of the backend infrastructure.

Figure 1-10 shows the same architecture described in Figure 1-8, where it was running on the regular EKS mode. But this time, it runs in the Fargate mode.

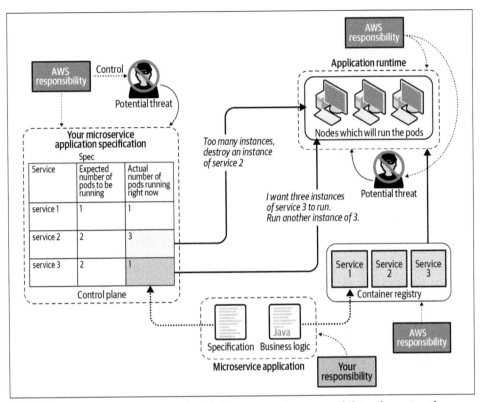

*Figure 1-10. In AWS Fargate mode, AWS assumes the responsibility of running the nodes, thus reducing your responsibility.*

You can see how the responsibility for the nodes that ran the Docker engine is now assumed by AWS in the cloud, thus reducing your security responsibility. You are, however, still responsible for the containers themselves as well as the business logic that runs on these containers. You can also redraw the application runtime stack, as shown in Figure 1-11. As mentioned, the Docker engine is run on the nodes; hence its responsibility is assumed by AWS. You are only responsible for using the right Docker container and the business logic that runs on it.

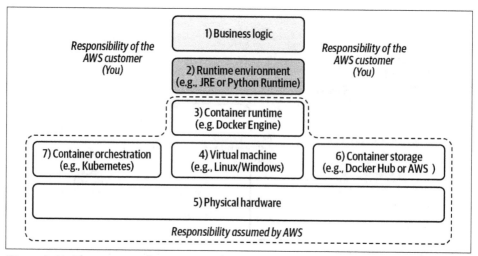

*Figure 1-11. The security of container orchestration, container storage, physical hardware, virtual machine, and the container runtime can be assumed by AWS in this model.*

## Function as a Service Using AWS Lambda

FaaS-based service is the final type of microservice that helps developers hit the ground running by assuming the responsibility for all types of security around running the service; therefore, developers can focus on the business logic instead of anything else. On AWS, AWS Lambda enables developers to run their function in a FaaS environment.

On AWS Lambda, the responsibility of implementing a majority of controls is assumed by AWS. However, you are still required to configure access and set up networking controls and other configurations to ensure that AWS can enable security on your behalf. AWS bears the responsibility of provisioning a server and running your code in a sandboxed environment, as long as it is written to the AWS Lambda specifications (*https://oreil.ly/ct7qf*). AWS Lambdas are a powerful, scalable, and most importantly, secure way of running microservices on AWS.

The runtime architecture stack of microservices running on AWS Lambda can be seen in Figure 1-12. As mentioned, the customer is only responsible for the business logic while everything else is managed by AWS. In a Lambda-based architecture, you do not have to worry about patching the operating system, Docker versions, or anything related to the infrastructure.

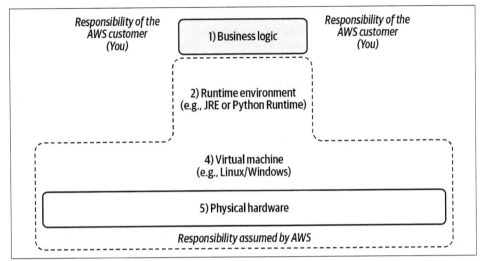

*Figure 1-12. The responsibility of everything except the business logic and its configuration is assumed by AWS.*

At the time of writing this book, AWS also allows you to run Docker containers on AWS Lambda. However, for the purposes of this book, I am restricting the scope only to running functions (FaaS).

## Microservice Implementation Summary

Figure 1-13 illustrates how your security responsibilities change depending on your choice of microservice implementation.

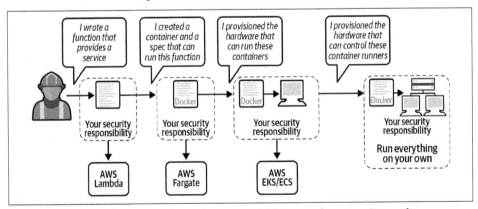

*Figure 1-13. AWS provides different ways to run the same function. Depending on your choice, you can trade off cost, flexibility, and configurability for security responsibility.*

As an architect, you should decide how much responsibility you want to take upon yourself, in return for the flexibility you gain from running the application on your own terms.

# Examples of Microservice Communication Patterns

Let's go back to the LEGO analogy of microservices. What can you do with a single LEGO brick? Perhaps not much. How about 10 of them? Now you can make a few different shapes. A hundred LEGO bricks give you lots of possibilities. Most large applications will be created by composing hundreds of smaller microservices, all working with one another and, more importantly, communicating with one another. Since communication links are the weakest links in any application, this interservice communication adds to the aggregate risk of the application. You have to secure new channels of external communication instead of the familiar in-memory calls, as may happen with monoliths. As a result, much of this book is dedicated to securing interservice communication. To illustrate how security concepts will be applied throughout this book, I would like to briefly discuss some of the many patterns that architects use in microservice communication. These examples do not constitute an exhaustive list, and many other communication patterns are followed in the industry. The Microservices.io (*https://oreil.ly/uSPHX*) blog or the Microsoft architecture ebook (*https://oreil.ly/9TEKt*) are great resources if you're interested in other microservice communication patterns.

---

### Loose Coupling

Whenever someone brings up microservice communication, a lot of developers automatically think of synchronous representational state transfer (REST) (*https://oreil.ly/dvMaz*). In the early days of the microservice movement, this was indeed the method of choice used for communication. However, in this book, I would like to remind readers that the microservice community seems to be moving away from synchronous communication. An important aspect of microservice communication is the *loose coupling* that is required between different bounded contexts. This means scaling and health of services within one bounded context should never affect the health of any other service in any other context.

As an example, say you have a checkout service as part of an ecommerce company that handles customer checkouts. As part of this checkout service, you are required to call an email service to send an email notification to the user. Loose coupling dictates that if this email service is under some sort of a security attack and goes down for any reason, the checkout service should not be affected and should continue to function as before, with the sole exception of not being able to send the confirmation email.

---

# Example 1: Simple Message Passing Between Contexts

The simplest way of communicating between contexts is by directly sending messages to each other (generally through HTTP requests). In this example, whenever a customer checks out an item, the checkout service will send out two messages. The first would be to the products domain, informing it to reduce the stock of inventory to reflect this purchase. The second would be to the finance service, informing it to charge the customer's credit card on file.

Figure 1-14 shows an example of direct communication.

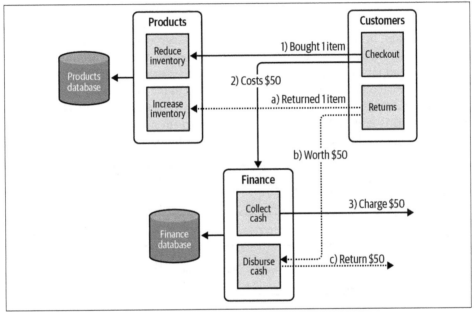

*Figure 1-14. There are many ways in which these messages can be passed.*

The traditional way of passing messages is by using synchronous REST endpoints. Even though it does not fit my definition of microservice-based communication, companies all over the world use it. Whenever a purchase is made, the checkout service will call a POST endpoint on the collect cash service and consequently call a POST endpoint on the inventory domain. However, synchronous communication using REST will mean the checkout service will wait for the two synchronous operations to complete before it can complete its job. This adds a strong dependency and increases coupling between the finance, inventory, and customer domains.

In such situations, the job of the security professionals is to secure the REST endpoints and the HTTP infrastructure in the application. Chapter 7 talks about the fundamentals of setting up security in transit.

It is my opinion that synchronous communication in this way goes against the very essence of microservices, since the resulting microservices are no longer independent and will continue to maintain a strong relationship. Although some microservice architectures still use synchronous REST communication, most architectural models for microservices dissuade microservice services from using synchronous communication (*https://oreil.ly/JTa0v*).

## Example 2: Message Queues

Message brokers or queuing systems are commonly used for cross-domain communication in microservices. A service that wants to send a message will put it on a persistent medium. In contrast, the recipient of the message will read from the persistent medium. Communication through message queues occurs asynchronously, which means the endpoints publishing and consuming messages interact with the queue, rather than each other. Producers can add messages to the queue once they are ready, and consumers can handle messages only if they have enough capacity. No producer in the system is ever stalled waiting for a downstream consumer or affected by its reliability. Figure 1-15 illustrates a queue-based communication.

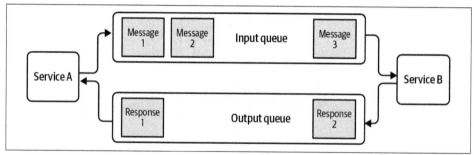

*Figure 1-15. Using message queues for communication between microservices*

You can see how the role of a security professional increases slightly in this example. Since queues use a persistence layer, security professionals must secure both the queues and the endpoints that service A and service B use to connect to the queue.

## Example 3: Event-Based Microservices

The event-based communication paradigm is another popular way of designing microservice communication. An event-based system works on the premise that every state-changing command results in an event that is then broadcast (generally using an entity known as an *event broker*) to other parts of the application. Other services within other contexts subscribe to these events. When they receive an event, they can update their own state to reflect this change, which could lead to the publication of more events. Figure 1-16 illustrates a sample event-based microservice application. To learn more, check out *Building Event-Driven Microservices* (*https://oreil.ly/gFZzV*) by Adam Bellemare (O'Reilly), an entire book dedicated to such an architecture.

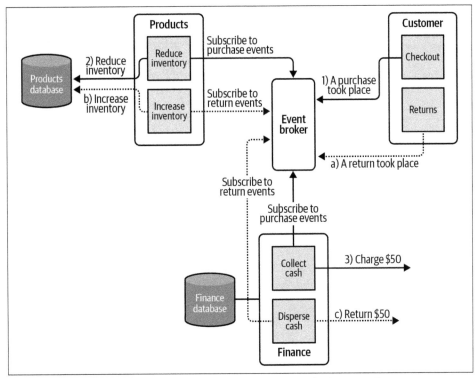

*Figure 1-16. Event-based microservices offer a choreographed approach to microservices.*

In this example, security professionals must secure the event broker, along with all the necessary infrastructure needed for storing, broadcasting, and hosting the events.

## Summary

This chapter introduced the basic concepts of threats and risk, and then explained the concept of control and countermeasures. In a cloud environment, the responsibility of implementing controls is shared between the customer and AWS. Understanding where this split lies is the main idea behind cloud security. Even if AWS assumes the responsibility for certain controls, it may still be the customer's responsibility to configure the controls in such a way that AWS can protect against potential attacks. The chapter also introduced some of the common microservice architecture patterns and their implementation on AWS. The next chapter goes deep into authentication and authorization, two of the most basic controls available that reduce the risk of your application from potential threats.

# Authorization and Authentication Basics

In Chapter 1, I talked about how security professionals may employ certain measures called *controls* (also known as *countermeasures*) to reduce the aggregate risk of any application. Some controls are better than others at applying nuanced security logic, to block only the unauthorized requests without affecting the experience of authorized users. Controls that are effective at identifying unauthorized requests and denying them access are said to be *precise* or *sharp*. The objective of this chapter is to examine two of the most precise security controls that an organization can employ on AWS:*authorization* and *authentication*. The level of granularity at which these controls work allows them to be sharpened enough to incorporate organizational nuance, resulting in well-tuned precision. This sharpening makes these controls your strongest and most targeted defense against potential threats.

 The concepts from this chapter are applicable to all applications running on AWS, not just microservices. Identity and access controls are the fundamental building blocks of every secure system. However, throughout the chapter, I will point at places where these controls benefit from the modularity that is provided by microservices.

To begin introducing these controls, let me define some terms. Each interaction or request within the cloud infrastructure can be thought of as initiated by some calling entity, called a *principal*. A principal can be a user or a service within or external to the organization. On the receiving end of this request may be a data store or another service that the principal wishes to interact with, called a *resource*. Thus, principals perform various *actions* on cloud resources.

I will now use these terms to define authorization and authentication in more detail:

*Authorization (access control)*
Authorization is the process through which access to particular resources is defined. In determining whether access may be granted to a request, factors such as the principal's identity, the target resource, the circumstances under which the request is made, and the location of the request may be considered. In most cases, prior to evaluating requests, access control systems require that the principal's identity be known to them.

*Authentication (identity management)*
Authentication is the mechanism by which principals are able to identify themselves and prove their identities to the target system, thus distinguishing themselves from any impostors. Cloud systems can map an end user's identity to a predefined set of known identities after a user has been authenticated. This enables cloud systems to control access to all incoming requests from this user through the authorization process.

Authentication and authorization work together to provide you with granular controls that guard against potential threats. The authentication process ensures that legitimate principals can identify themselves to the access control (authorization) system. Upon identification, the access control system can determine if the request is authorized or needs to be blocked.

As one might imagine, in a microservice architecture there are many principals and many resources. Thus, there are many ways a malicious actor could exploit vulnerabilities to compromise the system. As a result, the access policy and, overall, the general security policy of a microservice architecture may get quite complex. This is where identity and access management (IAM) comes into play. The IAM system within an organization is used to specify rules as prescribed by the organization's access policy. Each request is evaluated against these rules to identify if the sender of the request is permitted access. Each IAM access policy evaluation boils down to deciding whether to allow or deny a request.

 The way I think about IAM is that by using IAM policies, you write business logic for AWS. AWS refers to this business logic to enforce access control and thus enhance the security posture of your organization. This way, you can help AWS in sharpening the controls you have on your assets.

# Basics of AWS Identity and Access Management

Although IAM does not apply specifically to microservices, it lays the foundation of any architecture that you may implement on AWS. As opposed to monoliths, where most communication happens in memory, microservices utilize external communication channels. AWS IAM can intercept each of these requests and evaluate them against the access policy of the organization. Hence, the role played by AWS IAM as an arbitrator of access control and authentication is crucial in securing a microservice architecture.

IAM was designed to be a global and fully managed service. Instead of scattering access control policies and authentication logic across the cloud, IAM allows cloud architects to centralize access policies in one place. AWS was also able to implement some of the best practices in security engineering by taking on the responsibility of protecting the access control mechanism. AWS IAM can be assumed to be highly available, highly scalable, and completely managed by AWS as part of the AWS Shared Responsibility Model (SRM).

Figure 2-1 illustrates a typical microservice application for an ecommerce company with AWS IAM providing centralized authorization services for each of their requests. AWS IAM is programmed to allow legitimate communication requests. As seen in the figure, requests 1 and 2 are allowed to proceed, while request 3 is denied since it is not allowed by IAM policy.

IAM also provides authentication services. So, when an imposter—"Hacked microservice"—tries to communicate with the purchase service (request 4), IAM denies the request.

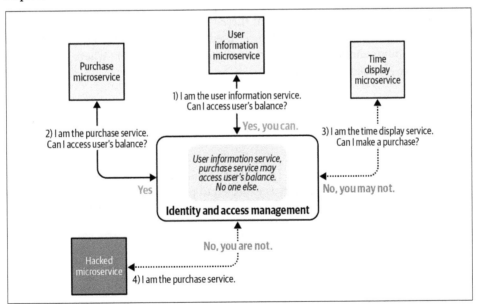

*Figure 2-1. AWS IAM acts as a centralized service that provides authentication and authorization services for all of your microservice architecture.*

As seen in Figure 2-1, there is no reason why the "Time display microservice" should ever be allowed to make a purchase. Microservices can run securely on the cloud when such rules are configured in AWS IAM.

To sum up, it is the responsibility of the security professionals to come up with the security policy (more specifically, the access policy) that dictates which users and microservices are allowed to interact with one another within the application. This policy needs to be designed in such a way that potential threat actors are not able to exploit vulnerabilities. Once created inside AWS IAM, AWS then assumes the responsibility of enforcing this access policy as part of the SRM.

## Principals on AWS

Before I go into the details of securing cloud resources through access control, let me briefly explain the major types of principals that exist on AWS:

*IAM users*
> These are your day-to-day users (employees, contractors, guests) who log in to your account with their individual credentials and interact with your cloud infrastructure.

*Root users*
> These are special types of IAM users that exist on AWS. These are account owners who have full control and superuser privilege over an AWS account. Given the near universal permissions that these users get on your AWS accounts, these accounts should be secured and never used for day-to-day activities. Ideally, root user accounts should only be used to create other IAM users where permissions are more granularly defined.

*IAM groups*
> An IAM group is a collection of users that can be attached to a common permission policy, making it easier to manage organizational growth.

*IAM roles*
> IAM roles are very similar to IAM users. An IAM role maps to a set of tasks or job functions that each identity is expected to perform. IAM roles can be thought of as IAM users without access credentials. (I cover roles in detail later in this chapter.)

## IAM Policies

Access control on AWS is governed by IAM policies, which are JavaScript Object Notation (JSON) documents that codify permissions regarding access control for each principal in an account. AWS consults these policies when determining whether to grant access to requests.

An access control policy involves two types of actors: principals and resources. A principal is an actor that requests access. This actor could be an employee or, at times, another cloud service. A resource represents the service being accessed. This resource could be a database, an Amazon Simple Storage Service (S3) bucket, or any other cloud service that is being provided by AWS.

Figure 2-2 illustrates the difference between identity-based policies and resource-based policies:

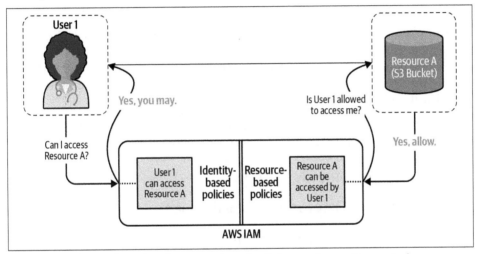

*Figure 2-2. Identity-based and resource-based policies can be used to control access.*

There are two ways to implement an access control policy in AWS IAM:

- Access can be limited by limiting what each principal can do within the cloud system. These policies are called *principal-based policies* (or *identity-based policies*).

- A resource's actions can be restricted based on the principal that is requesting to perform them. These policies are called *resource-based policies*.

IAM policies can be found in the Policies tab inside the Identity and Access Management tab in your AWS Management Console. IAM policies exist independent of the principal or the resource that they are applied to and can be applied to multiple principals to enable reuse.

## Principle of Least Privilege

Now that I have introduced you to the tool that will aid you in defining controls to protect your microservices, I would like to introduce you to the process you can follow to build these controls. This process is called *need to know*. In complex environments, the security architect creates a list of all the principals in the organization and determines what resources each principal needs access to. The list is then used to determine which policies will be applied to each principal or resource.

"Need to know" is the first step to applying what is known as the *principle of least privilege*, or PoLP. The PoLP was originally formulated back in 1958 by the Association for Computing Machinery as the following: "Every program and every privileged user of the system should operate using the least amount of privilege necessary to complete the job."

A great way of visualizing the PoLP can be to follow the four rules highlighted in Figure 2-3 as demonstrated by AWS (*https://oreil.ly/8gYDk*).

Give the Right access

Only to the Right individuals

To perform the Right action

Only when it is the Right time

...And nothing more...

*Figure 2-3. A great quote for remembering the PoLP.*

PoLP helps ensure that vulnerabilities in one area of the system can't affect other areas. Policies should be assigned using PoLP, which means a principal should be assigned the most restrictive policy possible while still allowing them to do their job.

## PoLP and Blast Radius

In Chapter 1, I discussed the concept of blast radius and how modular applications are advantageous because they minimize the impact of security incidents by locking attackers into specific modules. It is through the use of PoLP and access control that this advantage can be achieved.

Figure 2-4 compares two applications for an ecommerce company. One is built using a monolithic architecture and the other using a microservice-based architecture. The application connects to three different databases: Marketing DB, Finance DB, and User Profile DB for different business needs.

If PoLP is applied, in the case of a monolith, the application's runtime identity (the user or role that the application runs as) will require access to all three of these databases. In the case of microservices, the application's identity will have access to the specific database that it needs to connect to.

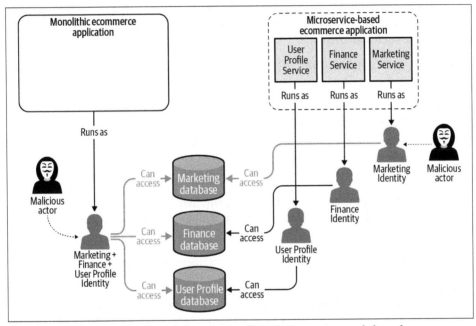

*Figure 2-4. A comparison of access control policies between a monolith and a microservice-based application. A microservice provides better incident isolation than a monolith due to its modular structure and the ability to grant more granular access to applications.*

As you can see in Figure 2-4, in the case of a monolith, the application runtime identity ends up requiring access to all three of the databases to perform its job properly. Hence, the access policy for this identity is wide. Now compare that to a microservice-based application. Each microservice has to connect to one specific database. Therefore, the PoLP dictates that each identity has access only to the specific database it needs to perform its job. Now if a malicious actor were to compromise any of these identities, the impact is different.

An attacker who compromised the monolith's identity could access all the databases. However, for microservices, malicious actors would gain access only to the marketing database, as shown in Figure 2-4. Technically speaking, in case of an incident, the blast radius in a microservice application is smaller than that of a monolith. This is, however, only true as long as PoLP is applied while designing the permissions for all identities and resources.

## Structure of AWS IAM Policies

Now that I have conceptually defined access control, it is time to look at how it is configured on AWS IAM. As a reminder, the purpose of every statement within an IAM policy is to state which *principal* is *allowed* (or *denied*) access to which *resource* under which *conditions* and for which specific *action*. On AWS, each policy can make one or more such statements.

PARC-E is a handy acronym to remember the components of an access policy statement:

*Principal*
> The principal that the statement is prescribing permissions for. This may be explicitly mentioned in the policy or implicitly assumed if the policy is attached to a principal.

*Action*
> The action that the statement applies to, whether it is the ability to read the data or write to a table or any other action that the resource is able to perform.

*Resource*
> The resource or set of resources that the statement is applicable for.

*Condition (optional)*
> The conditions under which this statement should even be evaluated. Or the conditions under which the effect prescribed in the policy should be applied to the action.

*Effect*
> Whether the statement should allow or deny access.

 All principals and resources within AWS are clearly identified by a unique ID assigned to them by AWS called the *Amazon Resource Name (ARN)*.

All policies are written in a JSON format. Here is an example of a customer-managed policy:

```
{
    "Version": "2012-10-17",
    "Id": "key-default-1",
    "Statement": [
        {
```

```
    "Principal": {
                "AWS": "arn:aws:iam::244255116257:root"
        },
        "Action": "kms:*",
        "Resource": "*"
        "Effect": "Allow",
        "Sid": "Enable IAM User Permissions",
    }
  ]
}
```

The statement within this policy says, *the principal with ARN* (arn:aws:iam::
244255116257:root) *is allowed to perform all the activities related to AWS KMS*
(kms:*) on all of the resources that this policy is applied to.

I demonstrate how the policy statements can be used to apply PoLP
in large organizations in Appendix D.

## Principal-Based Policies

Principal-based policies are applied to a principal within an account, determining the
level of access the principal in question has. A principal can be either a user, a group,
or a role that lives within the account. The resource being accessed can be within the
same account or a different account.

If you have the answer to the question *What resources is this user/
role/group allowed to access?* principal-based policies are best suited
for your needs.

IAM follows a *default deny* rule. By default, whenever a user or a role is added to an
account, they will have no access to any resources within that account until an IAM
policy is created by an administrator or a root user of the particular account to allow
access.

Policies that are principal-based apply to the principal in question; you don't need to
specify the principal explicitly in a policy statement (and AWS won't allow you to).
The principal of the policy is always the entity to which the policy is attached.

When the policy is attached to an IAM group, the principal is the IAM user in that group who is making the request.

## Resource-Based Policies

As the name suggests, resource-based policies are applied to specific supported resources. AWS maintains a list (*https://oreil.ly/fAo9L*) of resources that support resource-based policies. These policies are inline only. They are not bound by AWS accounts, so they may include principals from any AWS account, not necessarily the one the resource belongs to.

If you have the answer to the question *Who (which principal) is allowed to access this resource?* resource-based policies are best suited for your needs.

Here is a sample resource-based policy. This policy allows a specific user (`arn:aws:iam::AWS-account-ID:user/user-name`) to invoke the Lambda function (`my-function`):

```
{
    "Version": "2012-10-17",
    "Id": "default",
    "Statement": [
        {
            "Sid": "sample-resource-based-policy",
            "Effect": "Allow",
        "Principal": { "AWS": "arn:aws:iam::AWS-account-ID:user/user-name" }
,
            "Action": "lambda:InvokeFunction",
            "Resource": "arn:aws:lambda:us-east-2:<account>:function:my-function"
        }
    ]
}
```

## The Zone of Trust

In a single account setup, resource-based policies may provide an additional layer of protection on top of principal-based policies.

Principals from one account may be allowed to call resources in another. Consider a scenario where Principal B in Account B would like to access Resource B in Account B (resource and principal being in the same account). Under a single-account configuration, an IAM policy that permits access to Resource B will provide the right access to Principal B.

Essentially, Principal B can be granted access to any resource in its own account by simply attaching an identity-based IAM policy to it that grants this access without requiring a resource-based policy.

Let's consider a slightly different situation. Resource B is still in Account B, but Principal A is in Account A (resource and principal being in different accounts). Principal A has an identity-based policy that allows it to access Resource B. However, you will realize, simply adding an identity-based policy is not enough for cross-account access. A resource-based policy is required in Account B on Resource B, in addition to any identity-based policy to enable this access. Figure 2-5 illustrates this evaluation logic.

In other words, even if Principal A is granted access to Resource B within Account A, AWS will not allow Principal A to access Resource B *unless* there is a resource-based policy within Account B that allows this access.

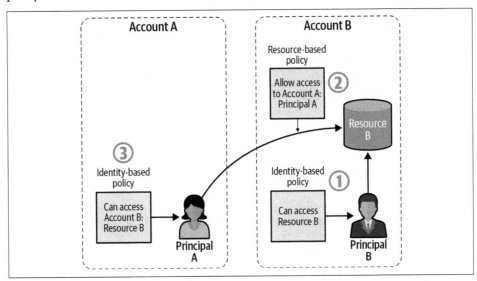

*Figure 2-5. For Principal B to access Resource B, only IAM policy (1) is required. For Principal A to access Resource B, though, both resource-based policy (2) and IAM policy (3) are required.*

Any internal request for a service from within an account is said to have come from within the *zone of trust* for that service. That's not the case for external access. Resources have to explicitly mention the principals that they trust outside their zones of trust (in this case, their accounts). A zone of trust dictates whether a resource-based policy is required to access a particular resource.

Figure 2-6 shows a Venn diagram that sums up how the concept of a zone of trust fits in with the policy evaluation algorithm. Consider a scenario where Principal A, defined in an AWS Account A, requests access to Resource B.

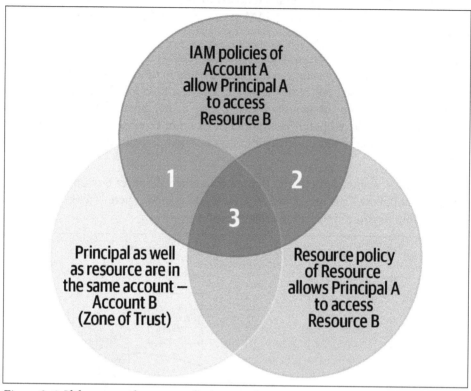

*Figure 2-6. If the request happens to lie in any of regions 1, 2, or 3, access to the resource will be granted. For all other requests, access will be denied.*

In evaluating whether access should be allowed, we can ask three questions:

- Is Principal A in the same account as Resource A within the zone of trust?
- Does the IAM policy in Account A allow Principal A to access Resource B?
- Is there a resource policy on Resource B that allows Principal A to gain access?

The request will be granted only if it falls into one of the three scenarios labeled in Figure 2-6.

In AWS, principals from one account are allowed to assume roles in other accounts and make requests to resources in the latter account. In such cases, the policy evaluation logic will assume that the request is originating from the target account's role, and thus assume that it comes from within the zone of trust. There is no requirement for such a request to be accompanied by a resource-based policy.

## Evaluation of Policies

For any given request, there may be multiple policy statements that need to be evaluated in conjunction with one another. After evaluating the request, AWS must decide whether to allow it to proceed or deny it access to the resources or services to which the original request specified access.

In making its decision, AWS follows a standard evaluation algorithm (*https://oreil.ly/yLeID*):

1. Start with the intent of denying the request by default (implicit deny).

2. Go through all the policies and statements that are applicable. If there are conditions, only retain statements where conditions are satisfied.

3. If there is a statement in a policy that explicitly denies this request, deny the request. *Explicit "denies" always override the "allows."*

4. As long as there is a policy allowing the request, the request should go on to the next step. In the absence of any identity-based policies allowing this request, deny the request and terminate the evaluation.

5. If the principal is from the same account as the target resource, you can assume that the request is from within the zone of trust. Resource-based policies are not needed in such a scenario. Let such a request access the target resource.

6. If the request comes from a principal from a different account, a resource-based policy is needed within the resource's account allowing this request. Check to see whether such a resource-based policy exists.

Figure 2-7 illustrates this algorithm in a flowchart.

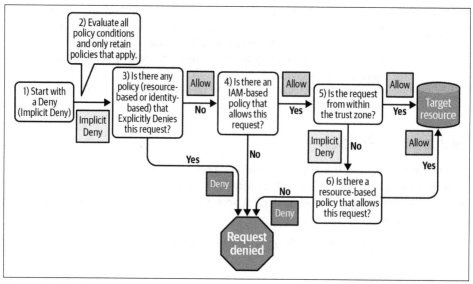

*Figure 2-7. Each request is evaluated against a workflow to determine if access should be granted or denied to the underlying service or resource.*

# Advanced Concepts in AWS IAM Policies

Microservices generally have a large number of principals and resources. Because of this, security professionals often realize that they can benefit from using some of the advanced tools AWS provides to better design their security policies. In this section, I will highlight some of the commonly used policy tools that can help in writing policies for large organizations.

## IAM Policy Conditions

Policies and statements within a policy can be evaluated on a conditional basis, adding more flexibility to the IAM process. AWS gathers context on each request it receives. This context includes information such as the following:

- The action that the request wants to perform on AWS
- The name and ARN of the resource that the request wants to interact with
- The principal or the identity performing this request

- Environment data that may be part of the request—this may include a variety of factors, such as the IP address of the requestor, the user agent, whether the request comes using a secure transport, whether the principal is another AWS service, and so on.
- More information associated with the target resource, such as any tags on a resource or any tables in a target database

A system administrator could then use all this information to formulate conditional logic to enforce one or more IAM policies. The conditional evaluation process relies on the ability to identify the policy context in which the policy applies and comparing this context with the actual request context when deciding eligibility.

For example, access may be granted to a resource only if the source of the request is from an IP belonging to your corporate office. This policy can be written like this:

```
{
    "Version": "2012-10-17",
    "Statement": {
        "Effect": "Deny",
        "Action": "*",
        "Resource": "*",
        "Condition": {
            "NotIpAddress": {
                "aws:SourceIp": [
                    "1.2.3.4/32"
                ]
            }
        }
    }
}
```

This policy will deny any request to all resources within the account. However, since this policy is only applicable if the IP address is not 1.2.3.4/32, it will restrict external access to resources without interfering with any other AWS policies related to requests originating from the IP address 1.2.3.4/32.

Here is another example where conditions can be used. To ensure that a particular resource can only be accessed using an HTTPS endpoint (secure endpoint), you can use this condition:

```
"Condition": {"Bool": {"aws:SecureTransport": "true"}}
```

This condition will evaluate to true if the incoming request to access a resource comes by way of a secure transport such as HTTPS. AWS maintains a list (*https://oreil.ly/FaBG9*) of all conditions that it supports within AWS policies.

# AWS Tags and Attribute-Based Access Control

When physical data centers were the primary mode of deploying applications, connecting wires and boxes used to be color coded to identify their purpose and the level of sensitivity of the data that was present in these boxes. Access was granted to employees based on the levels and the color codes. Each server had stickers on it that allowed them to record basic metadata (such as the sensitivity of the data that the server dealt with). This way, teams could identify their resources. This process of marking resources based on teams is called *server tagging*.

You can assign metadata to your cloud resources using tags on AWS. Tags are simple labels composed of a key and an optional value that can be used to manage, search for, and filter resources. You can categorize resources based on purposes, owners, environments, bounded contexts, subdomains, or other criteria. In the case of microservices, with the increased fragmentation of services, tags can prove to be a great resource managing all of your cloud resources and, more importantly, controlling access to them.

Assigning attributes (tags) to various resources allows your administrators to specify the sensitivity level of the data and the minimum clearance level required for accessing the resource. You can also specify the tag that a principal should have in order to gain access to this resource. So you may have conditional policies such as "only a manager can access resources that have a *level-manager* set on them" or "only a person from Team X can access a resource that has a tag *team* set to *team x.*" Such a system is called *attribute-based access control (ABAC)*.

IAM policies have access to the tags in the request's context and thus can be used to compare the tag present on the resource to determine whether the request should be allowed:

```
"Condition": {
            "StringEquals": {"aws:ResourceTag/project":
              "${aws:PrincipalTag/project}"}
        }
```

As you can imagine, microservices are great environments for using ABAC.

# "Not" Policy Elements: NotPrincipal and NotResource

Two commonly used exclusion policy statements are `NotPrincipal` and `NotResource`. Since both statements are similar in structure and have a somewhat similar effect, I have bundled them together.

They are both used to specify a list of items that the specified policy does not apply to. Let's say you want to create a policy that denies access to S3 buckets to everyone except for a few users in the organization. You can use `NotPrincipal` to specify a deny policy that applies to everyone in the account except the users specified in the policy:

```
{
    "Version": "2012-10-17",
    "Statement": [{
        "Effect": "Deny",
        "NotPrincipal": {"AWS": [
            "arn:aws:iam::<accountid>:user/<username>",
        ]},
        "Action": "s3:*",
        "Resource": [
            "arn:aws:s3:::<BucketName|>"
        ]
    }]
}
```

NotResource can be used in a similar way; it can be used with a deny policy if you want to deny access for one user to all buckets except one S3 bucket:

```
{
    "Version": "2012-10-17",
    "Statement": {
        "Effect": "Deny",
        "Action": "s3:*",
        "NotResource": [
            "arn:aws:s3:::<theonlybuckettoaccess>"
        ]
    }
}
```

## Wrapping Up IAM Policies

It is impossible to overstate the importance of IAM in any cloud application and, specifically, in a microservice application. Due to their nature, in a microservice environment you may end up requiring significantly more IAM policies in order to control each and every service. This proliferation of policies may add to the complexity of the application.

However, what you lose in complexity, you may gain in configurability. Microservices afford better control due to their modular nature. With a domain-driven design (DDD), it is possible to frame IAM policies that are targeted and hence can provide preventive controls against potential threats. In order to target attacks, AWS provides you with many different conditions that can help in tailoring these IAM policies to better suit the needs of the service. AWS provides great documentation (*https://oreil.ly/cAyea*) on how you can tailor these policies further.

Even so, for large organizations, IAM policies may end up causing friction between developers and microservice security architects. In Chapter 8, I will attempt to introduce you to some other techniques that aim at reducing the burden of complexity that microservices bring with them.

# Role-Based Access Control

Because microservices involve a lot of services running with different identities, IAM policies may get complicated very soon, mainly due to their sheer volume. In such a situation, AWS roles aim to simplify the development of these identities while keeping the security policy simple and scalable. The concept of roles has been borrowed from social sciences. *A role is a set of permissions, behaviors, identities, and norms as defined by people in a specific circumstance.*

For example, a student attending a class and the same student at a party are the same person, yet that person plays two different roles. In class, the student may not be allowed to play loud music. However, at a party, the same student may be able to blast their stereo. Using role-based access control (RBAC), it is possible to place different restrictions on the same individual depending on the role they currently play.

RBAC is an access control paradigm and a fascinating topic in the field of security. For readers interested in learning further, I recommend *Role-Based Access Control* by David Ferraiolo et al. (Artech House).

 RBAC is not the only way of organizing access control across complex organizations. There are many others, such as ABAC, mandatory access control (MAC), graph-based access control (GBAC), and more. Every organization needs to find the access control paradigm that best suits its security needs; each has their advantages. Since RBAC is widely used and ties well with other microservice concepts, it's covered in this chapter.

If I am working for an organization and would like to access a resource, RBAC dictates that my responsibilities be converted to a role that I am allowed to assume. The role that I will be assuming can have a lifecycle that may not be tied to my lifecycle in the company. In this way, if I get replaced in the organization, the person who replaces me can still use the same role and access the same resource.

Figure 2-8 shows how access to a resource modeled after a role instead of an individual user helps in enforcing a similar access control policy. In this case, user Gaurav Raje does not have access to a resource. However, the same user is able to access the resource when he assumes a system administrator role.

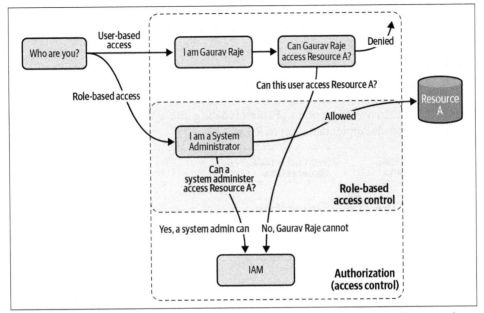

*Figure 2-8. In RBAC, the same user can request access to a resource either by using their individual identity or by using a role that they are authorized to perform within the organization.*

Organization-wide paradigm shifts like RBAC require top-down alignment when it comes to implementation. The transitions can be a challenge at times, especially in large organizations. But once implemented, RBAC leads to reduced complexity, improved access visibility, improved compliance, and an easy-to-manage security infrastructure.

# RBAC Modeling

In RBAC modeling, the first step is to identify the various resources and the actions that are authorized to be performed on these resources:

1. An inventory is taken of each and every action that needs to be performed on these resources.

2. After that, the organization is analyzed to identify the different employees and the actions they perform on each of the resources within the organization. This may include grouping actions based on the employees, their positions, their titles, and their access privileges.

3. Roles are then created to reflect the individual access pattern that employees within the organization use to perform their jobs, as reflected in Step 2.

4. Roles are then assigned IAM policies to control their access. A rule of thumb here is to follow PoLP by providing access only to the bare minimum resources and actions to each role.

5. Finally, individual users are allowed to assume these roles, whereas direct access to resources (without using roles) is disabled for all users.

Figure 2-9 illustrates this process of role modeling and compares the access patterns before and after an implementation of RBAC.

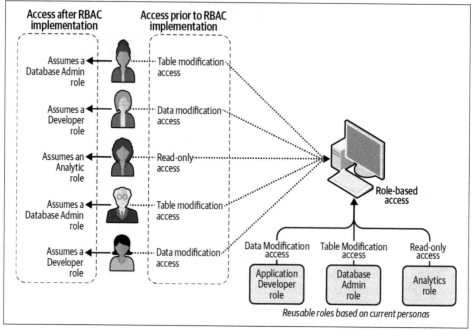

*Figure 2-9. How an organization can transition from user-based access to role-based access by modeling the user access patterns into roles.*

After completing the RBAC model, access to resources for each user should be restricted through roles rather than direct access.

 RBAC can be useful only if the PoLP is applied within the organization. Overly permissive roles may compromise the security of the application. On the other hand, excessively restrictive roles may deter legitimate users from doing their jobs.

## Securing Roles

Assuming your application has already implemented the roles required for every employee and microservice in the organization, the next step is to allow these principals to assume these roles. AWS has many ways that users or other services can assume the roles necessary to accomplish what they need to do. Under the hood, AWS uses the AWS Security Token Service (AWS STS) to support all these methods of switching roles. For a principal to be able to switch roles, there needs to be an IAM policy attached to it that allows the principal to call the `AssumeRole` action on STS:

```
{
  "Version": "2012-10-17",
  "Statement": {
    "Effect": "Allow",
    "Action": "sts:AssumeRole",
    "Resource": "arn:aws:iam::ACCOUNT-ID-WITHOUT-HYPHENS:role/<Role>"
  }
}
```

In addition, IAM roles can also have a special type of a resource-based policy attached to them, called an *IAM role trust policy*. An IAM role trust policy can be written just like any other resource-based policy, by specifying the principals that are allowed to assume the role in question:

```
{
  "Version": "2012-10-17",
  "Statement": [
    {
      "Effect": "Allow",
      "Principal": {
        "AWS": "arn:aws:iam::<accountid>:user/<username>"
      },
      "Action": "sts:AssumeRole",
    }
  ]
}
```

Any principal that is allowed to access a role is called a *trusted entity* for that role. A trusted entity can also be added to a role through the AWS Management Console by specifying it in the Trust relationships tab on the Roles page within the Identity and Access Management setup, as seen in Figure 2-10.

> IAM role trust policy is like any other resource-based policy and allows principals to be from external accounts. Assuming a role within the current account is a great way of sharing access to AWS resources across accounts in a controlled way.

*Figure 2-10. New principals can be added into the resource policy for IAM roles by editing the trust relationships of the role.*

 As with any policy evaluation, trust relationships and identity-based IAM policies are evaluated simultaneously when a user attempts to assume a role with IAM. To succeed in assuming a role, both these policies should allow the action to proceed. The user will not be able to assume the role if either of these policies leads to a denial.

## Assuming Roles

I have already mentioned that the process of assuming a role involves the use of AWS STS behind the scenes. Assuming a role involves requesting a temporary set of credentials from AWS that can be used in future requests. Figure 2-11 shows two users, Bob and Alice, attempting to assume a role (Role A) using AWS STS. Bob is not specified in the trust policy for Role A while Alice is.

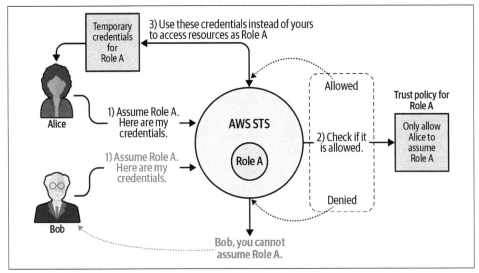

*Figure 2-11. AWS STS is used to issue temporary credentials to any user specified within the trust policy of the role that tries to assume that role.*

Root users are not allowed to assume roles using AWS STS. `AssumeRole` must be called with credentials for an IAM user or a role.

Roles allow access to resources. This is how roles are used to access resources:

1. IAM checks whether a user is allowed to make an STS request to assume a role.

2. A user makes a request to AWS STS to assume a particular role and get temporary credentials.

3. AWS STS checks with IAM to ensure that the target role allows the calling principal to assume this role in the trust policy of the target role.

4. The calling principal exchanges its own identity in return for temporary credentials of the target role.

Figure 2-12 illustrates this evaluation flow.

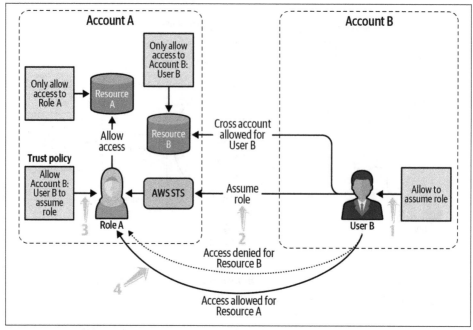

*Figure 2-12. AWS STS allows users from either the same or external accounts to exchange their identities for that of a role in a target account.*

In the event that the assumed role has access to a particular resource, the calling identity can access the resource in question by using the temporary credentials that it has of the assumed role. In Figure 2-12, because Role A has access to Resource A, User B can access Resource A by assuming Role A.

 Giving up original credentials and access while assuming roles may be problematic for certain use cases—such as where one role with access to one AWS S3 bucket would like to copy or compare files with another bucket that allows access only to a different role. In such situations, using resource-based policies to allow access to both buckets for such a role may be the best solution.

As the same user may access resources in different roles, it is sometimes difficult to remember the exact identity used to access a particular resource. You can find out which identity is being used when interacting with AWS through the AWS CLI.

If you run the following command, AWS will inform you of the user's current identity, as you can see in Figure 2-13. It could be a user or a role that you may have assumed:

```
aws sts get-caller-identity
```

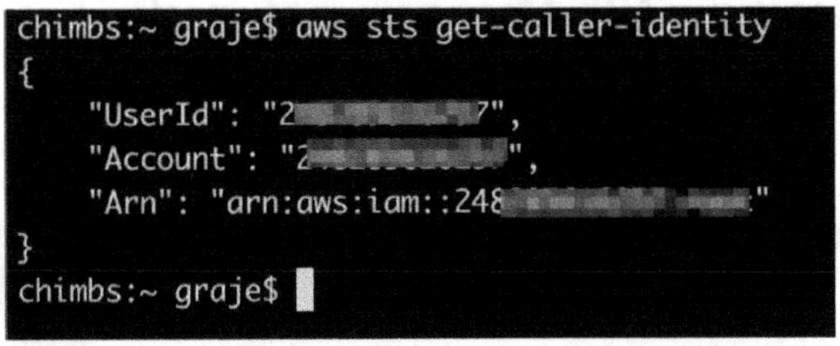

```
chimbs:~ graje$ aws sts get-caller-identity
{
    "UserId": "2       7",
    "Account": "2          ",
    "Arn": "arn:aws:iam::248           "
}
chimbs:~ graje$
```

*Figure 2-13. A call to sts get-caller-identity will return the current user ID, account ID, and the ARN of the identity of the current session.*

## Assume Roles Using the AWS Command-Line Interface (CLI)

The AWS CLI can be used to assume a role using AWS STS by running the following command:

```
aws sts assume-role --role-arn arn:aws:iam::123456789012:role/targetrole
  --role-session-name assumed-role-session
```

AWS responds to such requests by issuing temporary credentials that the caller can use to access AWS resources:

```
{
    "AssumedRoleUser": {
        "AssumedRoleId": "AXAISKDJSALA:assumed-role-session",
        "Arn":
          "arn:aws:sts::123456789012:assumed-role/
          targetrole/assumed-role-session"
    },
    "Credentials": {
        "SecretAccessKey": "9drTJvcXLB89EXAMPLELB8923FB892xMFI",
        "SessionToken": "AQoXdzELDDY//////////
        wEaoAK1wvxJY12r2IrDFT2IvAzTCn3zHoZ7YNtpiQLF0MqZye/
        qwjzP2iEXAMPLEbw/m3hsj8VBTkPORGvr9jM5sgP+w9IZWZnU+LWhmg+a5f
        Di2oTGUYcdg9uexQ4mtCHIHfi4citgqZTgco40Yqr4lIlo4V2b2Dyauk0eY
        FNebHtYlFVgAUj+7Indz3LU0aTWk1WKIjHmmMCIoTkyYp/k7kUG7moeEYKS
        itwQIi6Gjn+nyzM+PtoA3685ixzv0R7i5rjQi0YE0lf1oeie3bDiNHncmzo
        sRM6SFiPzSvp6h/32xQuZsjcypmwsPSDtTPYcs0+YN/8BRi2/IcrxSpnWEX
        AMPLEXSDFTAQAM6Dl9zR0tXoybnlrZIwMLlMi1Kcgo5OytwU=",
        "Expiration": "2016-03-15T00:05:07Z",
        "AccessKeyId": "ASIAJEXAMPLEXEG2JICEA"
    }
}
```

Temporary credentials are used for the same reasons as regular credentials, except that they expire after a certain date and time, and they are tied to a session. The credentials in the response can be used to access other resources.

## Switching Roles Using AWS Management Console

AWS allows users to switch to roles that the current logged-in user has access to, right through the AWS Management Console, as shown in Figure 2-14 and 2-15.

*Figure 2-14. A new role can be added to the list of roles that the logged user can switch to by selecting Switch Roles.*

*Figure 2-15. To add a new role, you can add the role name and account ID as well as a convenient nickname to the form; AWS will switch the console to the newly assumed identity of the role in the target account.*

Now that you can set up roles for everyone in your organization and ask users to assume roles to access resources, your IAM policies should be much cleaner, since each access can now be tied to a role instead of individual users. This also helps in decoupling user identities from their function within the application.

## Service-Linked Role

In a microservice environment, least privilege should be applied to the roles that microservices assume in order to run on the cloud infrastructure. To make this process easier, AWS allows the creation of a service-linked role for certain supported services. A service-linked role has its policies and statements prewritten by AWS. All service-linked roles are predefined by the service that assumes these roles. They include all the permissions that the assuming service needs to make calls to other AWS services. Service-linked roles can be created from the command line using the following command:

```
aws iam create-service-linked-role --aws-service-name <service name>
```

The service name in this case can be looked up in the AWS documentation (*https://oreil.ly/lhrIj*).

# Authentication and Identity Management

So far, it has been assumed that AWS knew the user's identity, without explaining how it could be accomplished. Access control tried to limit the amount of damage a known identity could inflict on a system. As long as AWS is aware of the real identity of the user, access control works effectively. But for an access control system, what makes you *you*? What should it base its decision on? Is it the way you look? Is it the identity card you possess that says who you are? This section shows the various ways in which this initial identity can be established, proven, and secured so that the rest of IAM is able to successfully apply controls around threats pertaining to unauthorized access.

---

### Basics of Identity

For microservices, the concept of identities can get a little complex. It may be desirable to identify a cluster of services that provide the same microservice with a common identity, even if they are running on different servers (and sometimes even in different regions). On the other hand, multiple users can interact with the same resources using the same workstation, so identifying each user uniquely may be required for the purpose of access control.

For the purpose of access control in information systems, the identity of a user is made up of three aspects, or basic building blocks:

---

*Entitlements*

Rights or privileges granted to a user for the purpose of performing their tasks. These may be due to their job positions, group membership, or something else. For example, Sruthi, who works for the finance department within your organization, may have full access to all the accounting databases simply due to the fact that she works in the finance department. To protect against unauthorized access, the system needs to make sure that Sruthi is part of the finance department. In fact, if I join the finance department, I may automatically gain this access as well, because of my position.

*Attributes*

Unlike entitlements, attributes are acquired over the lifetime of the identity. These may either be granted by administrators or be acquired by performing certain actions. Rather than being a right of the employee, the administrator grants attributes on a temporary basis, and they may be revoked easily. Anyone in your organization with a security clearance, for example, may be able to access sensitive data. To protect against unauthorized access, the system needs to ensure that the attributes are protected against tampering or spoofing. Therefore, George, who does not possess a security clearance, shouldn't be able to fool your access control system into believing he does.

*Traits*

Traits are inherent features of the subject. These may include biological features or any other identity information that belongs to the user, which access control systems may use to grant access. For example, if your building's security manager knows you personally, you may be able to enter your building without showing an access card since the security manager is able to identify you based on your physical appearance.

An access control system may use one or more of these aspects of your identity to enable you to perform tasks or prevent you from completing them. For example, when you buy alcohol from a liquor store, you may be asked to provide proof of age in the form of a driver's license. Your driver's license is an *attribute* that was granted to you by your local government. You have an *entitlement* to purchase alcohol because you are older than the minimum legal drinking age (that is, you belong to the group of people who are allowed to purchase alcohol). The picture on your driver's license matches your face, allowing the store to verify your identity—this is the *trait* aspect of your identity. As seen, all three aspects of your identity work together with one another to allow you to buy alcohol.

Identities are said to have been compromised if a malicious actor or an imposter is able to gain access to systems using the identity of a legitimate user.

# Basics of Authentication

Maintaining the integrity of identities ensures that access control systems can prevent unauthorized access by using these identities. For example, to prevent minors from purchasing alcohol, a liquor store may require every customer to show their driver's license (attribute). It is possible to have strong security guards to ensure that people without such a document cannot buy alcohol. However, if it were easy to fabricate a fake driver's license, minors could easily circumvent the access control system by creating fake proof of age, thus making such a system useless. It is the job of an authentication system to ensure that a compromise of identities is prevented. In the case of driver's licenses, this may mean the introduction of 3D holograms or computerized scanners that ensure the integrity of the document.

Authentication is the process of establishing confidence in user identities presented to an electronic system. An authenticating user or service must perform certain actions that your AWS account believes can only be performed by that particular user in order to establish their identity. In the case of AWS, these actions can be roughly classified into three buckets:

*Authentication using knowledge factors*
> In this bucket, AWS requires the user to prove knowledge of a secret that only a legitimate user is supposed to know. Typing in a password, using a passphrase, answering a security question, or using any secret pin code are all examples of knowledge factors.

*Authentication using a possession factor*
> In this one, AWS requires the user to prove the possession of an item that only that user may be in possession of. This might include the user's cellphone or a physical hardware authentication device (such as a YubiKey or a Google Titan key).

*Authentication using federated authentication*
> Instead of the AWS taking on the responsibility for authentication, a different system is designated to perform the checks. This enables an organization's existing authentication process to be reused. With federated authentication, AWS can delegate authentication tasks to established systems within the organization, such as Active Directory or any other mechanisms that the organization may already be using for registering identities.

 In most secure organizations, a possession factor is used in addition to any of the other mechanisms to add an extra layer of security. This is known as multifactor authentication (MFA). Throughout this book, I will keep insisting on the importance of using MFA.

# Identity Federation on AWS

A strong password requirement on the AWS Management Console is a good start to securing your cloud infrastructure, but the added liability of requiring users to keep their login credentials could result in friction within organizations. This may be further aggravated by having stricter password policies for IAM credentials. Employees may already have corporate identities within most companies, so requiring them to create new accounts on AWS (with strong password policies) could simply increase friction among employees.

AWS gives organizations the ability to integrate AWS Identity Services into their own identity management systems. This system of delegating the authentication aspect of AWS to a trusted third-party system is called *identity federation*. The key to federated identities is the fact that you have two identity providers—your on-premises system and AWS IAM—and the two providers agree to link their identities to each other (for more on this, see Chris Dotson's book *Practical Cloud Security* (O'Reilly) (*https:// oreil.ly/0JXCh*)). The third-party system that performs the actual identity check on behalf of AWS is called an *identity provider (IdP)*.

There are many ways to perform identity federation. Most involve the use of RBAC to map external third-party identities to established roles within the AWS account and allowing these third-party identities to exchange their credentials for an AWS role.

There are many ways of achieving identity federation, but they all follow a common theme (highlighted in Figure 2-16). Let us assume a user wishes to access a resource within AWS called Target Resource using federated identity. The on-premises system already has all of the users' identifiers. This system is the IdP and is capable of determining the levels of privilege or the role that this user should be allowed to assume to perform their task with the minimum privilege.

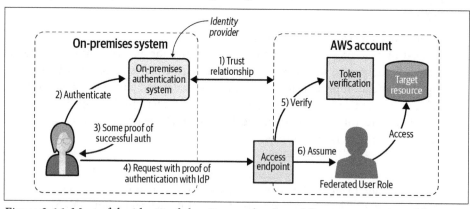

*Figure 2-16. Most of the identity federation mechanisms follow some version of this abstract flow when it comes to authenticating requests from federated identity sources.*

This is the flow shown in Figure 2-16:

1. The external identity management system will set up some sort of a trust relationship with an AWS account.

2. A user who wishes to access the target resource first authenticates with the on-premises system. (This on-premises system can use whatever combinations of factors it chooses to ensure the identity of the calling user.)

3. The on-premises authentication system responds with some form of an assurance that it believes will be able to convince AWS of a successful validation. AWS on its end is able to look at this token and determine its validity.

4. The user uses this token to make a request to AWS by saying, "Here is my request along with the assurance that I have been authenticated by the IdP that you agreed to trust."

5. AWS verifies the identity of the token (or the assertion that is present in the token) to ensure that the user is indeed validated by the IdP.

6. Upon verification, the end user can now exchange their identity within their target account for an AWS role, much like what was discussed in "Role-Based Access Control" on page 52. As opposed to being an external AWS account user that is authenticated by AWS, in this case the user is authenticated by a third-party system that you have instructed AWS to trust. Since the target role has access to the "target resource," the end user can access the target resource using the identity of the role it just assumed.

## Identity Federation Using SAML 2.0 and OpenID Connect

Security Assertion Markup Language (SAML) 2.0 is one of the most common standards used in exchanging identities between security domains. Many third-party IdPs are fully compliant with SAML 2.0; hence, being able to integrate with SAML allows your organization a wide array of third-party authentication providers.

Appendix B shows a hands-on example of integrating with a third-party SAML provider. If you're interested in setting up federated IdPs, you will find the exercise very worthwhile.

OpenId Connect (OIDC) is another tool you can use to add a trusted IdP to your AWS account. OIDC is built on top of OAuth 2.0 and allows AWS to verify the identity of the end user based on an HTTP-based exchange. Like SAML, OIDC also allows federated users to exchange their existing external identity for the purpose of assuming a role within their target AWS account. This role can be made to reflect the policy of least privilege and all the concepts discussed in "RBAC Modeling" on page 53.

This way, using either a SAML- or an OIDC-based IdP, AWS allows for the delegation of authentication to your existing IdPs, thus reducing the number of login credentials that your employees may have to keep track of.

 Because AWS trusts IdPs for authentication, it is important that the IdP that is used for authentication adhere to security best practices. This may include choosing strong password policies, enforcing MFA on users, and reviewing access regularly to eliminate users who no longer need access to AWS resources.

# RBAC and Microservices

This chapter has laid the foundation for IAM for any cloud system on AWS. IAM roles, authentication, and policies allow you to build secure microservices. Nevertheless, given that microservice applications have a greater number of services running and interacting with one another, it's likely that your IAM policies will grow complicated if you aren't careful. I would like to talk a little about some of the cloud infrastructure's architecture elements that you can leverage in order to preserve the complexity of a microservice application.

To start, I will assume that your application has a clean separation of services based on domain design. As a result, each microservice within your application is focused on a specific business responsibility. Given that the service is neatly aligned with business-level objectives, it may be easier to define the service in terms of a business role. RBAC can be a good approach for implementing access control for such use cases.

In most microservice applications, you can perform the exercise of role modeling on these services. You will have to document all the ways in which each of your services accesses AWS resources and assign roles according to the permissions required for such access, based on the contexts of these requests. With the exception of tying each role to a service instead of to an employee, role modeling done on microservices is very similar to it being done with employees.

So, after a successful implementation of RBAC, you can assume that each of your microservices can be mapped to a role that will have the right level of access within your infrastructure. By applying the PoLP to this role, you can ensure that your microservices will never stray from their defined roles.

# Execution Roles

Many supported AWS services run by assuming a certain default role called an execution role. These roles can be created identical to roles that users assume. RBAC brings in a huge advantage to microservices that I will demonstrate with an example. Let's say you have a microservice that is running a certain application that requires access to a certain sensitive cloud resource (say, a database). You may have multiple cloud environments where your service can be deployed. In a staging environment, you may have a database that has certain staged data, while in a production environment, you may have actual customer data.

Before execution roles and cloud deployments, access control used to be controlled primarily with passwords or other authentication mechanisms. These passwords either used to live alongside application code in the form of encrypted config files or needed access to other third-party configuration management services, adding to the complexity of the application. This problem is mitigated by the implementation of execution roles. All you need to do is create a role that has access to the database and make this role the execution role of your deployed microservice. The application code will now attempt to access the cloud resource by assuming that the role it runs as has the required access. If the code is deployed to the production environment, it will run by assuming the production role. Simply assuming this role gives this microservice the ability to access the production data without needing any separate authentication logic. In a similar vein, deploying the same service to a staging environment can give access to the staging database. Figure 2-17 illustrates this.

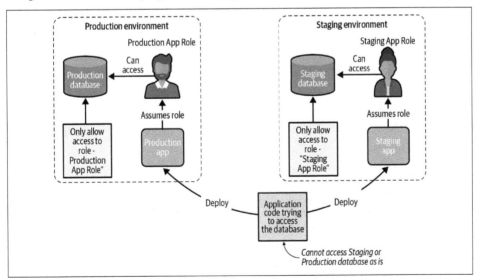

*Figure 2-17. Execution roles simplify the process of authenticating against cloud resources since you can use their identities (roles) in place of passwords.*

In such a setup, developers focus on writing business logic while security professionals can sharpen the execution roles to apply least privilege, clearly separating the duties. Application logic is never made aware of any security or access rules, making the process extremely elegant. Hence, it is a best practice for applications running microservices to use roles to access cloud resources rather than passwords, which may bring in concerns with respect to maintainability. Based on the type of microservices you're running for your organization, let's look at how to get microservices to assume these roles.

## RBAC with AWS Lambda

We'll start off with AWS Lambda functions since they require the least amount of effort in setting up. For serverless microservices using AWS Lambda, it is possible to specify the execution role while creating an AWS Lambda function. As seen in Figure 2-18, you can either create a new role or use an existing role while creating the Lambda function.

*Figure 2-18. You have the choice of either creating a role or specifying an existing role for Lambda execution.*

Using an execution role, it is easy to design an entire microservice application running on AWS Lambda with clean access control logic that doesn't violate the PoLP, since each Lambda function will have a role associated with it. As mentioned earlier in "Execution Roles" on page 67 any code deployed to a Lambda will already have assumed the execution role that was specified while creating the Lambda. To achieve clean access control, you merely need to grant this role access to any sensitive resource in the correct context. You can reuse your code across multiple environments by using different roles across different environments.

# RBAC with EC2 and the Instance Metadata Service

All AWS Lambdas come with an execution role, and if all of your microservices run on AWS Lambda, you may be lucky enough to get great RBAC without a lot of heavy lifting. But not everyone is as lucky, and chances are you may have different AWS compute services backing your microservice architecture. Let's consider AWS Elastic Cloud Compute (EC2), since it's one of the most popular compute engines.

Multiple applications may run on EC2 instances, unlike AWS Lambdas where functions run on their own. With AWS, your applications running on top of EC2 can use a slightly modified version of AWS Lambda's execution roles for gaining access to cloud resources called the *instance metadata service (IMDS)*.

On AWS, you can run an EC2 instance and attach a role to the running instance. Figure 2-19 shows an example of such an instance being created.

*Figure 2-19. IAM roles can be assigned to EC2 instances during their creation in the Configure Instance Details step.*

Every Amazon EC2 instance is equipped with the IMDS service, which allows applications running on top of these instances to access and find more information about their runtime environments. The role assigned to the EC2 instance is within this information. Through the IMDS, applications are able to access information such as their AWS access secret key and their AWS access key ID. The role-specific security credentials are used to grant the application access to the actions and resources you have assigned to the role. These security credentials are temporarily rotated automatically. So when you write your microservices and deploy them onto EC2 instances, the following steps happen:

1. The application contains no information around its identity. However, you can configure it to query the IMDS to find out about its identity.

2. Upon being queried, the IMDS can then respond with the identity of the execution role that the EC2 instance runs as.

3. Applications running on EC2 can use the temporary credentials that IMDS returns, thus assuming the execution role.

4. The applications can make requests to the resources using the temporary credentials returned in Step 3.

This way, applications can run without the need to have any secrets or config files within their code and rely solely on the IMDS to provide identity and access, as seen in Figure 2-20.

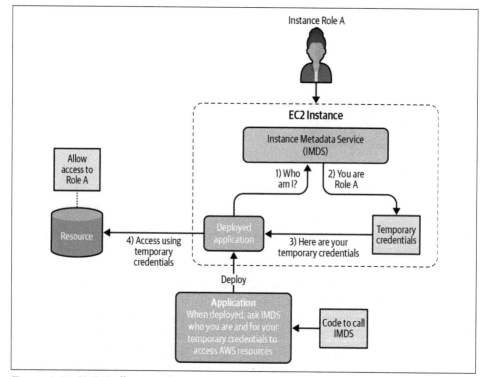

*Figure 2-20. IMDS allows applications to access the temporary credentials of the role that is attached to the EC2 instance.*

You can query IMDS by making a simple HTTP curl request to the endpoint *http://169.254.169.254/latest.*

So, if you have an application running on EC2, you can make the following request:

```
TOKEN=`curl -X PUT "http://169.254.169.254/latest/api/token"
    -H "X-aws-ec2-metadata-token-ttl-seconds: 21600"` \
    && curl -H "X-aws-ec2-metadata-token: $TOKEN" -v
    http://169.254.169.254/latest/meta-data/iam/security-credentials/
        s3access
```

This request returns an output similar to this:

```
{
    "Code" : "Success",
    "LastUpdated" : "2012-04-26T16:39:16Z",
    "Type" : "AWS-HMAC",
    "AccessKeyId" : "ASIAIOSFODNN7EXAMPLE",
    "SecretAccessKey" : "wJalrXUtnFEMI/K7MDENG/bPxRfiCYEXAMPLEKEY",
    "Token" : "token",
    "Expiration" : "2017-05-17T15:09:54Z"
}
```

Now that your application has the AWS access key ID and the AWS secret access key, you can use AWS STS to assume any role it wishes to and thus get access to resources that it wants, very similar to the way AWS Lambda does.

This means your code can assume a role on any environment of your choice. Depending on where it is deployed, it can call the IMDS and assume the role that the environment wants it to assume. Through IMDS, your applications can securely make API requests from your instances without having to manage the security credentials within the application code.

## RBAC with Amazon EKS Using IAM Roles for Service Accounts

IMDS works with EC2 instances, so any service running on EC2 can use RBAC to gain access to AWS resources. If each EC2 instance in your microservice application hosted only one service at a time, this design would work flawlessly for your use. However, if multiple applications run on top of the same EC2 instance, they will be tied to the same underlying instance's IAM role, making it harder to implement PoLP.

This is especially true for services running containerized microservices applications such as those running on AWS Elastic Kubernetes Service (EKS) nodes on EC2 instances. Containerized applications are known to have deployment transparency. Having the IAM role of the underlying node tied to each microservice makes sharing instances insecure from a security standpoint because multiple different microservices share the same instance. This means the resulting role is a union of all the permissions required by the underlying services. Since each service will have extra access, this goes against PoLP.

To make matters worse, Kubernetes also has its own RBAC mechanism where users are granted access based on Kubernetes identities and roles. So, in such a system, you have two sets of identities. On the Kubernetes side, you have the Kubernetes role bindings that may allow access to pods or users depending on your Kubernetes config. On the AWS side, you have IAM roles that you would like to utilize to control access to cloud resources such as AWS S3 buckets.

If this problem of having two separate identities in two different systems sounds familiar, you're right. It's very similar to the problem faced by organizations using multiple authentication mechanisms. I talked in depth about how identity federation helped resolve such a problem, and to synchronize identities between Kubernetes and AWS I recommend a similar approach.

In their words (*https://oreil.ly/4dqgB*), AWS decided to make Kubernetes pods first-class citizens in AWS. With Kubernetes service account annotations and OIDC identity providers, you can assign IAM roles to individual pods and use roles the same way you did with AWS Lambda. Figure 2-21 shows how IAM roles for service accounts (IRSA) works when a microservice running on a pod would like to access an AWS resource by assuming an AWS role.

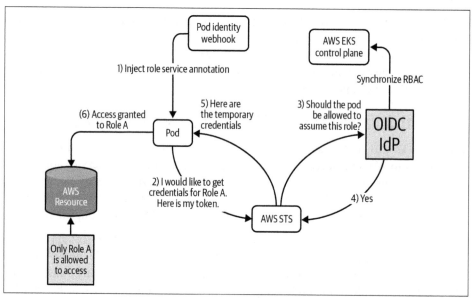

*Figure 2-21. Using IRSA, pods can use OIDC IdP and AWS STS to assume roles and access AWS resources without being tied to the underlying node.*

Let's examine this more closely:

1. Each pod starts with an annotation (*https://oreil.ly/wvoe3*) about a service account along with a token that it can use to exchange with AWS STS in return for a role within your organization. This is done by mutating the pod with information that EKS injects into it through the mutating webhook. It also injects the web identity token file that the pod can use to identify itself to an OIDC IdP in Step 2.

2. To fetch the credentials, the pod makes a request to AWS STS to assume the identity of the role along with the service account token that was injected in Step 1. This token will be exchanged in order to get temporary authentication credentials with AWS.

3. AWS STS makes a request to the OIDC IdP to verify the validity of the request.

4. OIDC IdP responds with an affirmative response.

5. AWS STS responds with temporary credentials that the pod can use to access AWS resources using the role that it wanted to use.

6. The pod accesses the AWS resource using the temporary credentials provided to it by AWS STS.

By creating roles and assigning those roles to pods, IRSA also provides RBAC for Kubernetes pods. Once assigned to pods, these roles can be used to design access control using RBAC similar to how execution roles were used with AWS Lambda.

# Summary

Authorization and authentication are the two most important controls that security architects have for reducing the aggregate risk of any secure system. Getting a good grasp on both of these mechanisms will help every security architect design better systems. Since microservices are made up of modular services that have a very specific purpose for their existence, it is easier for security architects to frame the security policies around microservices using the PoLP. The security policies can be added to the AWS IAM, a service specifically designed for providing identity management services. On AWS, authorization and authentication generally provide you with the most comprehensive and granular protection against potential threats when combined with encryption controls. This interplay between authorization, authentication, and encryption will be covered in great detail in Chapter 3.

# Foundations of Encryption

Cloud resources are backed by physical infrastructure that is often shared among multiple clients. AWS resources and data can be isolated by either restricting unauthorized access to them (*authorization* or *access control*) or by encoding sensitive information into a format that can be read only by its intended audience (*encryption*). In most cases, both are combined to secure user data, which is why encryption is an essential topic in cloud security. Ideas discussed in this chapter are not specific to microservices, but they will provide a general overview of security in the cloud. Later chapters will apply concepts covered here to different use cases that focus on microservices.

I have already introduced you to the CIA triad (*https://oreil.ly/ORJKw*) of information security impact. Encryption provides protection against a specific class of potential threats where malicious actors either want to read sensitive data (thus affecting the *confidentiality* of the data) or want to alter the content of this data (thus affecting the *integrity* of the data) without having the right access.

Users require a key to read encrypted data, even if they have already been authenticated and authorized.

 Encryption can serve as a great *fail secure (https://csrc.nist.gov/glos sary/term/fail_secure)* mechanism in secure systems. When other threat-prevention controls such as authentication and authorization fail, encryption protects your sensitive data from being read or modified by unauthorized users who don't have access to the encryption key.

To use security terminology, encryption protects your data by identifying its intended user using a *knowledge factor* (a specific attribute that only the intended recipient should be aware of). In this case, the encryption key is the knowledge factor. A cryptographic algorithm assumes that a key is known by only those who are permitted to read this data.

# Brief Overview of Encryption

Here are definitions for some terms that I will use for the rest of the chapter:

*Plaintext item*
> This is the file or item that you want to encrypt. *Plaintext* means that this item can be read by either a human or a machine. Here, I use the term *item* to denote that the target may not always be a file and could be anything from a row in a database to an image or a binary large object (blob).

*Data key (plaintext data key)*
> This is the input to an algorithm (similar to a password) that is used to encrypt the information present in the plaintext.

*Ciphertext item*
> This is the encrypted data that is stored on the AWS system. This data cannot be read in a meaningful way (by a human or by a machine) without being decrypted first.

In simple terms, Figure 3-1 shows the process of encryption and decryption.

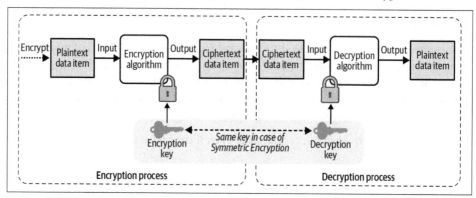

*Figure 3-1. How encryption works.*

So to encrypt something you need two things:

- The plaintext item
- An encryption key that will be used to encrypt or decrypt this item

If the same key that is used during the encryption process is used for decrypting the ciphertext, the encryption is called *symmetric encryption*. In this case, it is the responsibility of the encryptor to securely and separately transmit the key to the receiver. If a different key is used for decrypting the ciphertext, the encryption is called *asymmetric encryption.*

## Why Is Encryption Important on AWS?

The short answer is the concept of *defense in depth* as I discussed in Chapter 1—multiple redundant defenses are better than a single all-powerful defense against potential threats.

As you already might be aware, nothing is physically isolated on the AWS environment. Your storage or computing resources are shared with other cloud customers. A cloud computing provider, by definition, assumes responsibility for protecting and isolating sensitive data for their customers. Although AWS provides its own guarantees with regard to the logical isolation of your data and services, it is always in your best interest to have additional layers of protection on the data you hand over to the cloud provider. Hence, locking your sensitive data (in the form of encryption) with a key that only you have access to will ensure that your data is protected logically from unauthorized access when it is handed over to AWS. In this way, our inability to physically control data access is compensated for by the logical isolation we gain from encryption.

## Why Is Encryption Important for Microservice Architectures?

Now that I have mentioned why encryption is so important on AWS, it can be quite easy to see why microservices take the need for encryption a step further. The basic value proposition behind microservices has been the modularity and the isolation they offer to your entire architecture. Instead of having one giant application where the data is shared by multiple identities, microservices encourage you to partition your application based on business domains. Security strategies like the zero trust network strategy draw their strength from your ability to modularize and isolate these modules. In physical environments, this would have been easy to achieve. Think of traditional data centers where you could have simply provisioned storage for different bounded contexts in different physical rooms within the data centers and possibly locked these rooms up with state-of-the-art security. On cloud environments, encryption is the best bet you have to make this isolation reliable. Encrypting different sources of data with different encryption keys gives you the same benefits that locked rooms provided in physical data centers.

## Encryption on AWS

Government organizations such as the National Institute of Standards and Technology (NIST) frequently standardize open source algorithms. Many regulatory bodies rely on the expertise of the NIST when it comes to formulating security policies. As a result, replacing existing cryptographic algorithms with their own (even if a newer algorithm may be more secure) is not a path AWS can take if it wants its clients to continue to maintain regulatory compliance. More importantly, writing your own cryptographic algorithm is never a good idea, in my opinion, even for companies as big as Amazon, since it can easily create security vulnerabilities. AWS does provide users with tools that support existing standardized cryptographic procedures. These tools make the process of encryption and all the activities surrounding the encryption process simple and secure. This includes the process of public key sharing, access control for the secret keys, key rotation, and key storage.

AWS supports both types of common encryption algorithms, symmetric as well as asymmetric, for most common use cases.

## Security Challenges with Key-Based Encryption

In a cryptosystem, the encrypted data is considered secure up to the point where a malicious actor is not aware of the decryption key. Therefore, the burden of protecting the data lies in securing the decryption key. If we are to assume that all the other information about the system is already public knowledge, knowledge of the key may be the only thing that stands in the way of an attacker getting their hands on sensitive data.

A good principle to keep in mind while designing a cryptosystem is Kerckhoffs's principle: a cryptosystem should be secure even if everything about the design of the system, *except* the encryption key, is public knowledge. An analogy is that of physical locks. The fact that everyone has the same brand of lock as yours doesn't mean they can open yours without the key.

Considering the key's importance to the decryption process, securing access to it becomes an important aspect of maintaining data security. In addition, the ability to monitor access to this key is vital for detecting unusual activity. Also, periodically rotating a key will reduce the possibility that it decrypts sensitive data and causes security issues if it is leaked.

In a microservice application, across different contexts there may be hundreds of items to encrypt, all with separate encryption keys, creating an organizational nightmare. Security breaches, disgruntled employees, phishing software, and other security threats are harder to monitor or prevent if the complexity of the application is high.

## Business Problem

Let's say you need a centralized platform that holds the encryption keys for all of your microservices. This platform is highly available and accessible by each of your microservices.

Suppose you have two services, Service A and Service B, and AWS Key Management Service (KMS). Service A wants to send encrypted data to Service B. Service A can authenticate with the KMS. Once authenticated, Service A wants to ensure that the key used to encrypt and decrypt this information is only available to Service B. Once Service A encrypts data, it transmits it to Service B. Service B can now call the KMS to decrypt it.

Therefore, KMS acts as some sort of wrapper around the key to provide standardized authentication and access control. In this scenario, even if a third party were to gain access to this encrypted data, it could not decrypt it as long as your KMS ensures that the only two parties with access to this key are Service A and Service B. Figure 3-2 illustrates this flow.

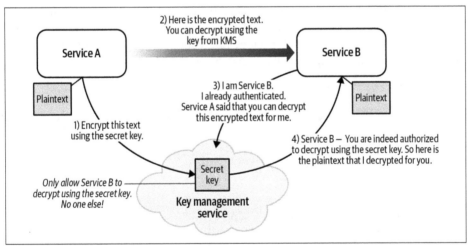

*Figure 3-2. Sharing encryption keys using a key management service.*

# AWS Key Management Service

In the past, safeguarding the key involved the purchase of a hardware security module (HSM), which provided a fail secure (*https://oreil.ly/ZCQHg*) way of keeping this key safe. The prohibitively high cost of acquiring an HSM meant most small organizations ended up thinking twice before making such an investment. However, through AWS KMS, organizations can avail the advantage of an HSM without the high capital investment. AWS KMS is the set of utilities AWS provides to safeguard this encryption key. AWS KMS is backed by an HSM that is maintained and secured for you by AWS as part of the AWS Shared Responsibility Model (SRM). With KMS, you can keep a log and an audit trail of all the actions performed with the key, whether it's for encryption, decryption, or simple access. It enables you to pinpoint and record who has tried to access your data—intruder or otherwise.

You can use AWS KMS to encrypt data blobs of small sizes using the AES-256 encryption algorithm. KMS is a managed service that makes it easy for you to create, manage, and control *customer master keys* (CMKs).

With AWS KMS, you get the following:

- A safe and durable place to store the CMK
- Access control for the CMK
- High availability for the CMK

## Basic Encryption Using CMK

If the size of the data to be encrypted is small (less than 4 KB), AWS KMS can be used to directly encrypt or decrypt it using the AES-256 algorithm. I will talk about how you can encrypt larger items in "Envelope Encryption" on page 82. Figure 3-3 shows the basic flow of encrypting a small payload using a CMK.

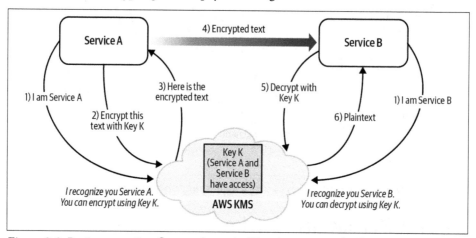

*Figure 3-3. Basic encryption flow as shown in "Envelope Encryption" on page 82. Figure 3-2 using the CMK implemented using AWS KMS*

Payloads of size less than 4 KB can be encrypted this way. With larger payloads, envelope encryption can be used (don't worry; more on that later). The process of securing the CMK is the same with either type of encryption.

Here are the steps, shown in Figure 3-3, for how AWS KMS makes the process I just described so elegant and smooth:

1. We can assume Service A and Service B have authenticated with our AWS setup. A CMK is created inside AWS KMS and access is granted to Service A and Service B.

2. Service A decides to encrypt the data it wants to send to Service B, so it makes an encryption request to AWS KMS.

3. KMS notices that Service A has already authenticated with an auth provider that it trusts and has access to Key K. Hence, it encrypts the data with K and responds with the encrypted text.

4. Service A transmits this encrypted text to Service B, which it receives.

5. Service B asks AWS KMS to decrypt the text.

6. KMS notices that Service B has already authenticated with an auth provider that it trusts and has access to K. Hence, it decrypts the data with K and responds with the plaintext.

If a third party—say, Service C—gets access to the encrypted data and tries to get the decryption key from AWS KMS, KMS will realize it has no access to the data and turn away any such unauthorized requests as part of Step 6.

Two important aspects of the encryption process that keep data safe are worth noting:

- Whenever the CMK is secure from unauthorized access, sensitive data can be considered safe since an attacker will not be able to decrypt it unless the CMK is present.

- If access to the CMK is granted to a service, the service will then be able to decrypt the encrypted text (also called *ciphertext*).

There was no communication of the plaintext key between the two services, but rather each of them had access to the same key in the cloud, which made our encryption process so strong. As part of the SRM, AWS guarantees high availability of the keys, so you don't have to worry about the key server going down or your authentication process failing.

## AES-256 and its Keyspace

For a cryptographic algorithm, a *keyspace* is defined as all the possible values that a key belonging to that algorithm may have. An algorithm with a larger and more randomized keyspace is naturally better at protecting your assets since it is harder to guess the encryption key through brute force algorithms.

It is estimated (*https://oreil.ly/pUQOG*) that the world's fastest supercomputer (as of 2018), Sunway TaihuLight, will need 27,337,893,038, 406,611,194, 430,009,974, 922,940,323,611,067,429,756,962,487 years (27 trillion trillion trillion trillion trillion years) to brute-force each of the keys present in the keyspace for AES-256, the algorithm used by AWS-KMS.

Basic encryption using KMS is restricted for very small chunks of data or for extremely basic situations where throughput and latency issues are not a problem. For almost anything else, envelope encryption is what will be used. Envelope encryption builds on top of the basic encryption services that KMS provides us, so I will introduce KMS first.

> Whereas KMS has high availability, KMS has an account-wide throughput restriction (*https://oreil.ly/zVnVj*) that may be shared across all services within the same region and account. When you exceed the throughput limits, calls to KMS may be throttled, resulting in runtime exceptions in your application.

Behind the scenes, AWS uses an HSM that performs cryptographic functions and securely stores cryptographic keys that cannot be tampered with. AWS KMS generates and protects the master keys that you provide to the FIPS 140-2 validated HSMs. The responsibility of the security of these HSMs is assumed by AWS as part of the SRM.

> Each CMK is created for a specific region. This means that if certain governmental regulations require you to hand over the CMK, you can continue to service other customers without violating any privacy requirements.

## Envelope Encryption

In envelope encryption, you break the encryption process into two stages:

- In the first stage, you use a key called the *data key* to encrypt your large data objects.
- In the second stage, you use your CMK to encrypt the data key and store this encrypted data key next to your ciphertext data while deleting the plaintext data key.

The application can then transmit the ciphertext data as well as the encrypted data key to the end recipient. Figure 3-4 shows how envelope encrypted ciphertext (encrypted data key and data-key-encrypted sensitive data) is protected from unauthorized access by properly protecting the CMK.

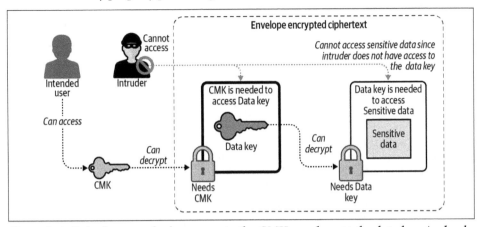

*Figure 3-4. Only the user who has access to the CMK can decrypt the data key. And only a decrypted (plaintext) data key can decrypt the sensitive data. Therefore, an attacker without access to the CMK cannot access the sensitive data.*

Envelope encryption is not a different type of encryption. It simply builds on top of basic encryption by adding an extra step of encrypting a data key and then using this data key to encrypt the plaintext data. The best practices for basic encryption are also applicable to envelope encryption, and almost every other aspect of encryption remains the same.

If the reading application has the master key to decrypt the encrypted data key, then all items can be decrypted within the same microservice, without having to make a call to a centralized key management server.

It is important to note that the only difference between the two is the output of the KMS decryption process. In basic encryption, you obtain plaintext sensitive data immediately after decrypting the encrypted payload. In contrast, when using envelope encryption, during the first step you obtain the plaintext data key, but the data is still encrypted. You have to use the plaintext data key to further decrypt the payload from the previous step. Apart from this added step, there are no differences from a security standpoint. In both cases, protecting the CMK protects data from being accessed. Figure 3-5 compares the two encryption methods.

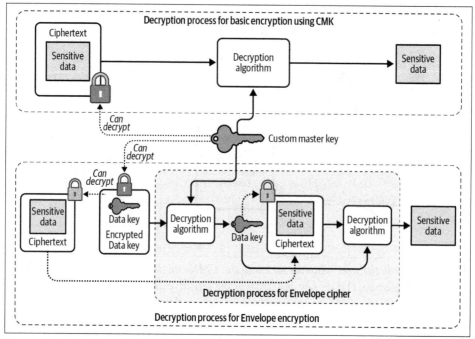

*Figure 3-5. A comparison of the decryption process when sensitive data is encrypted using the CMK as opposed to using a data key (envelope encryption).*

The two aspects of security that applied to basic encryption also apply to envelope encryption:

- As long as the CMK is secured from unauthorized access, the sensitive data can be considered to be safe from unauthorized access, since an attacker will be unable to decrypt the encrypted data key, which is then required to decrypt the ciphertext.
- If access to the CMK is granted to a service, the service will then be able to decrypt the encrypted ciphertext, since access to the CMK will allow the service to decrypt the encrypted data key, which can then be used to decode the ciphertext.

In basic encryption, you want to encrypt the table directly using the CMK. Given the 4 KB limit on using CMK, you will most likely make millions of calls to the CMK to either encrypt or decrypt each row in the table. The added latency due to encryption will thus rise significantly with each additional row because of the added step of calling KMS.

In contrast, envelope encryption requires you to first create a data encryption key (DEK), and then the entire table can be encrypted using this key. This key can be

---

stored in memory by the encrypting application. Once the data encryption process is completed, the key can then be encrypted using a CMK, by calling the encrypt function on AWS KMS. While decrypting large amounts of data, a similar in-memory caching of the data key can result in significant efficiency gains.

Most importantly, since the data key can be cached in memory, the latency of the encryption step will not increase with the number of rows in the table. Figure 3-6 shows an example of how a cached data key can be used to decrypt multiple rows in a table.

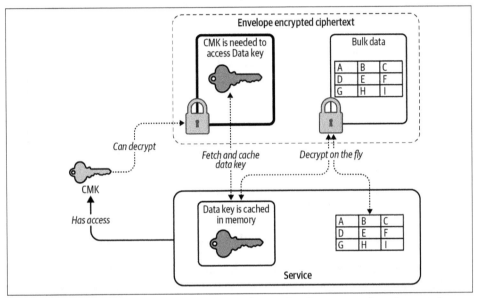

*Figure 3-6. In cases where large amounts of data need to be encrypted or decrypted, some services may choose to cache the data key in memory for subsequent encryption or decryption processes.*

## Envelope Encryption in Action

Let's look at how envelope encryption behaves in the real world when communicating encrypted data between two services.

We'll compare the end-to-end process of envelope encryption with the end-to-end process of basic encryption, as highlighted earlier in Figure 3-2. Since envelope encryption involves the added steps of encrypting and decrypting the data key, Figure 3-2 has to be slightly modified to reflect these changes. Figure 3-7 outlines how envelope encryption works in an end-to-end flow.

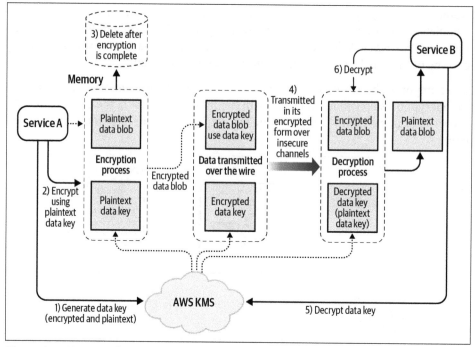

*Figure 3-7. How envelope encryption works.*

Here are the steps in the envelope encryption process:

1. Call KMS to generate a plaintext data key as well as a KMS encrypted version of this data key that is encrypted using the CMK. (This can be done in one call to KMS where KMS responds with both of these keys in its response.)

2. Encrypt the plaintext item with the plaintext data key from Step 1.

3. Delete the plaintext data key.

4. Send the encrypted data key and the encrypted data blob over the wire to the receiving service. (The plaintext data key or the data blob is never persisted and never leaves the sending service.)

In this way, only encrypted text traverses the insecure channel while the plaintext keys are deleted as soon as the encryption process is complete.

And here is the decryption process:

5. Take the ciphertext data key and use AWS KMS to produce a plaintext data key.

6. Use the plaintext data key in memory to decrypt the ciphertext blob.

By doing the encryption in this way, you control a few things:

- Data can be stored independent of the key storage.
- A leak of the encrypted data that is sent over the wire (encrypted data key + encrypted data blob) can still protect you from a leak of the data because the data is useless without the plaintext data key. And the plaintext data key cannot be retrieved unless the consuming service has access to the CMK.
- Because the encrypted data is available locally, you can cache the plaintext data key in memory if you want to repeatedly encrypt or decrypt data, making the whole process fast.
- Because the only thing that you use the CMK to encrypt is the data key, the size limitation of the KMS encryption process no longer applies to your encryption process.

You can create a data key using the AWS CLI with the `generate-data-key` command. Luckily, AWS understands the importance of this use case and provides a simple method of creating a data key using KMS:

```
aws kms generate-data-key \
--key-id <key-id> \
--key-spec <key spec for e.g. AES_256>
```

This command creates a data key that you can use to encrypt your data. The plaintext part of this response can be used to encrypt your plaintext data blob. You can then use tools such as OpenSSL to encode your data with the plaintext key and store or transmit this encrypted data. It also returns the ciphertext data key that you can save or transmit along with your encrypted blob.

Here is a sample response:

```
{
    "CiphertextBlob": "<Base 64 encoded cipher-text  data-key>",
    "Plaintext": "<Plain text data-key>",
    "KeyId": "arn:aws:kms:us-east-1:248285616257:key/
                        27d9aa85-f403-483e-9239-da01d5be4842"
}
```

# Security and AWS KMS

This section covers how you can leverage KMS to protect data and information within your microservice architecture.

# KMS Contexts and Additional Authenticated Data

A common security mechanism generally used in encryption is called *additional authenticated data* (AAD). AAD is any nonsecret plaintext string that you pass to KMS as part of an encrypt or decrypt request.

For example, imagine an application that lets users maintain a private journal. In the case where a user needs to view a private entry, the application can use the username as the AAD to explicitly detect the user.

The AAD is used as an additional integrity and authenticity check on the encrypted data. Typically, the decryption process fails if the AAD provided to the decryption process does not match the AAD provided to the encryption process. AAD is bound to the encrypted data since it is used in decrypting the ciphertext, but this extra data is not included as part of the ciphertext.

A tuple describing a cryptographic context is supposed to contain a descriptor (a key) and a value for the descriptor. It is crucial that the context (the key and its value) used during encryption is reproducible during decryption.

AWS KMS cryptographic operations with symmetric CMKs accept an encryption context in the form of a key value pair, which functions as AAD for the purpose of supporting authenticated encryption.

The contextual information cannot be considered secret. It appears in plaintext within AWS CloudTrail logs so you can make use of it to recognize and categorize your cryptographic operations. This context can have any information as a key value pair, but because it is not secret, you should not use sensitive information as part of your context. Here is an example of how the encryption context can be set as a Java-Script Object Notation (JSON) string:

```
"encryptionContext": {
    "username": "gauravraje"
}
```

The same username has to be passed during encryption and decryption.

# Key Policies

As mentioned at the beginning of this chapter, the true power of encryption comes with the ability to control access to the CMK. And as you may have guessed, that means the ability to use resource-based policies on the CMK.

As discussed in Chapter 2, key policies can be classified as resource-based policies. The basic format of key policies is as follows:

```
{
  "Sid": "Enable IAM User Permissions",
  "Effect": "Allow",
```

```
      "Principal": {"AWS": "arn:aws:iam::111122223333:root"},
      "Action": "kms:*",
      "Resource": "*"
}
```

A key policy applies (*https://oreil.ly/mJ9cZ*) only to the CMK it is attached to. Given that your CMKs are being used to protect your sensitive information, you should work to ensure that the corresponding key policies follow a model of least privilege.

If you do not explicitly specify a key policy at the time of creation, AWS will create a default key policy for you with one policy statement giving the root user full access to the CMK. You can grant more access by way of identity and access management (IAM) policies that are attached to individual users. However, if you add a policy either to this CMK or on the user attempting to access this key that says explicitly, "Deny," then access will be denied. In other words, an explicit denial will always take priority over an allowance.

 As you have noticed, the root account *has* to be given access separately to this CMK. It is not assumed that your root account automatically has access to the key. And taking access away from the key could make the key unusable. AWS requires you to create a support ticket in cases where the root account does not have access to the key.

## Grants and ViaService

There are many situations where you want even more granular access while accessing encryption keys. That is, you want certain external services to be able to encrypt or decrypt your data only in some very specific contexts.

The next sections briefly introduce two tools that AWS provides that enable us to achieve a granular level of access control, without compromising on security. You'll then see examples of how these tools can be incorporated in your architecture design a little later in the chapter.

### KMS grants

KMS grants are one way of enabling controlled and monitored access to KMS keys. I will elaborate on situations when such a use case is required, but for now we'll assume there is a legitimate case like the following example.

You have a service—Service A—that has complete access to a particular KMS CMK—K. This service can encrypt or decrypt certain data using K. You also have Service B, which wants to perform these same operations. Instead of asking Service A to do this, your Service A wants to allow Service B the ability to access and use K (temporarily).

This is where KMS grants come in. A principal with a grant (in this case, Service B) can perform operations (encryption or decryption) on a CMK (K) when the conditions specified in the grant are met. Grants are applied per CMK and can extend beyond accounts if necessary (your services can give out grants to principals from other accounts). Grants can only allow access but not deny access. So if a principal already has access to the key, a grant is redundant and has no net effect on the security boundary of your keys. Principals can use grant permissions without specifying the grant, just as they would with a key policy or IAM policy. So after receiving a grant, it is as if the calling principal has access to this KMS key through its IAM or key policy.

 It is important to note that AWS grants rely on the principle of *eventual consistency*. In other words, the creation or revocation of a grant on a KMS key may not take effect immediately—it may take a few seconds (usually less than five minutes) to take effect.

You can create a grant using the AWS Console tool by running the following:

```
aws kms create-grant \
    --key-id <Key ID that you want to create a grant on> \
    --grantee-principal <arn of the target principal recipient of the grant>  \
    --operations Decrypt
```

This command creates a grant that will allow the target principal to decrypt any items that were encrypted using the key that is specified using the Key ID.

You can also apply constraints to your grants so that you can have more granular permissions in your grants:

```
aws kms create-grant \
    --key-id <Key ID that you want to create a grant on> \
    --grantee-principal <arn of the target principal recipient of the grant>  \
    --operations Decrypt
    --constraints EncryptionContextSubset={Department=IT}
```

This will ensure that your grant is given to the principal only as long as the condition related to the encryption context is met. This combination of encryption contexts and grants can further help you in assigning more granular permissions.

## KMS ViaService

Similar to grants, the ViaService condition in key policy can be another tool in providing external services access to your key without compromising on your domain security infrastructure. Though grants are a good way of giving out temporary access to external services, there are times when this access needs to be permanent. I don't mean you want to increase coupling between these contexts; you just want to have the ability to extend your encryption security boundary beyond your domain under very specific circumstances. When such circumstances are easy to define, you can use the key policy to formally codify such exceptions.

The `kms:ViaService` condition in a key policy constrains the use of a CMK to requests from specified AWS services.

Let's look at an example of a ViaService condition where you will restrict the KMS operations to a specific principal as long as the call to use the keys comes from a lambda and not any other service:

```
{
  "Effect": "Allow",
  "Principal": {
    "AWS": "<ARN of calling entity>"
  },
  "Action": [
    "kms:*"
  ],
  "Resource": "*",
  "Condition": {
    "StringEquals": {
      "kms:ViaService": [
          "lambda.us-west-2.amazonaws.com"
      ]
    }
  }
}
```

It is worth noting that the ViaService condition can also be used to deny permission to your keys just as it can to allow:

```
{
  "Effect": "Deny",
  "Principal": {
    "AWS": "<ARN of calling entity>"
  },
  "Action": [
    "kms:*"
  ],
  "Resource": "*",
  "Condition": {
    "StringNotEquals": {
      "kms:ViaService": [
          "lambda.us-west-2.amazonaws.com"
      ]
    }
  }
}
```

This statement will ensure that any service that is not a lambda function will not be able to access your KMS resources for the principal mentioned in the policy. These two policies combined together will restrict KMS access for the user to the lambda.

## CMK and Its Components and Supported Actions

Until now, I have been referring to the *key* as one logical entity, but in reality, a CMK is made up of different parts:

*Key metadata*

These are the attributes of the key that help in identifying and describing the key. They include the usual key ID, key Amazon Resource Name (ARN), key tags, and so on.

*Key alias*

This is a logical reference to a key that exists outside your actual key. An alias can be used interchangeably with the CMK within your application.

*Key material*

This is the backing cryptographic data that constitutes your actual key. This is where the meat of your cryptographic knowledge lives. The *material* is what your encryption or decryption algorithms will use as input for the encryption process, so it is what is eventually responsible for encrypting or decrypting your data.

For most use cases, Amazon creates the key material for you whenever you create a key and are offered a seamless use experience. However, knowing the material is stored separately from the rest of the metadata can be useful for some advanced use cases, especially related to compliance.

### Importing key material

As mentioned previously, KMS generates and maintains the key material independently of the key. When you create a new CMK, KMS stores the key material and all related metadata inside an HSM. However, KMS also allows you to import your own key material into KMS. This can be useful for two reasons:

- For regulatory reasons, organizations like to control the lifecycle of their keys, and importing key material enables this control.
- KMS does not allow immediate deletion of keys as a way of safeguarding objects from accidental deletion. Importing key material, however, is a way of getting around this limitation.

Key material can be imported through the UI or the API.

## Types of CMK

There are several types of CMKs within AWS:

*AWS managed CMKs*
> AWS managed CMKs are the keys that back the encryption of AWS services that are created on your account. You still own these CMKs, but they are managed for you by AWS. This way, you do not have to maintain them as part of the SRM.

*Customer managed CMKs*
> These are the CMKs that you created for your applications or encryption needs. As the name says, you have to manage these keys even though AWS provides tools that make the management process easier. You can use a customer managed CMK to back most AWS services as well, but with this control comes certain responsibilities that you have to take up and move away from the SRM.

*Customer managed CMK with imported key material*
> This is more of a subtype of the customer managed CMK than a different type of its own, but it deserves special mention here. These are keys where you import your own key material and thus have even more control over the process and the lifecycle of the key.

## Automatic key rotation

Along with key generation, key exposure is a big problem that almost all security systems face. Most security scientists agree that key rotation ensures that your keys are safe and protected from abuse. For example, some industry standards, such as Payment Card Industry Data Security Standard (PCI DSS), require regular key rotations.

AWS provides you the ability to rotate keys either manually or automatically. *Key rotation* just means changing the backing key material that is used in the encryption process. Whether the CMK's backing material changes multiple times or not, it is still the same logical resource.

One way to change the cryptographic material for your CMKs is to create new CMKs and then change your applications or aliases to use the new CMKs.

AWS realizes how important this use case is for maintaining security and hence has made it easy to rotate keys. Customers have the ability to turn on automatic key rotation for an existing CMK.

A customer managed CMK is automatically refreshed every year with new cryptographic material when automatic key rotation is enabled. Additionally, AWS KMS retains older versions of the CMK's cryptographic material (previous key versions) until you delete the CMK. AWS KMS does not delete any older cryptographic material until you delete the CMK.

This means that at any given point there may be multiple versions of backing materials of keys that are represented by a single logical resource—the CMK. When you use a CMK to encrypt, AWS KMS uses the latest version of the backing key. But when you use the CMK to decrypt, AWS KMS is smart enough to identify and use the backing key that was used to encrypt this data in the first place.

Automatic key material ensures that the rotated key continues to have the same IAM and key policies and ARN as its previous versions, thus making the key rotation process easier. This also makes sure your application can continue to run without needing any code changes or deployments. Furthermore, a scheduled key rotation process ensures that your administrators can focus on other parts of the architecture without having to worry about the key rotation, which is handled completely by AWS.

In contrast, automatic key rotation has no effect on the existing data encrypted by the CMK. Thus, it will not re-encrypt data protected by the CMK, and by extension won't mitigate any damage done by a compromised data key.

KMS rotates AWS managed CMKs every 1,095 days with the exception of keys that are disabled or pending deletion. Customer-managed keys on the other hand can be optionally rotated every 365 days.

### Manual rotation

As mentioned, a new CMK can be created to replace a current one instead of enabling automatic key rotation, if more granular control over key rotation is desired. A new CMK has the same effect as changing the backing key in an existing CMK when the new CMK has different cryptographic material than the current CMK.

Of course, since the new CMK is a new logical resource, you have to change any references to this CMK. Hence, it is best to refer to a CMK by using an alias in your applications. When you want to switch to a different CMK, you can change the target of the alias without needing any application code level changes.

When decrypting data, KMS identifies the CMK that the data was encrypted with and uses the same one to decrypt it. AWS KMS can decrypt any data that was encrypted by either CMK as long as you have access to both the original and new CMKs. If you only have access to one of the CMKs, you won't be able to decrypt the data.

### Deleting a CMK

Whereas most other resources don't have a "Delete" section, CMKs deserve special attention. The reason is that, depending on the type of the CMK, outright deleting the CMK immediately may not be possible. Deleting a key deletes all its backing material and is an irreversible process. Deleting it also means any resource or data that was encrypted using this key is lost forever without any hopes of reviving it.

AWS understands the seriousness of deleting a CMK (and all its backing material). To protect us from ourselves, AWS provides a mandatory waiting period during which a scheduled CMK deletion can be overturned. You can set this scheduled waiting period from a minimum of 7 days up to a maximum of 30 days, during which the key can be revived. The default waiting period is 30 days. A CMK that is pending deletion cannot be used in any cryptographic operations and does not get automatically rotated.

The only exception to this waiting period rule is a CMK that has imported its key material. You can delete key material on demand. When you delete the key material, the CMK becomes unusable but can be restored by reimporting the material. In contrast, once you delete the CMK itself, it cannot be recovered.

## Regions and KMS

KMS being a regional service is generally not a problem, but it's important to remember in two unique situations that microservices face from time to time.

The first situation is where you have a globally replicated service that is backed by the KMS key. In such a service, global data replication may involve using the same key, and thus encryption may involve cross-region communication that may add to your billing.

The second situation is similar, where you may be required by regulatory agencies to ensure the geographic containment of your data. In such a situation, AWS will have to use a key from the same region of your geographic area. This is especially important if you have to send cryptographic material across multiple regions or even move your data from one region to the other.

> If you move any encrypted data to a new region, you may want to consider re-encrypting this data blob in the new region with a new set of data keys and a completely different CMK that is provisioned in the target region. This is to avoid cross-region calls and be fully compliant with certain regulatory frameworks and data security requirements that may be location specific.

## Cost, Complexity, and Regulatory Considerations

Although AWS KMS offers a great alternative to managing your own HSM, it does come with a few trade-offs that should be considered when designing a system that relies on it.

Costs associated with KMS can be divided into two parts. Users have to pay a flat fee for each CMK that is present on KMS. Additionally, there is a per-request charge associated with every request made to this CMK.

Actions associated with the CMK also have an account-wide throughput limit. At the time of writing this chapter, each account is restricted to 10,000 API calls per region per second. These calls include calls to encrypt, decrypt, create grants, or any other action associated with the CMK.

AWS KMS is designed so that no one, not even AWS employees, can retrieve your plaintext keys from the service. From a regulatory standpoint, AWS KMS is compliant with various compliance standards such as PCI-DSS Level 1, HIPAA, FIPS 140-2 Level 2, and so on. Companies interested in maintaining their current compliance levels should check with their regulator if using AWS KMS is permitted and compatible with their level of compliance. More compliance-related information can be found in AWS Artifact within the AWS Management Console. AWS manages the maintenance and uptime in AWS KMS.

AWS KMS firmware updates are controlled by a strong and very restrictive access control. Each access is heavily audited and controlled by independent auditors. Some customers, however, may not be satisfied with the idea of using a serverless, fully managed service for key storage without having much control over the underlying hardware. For those customers whose regulatory, compliance, or security policy does not allow the fact that AWS fully controls, manages, and shares the infrastructure that holds the keys, AWS offers a different solution in the form of AWS CloudHSM (*https://aws.amazon.com/cloudhsm*), which provides a more isolated key management setup. Additionally, CloudHSM can be deployed fully within your virtual private cloud (VPC).

> AWS CloudHSM is also more compliant with a wider range of standards. Nevertheless, AWS CloudHSM does not provide high availability by default, which means users will have to assume more responsibility in maintaining their key management infrastructure.

# Asymmetric Encryption and KMS

Asymmetric encryption is probably one of the most fascinating aspects of modern-day cryptography and is a topic worthy of an entire book by itself. A good place to start is Bruce Schneier's book, *Applied Cryptography* (Wiley). For our purposes, I only have room to summarize the essence of asymmetric encryption. In *asymmetric encryption*, instead of a single key, you have two keys (a public key and a private key) that are connected to each other with a unique bond:

*Public key*
> This one is widely available and freely distributed as nonsensitive, nonprivate data, similar to an email address. The public key is available for anyone who needs it.

*Private key*
> This one is secret, similar to an email password. It is never shared beyond the service that owns this key.

On AWS, you can use asymmetric key encryption in two use cases:

- Encryption and decryption
- Digitally signing data

## Encryption and Decryption

With asymmetric encryption you can encrypt plaintext using a public key and then decrypt the ciphertext using the corresponding private key. The advantage of such an approach is that if the data can be decrypted only using the private key, just about anyone can encrypt the data and be assured that only the intended recipient will be able to decrypt it, thus maintaining a secure channel of communication without having to exchange keys. AWS safely stores the private key for the recipient and maintains access control over it.

Figure 3-8 illustrates how asymmetric algorithms can be used by external services.

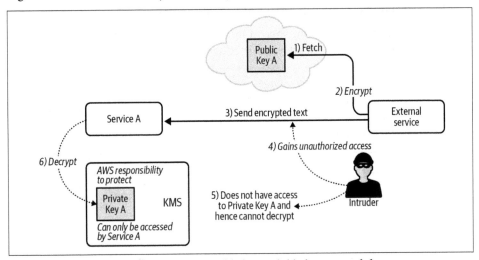

*Figure 3-8. An external service uses a publicly available key to send data to a microservice.*

To send data using an asymmetric algorithm, the sender follows these steps:

1. Retrieve the recipient's public key (which is public knowledge).
2. Encrypt the sensitive data using this public key.

3. Send this encrypted ciphertext to the intended recipient.

4. In this case, even if any intruder happens to gain access to the encrypted text, the intruder still will not be able to read the sensitive plaintext (the access control provided by AWS KMS will prevent the intruder from decrypting this text using the private Key A).

5. However, Service A will have access to private Key A and hence will be able to decrypt the text.

Because this data can only be decrypted using the private key, no "man-in-the-middle" attack is possible here. Furthermore, no keys are exchanged, so the recipient has close to no *coupling* (cross-module interdependence) with the sender.

Upon receiving the data, the recipient can decrypt it using their private key. In this way, sensitive keys never leave the intended recipient's service.

## Digital Signing (Sign and Verify)

It also works in reverse. Using asymmetric encryption, you can encrypt data using a private key and then decrypt using the public key. So if a recipient receives any data that is decryptable using the public key of a known entity, the recipient can be sure that the encryption process happened using the private key.

Figure 3-9 illustrates a situation where a microservice can use AWS KMS to digitally sign data that needs to be verified by other external services.

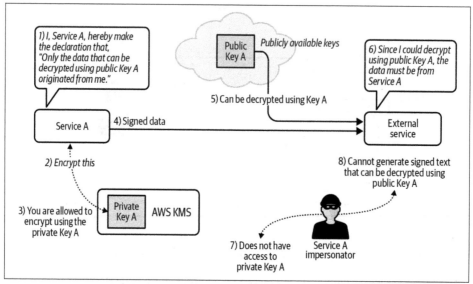

*Figure 3-9. AWS KMS can be used to transmit digitally signed data that can be verified from its originator using asymmetric key encryption.*

The process can be described using the following steps:

1. Service A makes its public key known to all external parties.

2. It then requests AWS KMS to digitally sign (encrypt using private Key A) the data that it needs to transmit.

3. AWS KMS identifies Service A (since they are both on AWS) and responds with encrypted data that is digitally signed using private Key A.

4. Service A then sends this data to any external service.

5. Public Key A can be used to decrypt this data sent in Step 4.

6. Since public Key A is able to decrypt this data, external services can be assured that it originated at Service A.

7. If any impersonator were to send data to the external service pretending to be Service A, it would not gain access to the private Key A, since it would not be able to identify itself as Service A to AWS KMS (due to any authentication control that you may have placed, as discussed in Chapter 2).

8. Since the intruder is not able to access private Key A, they are not able to encrypt data in a way that can be decrypted using public Key A. Hence, external services will not be able to trust any impersonator.

Figure 3-10 and 3-11 show how asymmetric keys work in the AWS Management Console.

*Figure 3-10. Asymmetric keys can be created in the AWS console in a similar way to creating symmetric keys.*

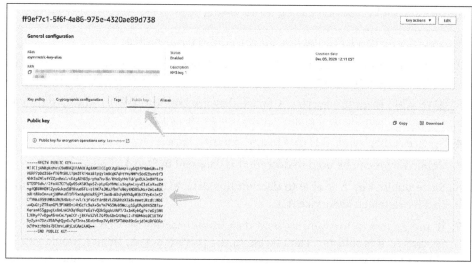

Figure 3-11. Once created, your public key can be accessed in the Public key tab of your asymmetric key.

One of the most common classes of algorithms used for asymmetric encryption is the Rivest–Shamir–Adleman (RSA) algorithm. The asymmetric keys in AWS allow the use of many RSA algorithms from this family along with a growing list of other commonly used ciphers. These keys can be used for both of the use cases discussed here for secure transmission of data and for digital signing of data.

# Domain-Driven Design and AWS KMS

Now that you've seen how AWS KMS and envelope encryption work, let's look at how you can modularize your encryption strategy to suit your domain design. There are some obvious design considerations in the context of encryption. Some typical advice includes the following:

- Use envelope encryption wherever possible and use CMKs only to encrypt or decrypt data keys.
- Do not reuse CMKs.
- Restrict access to CMKs to a bare minimum so that only the services that are designed to talk to each other will have access to these keys.
- Ensure that the data keys are not cached locally.
- Use KMS contexts to add extra layers on top of your usual authentication.
- Use IAM policies to restrict access to AWS keys using the principle of least privilege (PoLP).

These commonsense measures go a long way in avoiding potential breaches.

## Contextual Boundaries and Encryption

Unlike other systems in our application, sometimes (but not always) encryption mechanisms can be considered to be cross-cutting concerns, similar to logging and monitoring. This is where encryption is not the core of your service—far from it—but you still think that encryption should be present across various modules in various contexts. Furthermore, if this encryption transcends contextual boundaries, it means you cannot really modularize encryption based on your existing service boundaries.

For cross-context communication, it is really difficult to draw a service boundary because, by definition, you want to allow two different bounded contexts to understand and speak the language. Hence, where these CMKs should live (in which bounded context) is generally a question that most architects face while designing their cloud infrastructure.

## Accounts and Sharing CMK

Generally, it is a good idea to have different accounts for different domains in order to grant autonomy to your service contexts. Each of your domains can then use a CMK for each service, giving access only to its constituent services. This brings up the question of cross-domain communication, where you may require service from one context to send data or information to another service in another context and, hence, in this case, another account.

Luckily, AWS allows sharing of keys across accounts. You can grant trusted entities (IAM users or roles) in one AWS account permission to use a CMK in another AWS account.

As you might guess, these permissions are set using key policies. The CMK key policy must be set up to grant the external account permission to use the CMK. The key policy permissions in external accounts must be delegated to their users and roles by IAM policies in that account. In the words of AWS: "The key policy determines who can have access to the CMK. The IAM policy determines who does have access to the CMK. Neither the key policy nor the IAM policy alone is sufficient—you must change both."

# KMS and Network Considerations

KMS, being a managed service, resides fully in a centralized cloud network. That creates a unique issue.

In order to perform their cryptographic functions, your individual services now need the capability to connect to AWS KMS. The risk of security issues increases because services which might not otherwise connect to the internet will need to do so.

The issues around network security can also be resolved using VPC endpoints. VPC endpoints are covered in detail in Chapter 5.

# KMS Grants Revisited

As promised, let's return to talking about business use cases in domain-driven design (DDD) where KMS grants help you in providing better modularization to your services. Consider the following business problem.

Let's say you are working on an internal organizational system that keeps track of all your employees' benefits and compensation. You have two domains that communicate with each other in your application. One domain (and its constituent services) keeps track of the sensitive information related to employee salaries. As a responsible employer, you have done a good job in protecting employee salaries. Among other measures, you have used a strong encryption suite with the help of AWS KMS and restricted access to this key to only certain privileged services within this domain. The other domain is the reporting domain that generates a report of all of your employees. These services typically do not need access to privileged information about employee salaries. But in certain very specific situations, the service is required to aggregate sensitive information and hence has the need to decrypt the salary information.

Here what you are saying is, "No one should have access to this key except when they have to perform a certain very specific operation." This is a textbook example of where grants work well with your domain design. A grant allows you to control access to your keys without having to open up the key to any external contexts on a temporary basis. These grants can be revoked as soon as the business use case is over, and in this way the access is controlled.

# KMS Accounts and Topologies: Tying It All Together

Bounded contexts within AWS generally follow business-level domains. On AWS, as I mentioned in Chapter 2, different domains may find it prudent to create separate accounts to maintain operational independence. Although most microservices may be classified based on the domains they belong to, services that rely on encryption may find it harder to get classified since encryption generally involves communication between contexts, and hence may span across AWS accounts. Luckily, as mentioned in "Accounts and Sharing CMK" on page 101, the CMK is not bound by any account-level boundaries, and services from different accounts can continue to use the CMK.

This brings us to the question of where exactly a CMK should live. There are two options, and each has its merits as well as demerits:

*Option 1*
> You could put the CMK within the bounded contexts. In this case, the CMK will live alongside other services in a domain-specific AWS account.

*Option 2*
> You could treat the CMK as an independent entity and let it reside in a separate independent AWS account.

> Once you have made a choice, you can use basic account-level controls such as IAM policies and resource-based policies to control access, as described in Chapter 2.

## Option 1: Including the CMK Within Bounded Contexts

This option assumes that each bounded context has its own AWS account, and that each account and therefore each bounded context within your organization, has its own set of KMS keys. Since there is now a 1:1 relationship between AWS accounts and bounded contexts, it is easier to secure individual domains.

This still leaves the question of cross-domain communication and data sharing. As discussed, though, because KMS keys are not restricted by account-level constructs, in this particular topology you can leverage tools such as KMS grants to allow granular access to external services from accessing your cryptographic functions and keys. Figure 3-12 shows how you can have the CMK bundled with the rest of your services. For any cross-domain encryption or decryption, you can use KMS grants to allow temporary cross-domain access.

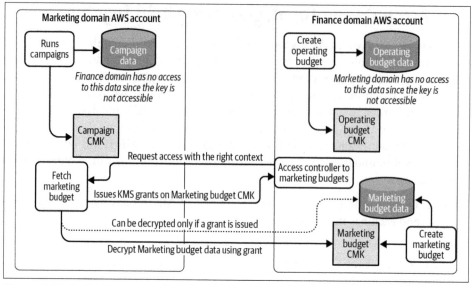

*Figure 3-12. In this case, you identify and separate out CMKs based on domains and only allow cross-account, cross-domain encryption using grants.*

The key advantage of such a system is the ability to cleanly separate out domains. There is no centralized orchestrator for encryption in microservices.

The disadvantage of such a system is the added complexity involved in cross-context communication where a grant-based communication protocol not only generates added logic that may be harder to debug but also brings the latency associated with KMS grants.

## Option 2: Using a Purpose-Built Account to Hold the CMK

A different approach to dividing your domains is to have a third account along with your existing two accounts that houses all of the infrastructure-related mechanisms. This is the account that will hold all the CMKs for all of your domains and services. As a result, all your encryption services will be granted access to these CMKs on a per-use-case, per-service basis, while the ultimate control of the encryption will still be maintained by a separate account where only users with higher access privilege will be allowed to make changes.

This cleanly separates the runtime operation of your microservices from the security-related infrastructure. This also ensures that if the root account on one of your domains is compromised, the encryption keys of that domain, and thus the data, can still be protected from intruders through the infrastructure account that holds the encryption keys. Using a new, purpose-built AWS account, your key administrators can collaborate and work from a secure, alternate infrastructure.

This infrastructure account can expose individual roles that can be used by "key admins" to perform admin-level tasks on these keys individually. So tasks such as changing IAM permission changes, key policy changes, and others can be restricted to these key admins without compromising the security of your CMKs.

Figure 3-13 shows such a structure where all the CMKs are kept outside of the business-level accounts, inside a third centralized account. The key policies of these CMKs can be used to grant granular access to domain-based services to perform tasks such as encryption and decryption.

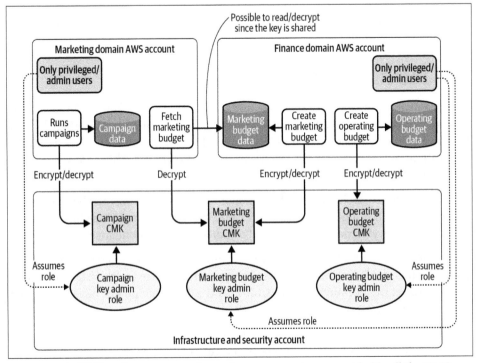

*Figure 3-13. KMS and account topology where a separate account holds all the KMS CMKs, while individual services are given granular access to the keys.*

The clear advantage of this approach is the ability to move some of your security infrastructure out of your domain logic into an infrastructure account. This also allows more granular access to data without needing KMS grants or any of the complexity associated with it.

On the flip side, however, maintaining a common infrastructure account within large organizations can be a nightmare in itself, requiring coordination at the security levels. This can be especially problematic if your organization does not have a clear security protocol in place for how much access should be given to which entity. Imagine a situation where you have a common infrastructure account where everyone has root access. Or even worse, an infrastructure account where only one person has access, and the entire company shuts down after this person leaves their job (sadly, this happens way more often than I would like to see in the industry).

 As mentioned, I am trying to be neutral about which choice works best and will let you decide what fits your use case. As long as you approach your architecture with careful thought and planning, both approaches have their advantages and disadvantages and can satisfy your requirements. I personally like the second option since, in my opinion, it is easier to harden and secure a centralized infrastructure account as opposed to encryption keys, which may be all over the place.

# AWS Secrets Manager

The problem of keeping secrets (passwords, credentials, or tokens) safe is an issue almost all companies have faced at some point. This problem is exacerbated by the presence of microservices. In a traditional monolith, where you had only a handful of applications, it was easy to store secrets in one location or, possibly, to just memorize all the secrets.

In a microservice architecture, the number of secrets is considerably higher. To ensure security, it is a good idea to also ensure that each microservice has independent access to any external service (shared or otherwise)—without any password reuse.

A very practical solution is to centralize the storage of all secrets. Storing them in one place and then providing certain access to a few sets of trusted administrators ensures efficient secret organization and control. This is a tempting policy, but it creates all-powerful administrators, which is not ideal.

Realizing this challenge, AWS introduced AWS Secrets Manager. Secrets Manager offers the illusion of a centralized repository but at the same time keeps it separated out and gives good access control over all the secrets. Secrets Manager also helps in rotating some of the passwords automatically for certain AWS-managed services. Secrets Manager has IAM control, which is completely independent of your running application, adding to the security since your secrets will still be protected even if someone gains control of your application.

AWS Secrets Manager is one example in which KMS can be used to provide security to the rest of your application. Secrets Manager transparently encrypts your secrets before storing them and decrypts them when you need them.

# How Secrets Manager Works

Figure 3-14 outlines a scenario where a microservice (Service 1) running on AWS using an AWS role wishes to access the password for a database (DB1).

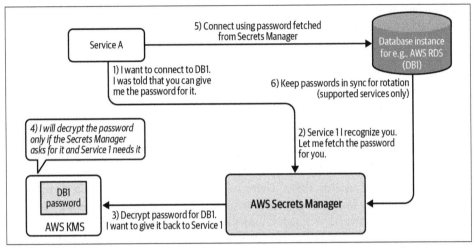

*Figure 3-14. An example of a use case involving AWS Secrets Manager used to store login credentials to a database instance.*

The process is as follows:

1. Service 1 makes a request to AWS Secrets Manager asking for the password.

2. Secrets Manager recognizes Service 1 (since they are both on AWS) and the role that it used to make such a request.

3. Secrets Manager has the password inside its storage, but it is encrypted. So it makes a request to AWS KMS to decrypt it.

4. AWS KMS is instructed to decrypt the password only if it is requested by Secrets Manager to be provided to Service 1. So no other service can gain access to the password.

5. Once this decrypted password from Step 4 is returned to Service 1, it can connect to DB1.

This way, no secrets are ever stored on the instance, and all the passwords can be implemented on the fly with absolutely no need to have any complex authenticated mechanism. AWS Secrets Manager also has the ability to rotate credentials to certain managed AWS services such as AWS Relational Database Service (RDS), AWS DocumentDB, and others, as shown in Step 6 in Figure 3-14.

To appreciate the elegance of this solution, let's take a step back and see what you achieve by doing this:

- You have a microservice application running an application.
- You attached a role to your microservice so external entities can identify you with an AWS role. (This took care of authentication for you.)
- You made calls to AWS Secrets Manager to fetch secrets for you. IAM policies and encryption here will handle access control for you.
- You made calls to your database or any other external resource that required credentials-based authentication.

All this was achieved without you having to store a single credential on your application side in a true almost password-less manner. I say *almost* password-less because you still use passwords under the hood to achieve this. But all of the password use is transparent to your microservice. There is no need for the application to maintain separate config files for storing secrets or using third-party encryption services. You can also rotate passwords regularly, and your application never has to know what changed. Each time it makes a call to AWS Secrets Manager, it is guaranteed to get the latest credentials for logging into your resource, keeping your environment highly secure.

AWS Secrets Manager is fully compliant with many different regulatory standards. It is rare to see a more perfect alignment of security initiatives with those of operational efficiency.

This way, your microservice can focus on its business logic while the security aspect is controlled by AWS for you.

## Secret Protection in AWS Secrets Manager

Every time you create or change the secret value in a secret, Secrets Manager uses the CMK that is associated with the secret to generate and encrypt a data key. Secrets Manager uses the plaintext data key to encrypt the secret value outside of AWS KMS, and then removes it from memory. The data key is encrypted and stored in the metadata of the secret.

The secret value is protected by the CMK, which remains encrypted by AWS KMS. A secret can only be decrypted by Secrets Manager if AWS KMS decrypts the encrypted data key. This is where the IAM permissions of your user can help in protecting your secrets. You can make use of all the concepts discussed in "Key Policies" on page 88, to ensure that the CMK has the most restrictive scope. This includes using the kms:ViaService condition on the keys to ensure that the decryption of the secret can only happen if the call is made from AWS Secrets Manager.

The IAM policy for the CMK can add a condition such as the following:

```
"Condition": {
            "StringEquals": {
                "kms:ViaService": "secretsmanager.us-east-1.amazonaws.com",
                "kms:CallerAccount": "<account number>"
            }
        }
```

That ensures that least privilege is applied to this key and that its use is restricted to AWS Secrets Manager.

Apart from restricting access to the CMK, the Secrets Manager has its own resource policy that can be used to further restrict access. It is considered a best practice to restrict access on both the AWS Secrets Manager as well as its backing CMK.

# Summary

This chapter laid the foundation for an understanding of encryption on the AWS cloud system. While being very conceptual, these concepts of encryption will inform many different resources that will be introduced in the next few chapters.

This chapter introduced both symmetric and asymmetric encryption. In symmetric encryption, you have a common shared secret key that the encryptor as well as the decryptor has to be aware of. The sharing and transmitting of this secret key can be done using KMS that, when coupled with proper authentication and authorization mechanisms, can provide you with a secure common cloud location from which your microservices can fetch the encryption key in a zero trust manner. This shared key is called the customer master key. The chapter then looked at a few ways to secure this CMK by adding additional layers of protection to ensure that the CMK will not be compromised.

Probably the most important takeaway from this chapter is to realize that the strength of the security of your application depends on the security protocols you put in place around your CMK. A compromised CMK does not protect anyone or anything, and hence most of the design around encryption revolves around ways to design the security of your CMK.

You also saw the limitations of KMS encryption using CMK and how the CMK should preferably be used in the context of envelope encryption. In envelope encryption, you can use the CMK to generate and encrypt a data key that is then used to encrypt the rest of your data. That way, you can go around the size limitation of CMK-based encryption.

# Security at Rest

When it comes to microservices, a lot of literature in the industry is focused on the design and development of the mechanisms that provide computing services to the end user. Despite this, it is widely known that microservices require us to fundamentally change the way we think about storage. Microservices are typically expected to be self-contained. This applies not only to their logic but also to their data storage mechanism. Unlike monoliths, where centralizing storage in a nonredundant manner is the guiding principle, microservices require architects to think of decentralization. In a real microservice environment, data is a first-class citizen and is to be treated in a similar way to any computing service. Microservice architects encourage (*https://oreil.ly/x6ulL*) data localization, in which data is kept close to the service that needs it, so the system can become less reliant on external databases. By avoiding shared and centralized databases, a microservice environment works only with the data available within the bounded context, thus ensuring autonomy and scale at the same time. Additionally, such a distributed storage design reduces the possibility of storage mechanisms becoming the "single points of failure (SPOFs)."

Security-wise, storing data can be very costly if you examine the risks involved. IBM and the Ponemon Institute publish an annual report (*https://oreil.ly/MlRMe*) detailing the average cost of a data breach for companies throughout the world, and as you can imagine, there are high costs associated with each breach. The average cost of a data breach, per this report, is $3.86 million. This is even higher if you are in a highly regulated industry where there may be regulatory or financial repercussions to data breaches. Thus, the microservice approach of polyglot (*https://oreil.ly/uanEe*) persistence (*https://oreil.ly/Z2xIu*) (using multiple data storage mechanisms) requires special attention to detail when it comes to security at rest.

Microservice architectures generally result in the creation of a collection of distributed storage mechanisms. These different storage objects are loosely coupled with one another, much like the microservices themselves. It is common for these distributed storages to follow the rules of the bounded contexts in which they reside. Figure 4-1 illustrates a sample domain-driven setup with distributed persistent storages that reside within the bounded contexts of the services.

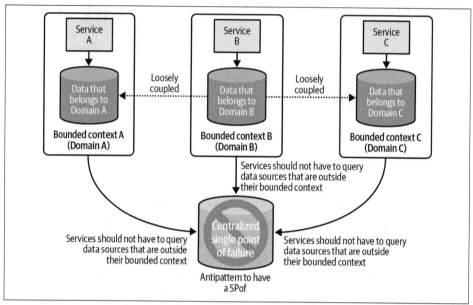

*Figure 4-1. In contrast to monoliths where data is created and stored from one application, microservices are fragmented, resulting in data that needs to be logically separated from one another, to conform to different data protection policies across the organization.*

 "Storage" could mean anything from a database system, application events, flat files, media objects, cached data, binary large objects (blobs), as well as container images. In fact, most microservice environments tend to use polyglot persistence (*https://oreil.ly/ xMVm4*) since each domain may have a different requirement out of its data storage platform. Some services may benefit from a NoSQL database, while some others may prefer to use a relational database management system (RDBMS). A distributed and localized storage mechanism ensures that you can use the best tool for the job.

In this chapter, I will focus primarily on the security at rest for microservices.

As I have mentioned in the previous chapters, security around data can be achieved through two ways:

- Preventing access to this data for unauthorized users through access control
- Encrypting this data so unauthorized exposure of data will not be readable

To secure a storage mechanism, the first task is to identify the permissions and security policies that govern access to it. In creating these policies, the principle of least privilege (PoLP) that I discussed in Chapter 2 is a good rule of thumb. To implement PoLP, AWS allows the use of identity and access management (IAM) policies for all of its cloud storage offerings, and I will use them often in this chapter.

Domain-driven environments, as opposed to traditional monoliths, have the natural advantage of being easy to secure using PoLP since data and business units are segregated already and hence access control can be streamlined.

Apart from access control, the data that is stored on AWS should also be encrypted. Encrypting this data provides an added layer of protection from unauthorized access, in addition to any existing access control that is added through IAM policies. Once the data is encrypted, it is important to control access to the encryption keys. On AWS, virtually all encryption can be handled by the AWS Key Management Servive (KMS) that I covered in depth in Chapter 3.

# Data Classification Basics

Although every manager likes to claim that all customer data should be protected, let's be honest: not all data is the same. There is an inherent hierarchy in terms of the sensitivity and importance of data. For example, personally identifiable data (PII), which can be used to identify the customers is more sensitive and has to be protected with more powerful controls than anonymized machine learning training data. In terms of the records that carry the biggest price tag when compromised, customer PII is the costliest (at $150), according to the IBM/Ponemon *Cost of a Data Breach Report*. Data classification is the step in security management that helps administrators in identifying, labeling, and realigning the organization's security to position itself to fulfill the needs of the sensitivity of the data. In this process, data types and sensitivity levels are identified, along with the likely consequences of compromise, loss, or misuse of the data.

It has been empirically proven (*https://oreil.ly/QKzpF*) that organizations that adopt strong data classification policies are better positioned to ward off potential threats. Government organizations have also prescribed various data classification levels in the past. For example, the US National Classification Scheme based on Executive Order 12356 (*https://oreil.ly/DLoFu*) recognizes three data classifications:

Confidential, Secret, and Top Secret. The UK government also has three classifications (*https://oreil.ly/K3Dnw*): Official, Secret, and Top Secret.

Each class of data may have a different security requirement while storing it. More importantly, the access that employees have may be different and hence, the data classification may dictate the identity management and access control structure within your organization. In my experience, companies have adopted innovative ways to systematically classify the resources that store sensitive data in physical data centers. Several companies implemented color coding of servers indicating the type of data that could be stored on each server. Other companies separated the servers that carried sensitive data and kept them in a separate location where only privileged employees had access.

 When I say "data storage," I mean intentional as well as unintentional persistence of data. Intentional persistence is the data that you wish to persist in an object store or a database. Unintentional persistence includes data that is persisted as a result of runtime operations such as log files, memory dumps, backups, and so forth. In my experience, many administrators tend to overlook unintentional persistence when they try to frame their data storage policy.

On AWS, data can be classified by using AWS tags that I briefly talked about in Chapter 2. AWS tags allow you to assign metadata to your cloud resources so the administrators will be aware of the type of data these resources store. Using these tags, conditional logic can be applied to access control to enforce security clearance checks while granting access. For compliance validation, AWS tags can also help identify and track resources that contain sensitive data. From a security perspective, you should tag each and every resource within your account, especially if it stores sensitive data.

# Recap of Envelope Encryption Using KMS

Envelope encryption is the tool that AWS uses frequently for encrypting all the data that is stored at rest. I have already talked in depth (Chapter 3) about how AWS KMS works, along with envelope encryption. But for those who need a refresher, here is a quick recap.

In basic encryption, whenever plaintext data needs to be encrypted, you can use the AWS-256 algorithm, which requires a data key as the input. This encrypted data (also known as the ciphertext) can be decrypted, accessed, and read by a recipient as long as they are in possession of the data key that was used to encrypt this data in the first place. Envelope encryption takes this process a step further. In envelope encryption, the data key that is used to encrypt the plaintext is further encrypted using a different key known as a customer master key (CMK).

Upon encryption, the ciphertext data and the ciphertext data key are stored together, while the plaintext data key is deleted. Access is restricted to the CMK and is provided only to the intended recipient of this data.

Figure 4-2 illustrates blocks of data that are stored using envelope encryption.

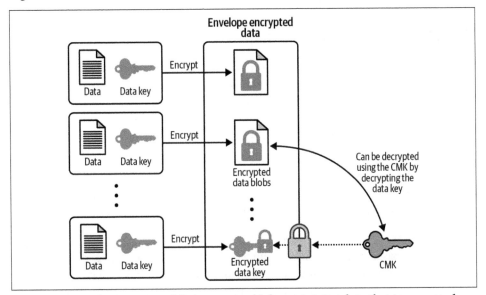

*Figure 4-2. Envelope encrypted data contains blobs containing data that is encrypted using a data key along with the encrypted data key that is encrypted using the CMK.*

To read the envelope encrypted data, the reader first has to use the CMK to decrypt the encrypted data key and obtain the plaintext data key. With this data key, the reader can then decrypt the encrypted data blobs and obtain the original plaintext data that was encrypted. Thus, the intended recipient can decrypt the data as long as they have access to the CMK.

Almost every encrypted data storage system on AWS will have three common themes:

- The CMK that you trust is securely stored away from unauthorized access, either on your own servers, on AWS KMS, or inside a hardware security module (HSM).
- You trust the encryption algorithm (*https://oreil.ly/ii9Pv*) to be unbreakable. In most of the AWS examples, AES-256 is generally considered to be a secure algorithm.

- There is a process of encrypting data. This may include encrypting data on the servers or enabling clients to encrypt this data before sending it to AWS. This process also specifies policies for how the data key is cached on the client side. Different storage systems on AWS use a different caching policy for data keys, which I will be discussing in detail in this chapter.

# AWS Simple Storage Service

In AWS Simple Storage Servive or Amazon Simple Storage Service (S3), storage "objects" are stored inside buckets. The most important responsibility of every security professional in the S3 environment lies in applying the PoLP to all objects and buckets within S3 that originate from different microservices. This means that only the users and resources that are required to access these objects should be allowed access.

Since AWS S3 is a managed service, any data that is stored in S3 may share its physical resources with other cloud customers. Hence, to protect your sensitive data, AWS gives you two options, which should be used together for any secure storage system:

- AWS IAM policies (specifically IAM principal-based policies and AWS S3 resource-based bucket policies), which I mentioned in Chapter 2, can be used to control access to these resources and ensure that the PoLP is applied.
- AWS KMS can be used to encrypt the objects that are stored inside AWS S3 buckets. This ensures that only principals with access to the encryption key used to encrypt this data can read these objects.

Encryption and access control play an equally important role in maintaining the security of data; both methods should be employed to protect it from unauthorized access. Figure 4-3 shows how you can leverage AWS KMS and AWS IAM policies to protect your data.

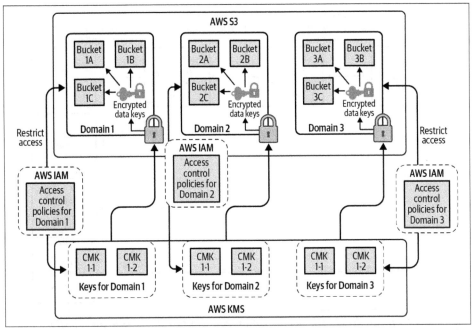

*Figure 4-3. Security professionals can employ AWS IAM policies to restrict access to the data inside AWS S3 buckets along with using AWS KMS envelope encryption for the data that is stored in these buckets. A good and secure solution effectively employs encryption and authorization to deter any unauthorized access.*

## Encryption on AWS S3

I will first talk about the techniques that you can use for encrypting data objects. There are four ways you can encrypt data objects on AWS S3. Each of these ways provides some flexibility and convenience to end users and hence, you can choose any of these methods that suit the needs of your organization. They are:

- AWS server-side encryption (AWS SSE-S3—AWS-managed keys)
- AWS server-side encryption KMS (AWS SSE-KMS—customer-managed keys)
- AWS server-side encryption with customer-provided keys (AWS SSE-C—customer-provided keys)
- AWS S3 client-side encryption (encrypting data on the client before sending it over to AWS S3)

Figure 4-4 shows a handy flowchart that can help you determine the type of encryption you need for your organization's needs.

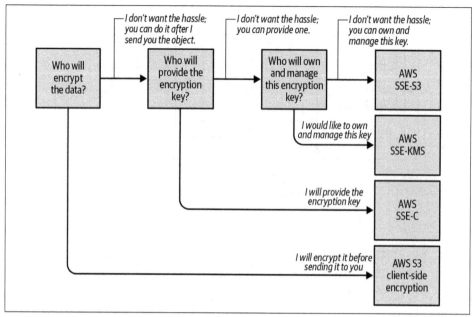

*Figure 4-4. You can decide which encryption you want by answering the questions in this chart.*

All of the encryption choices can use AWS KMS to achieve encryption on AWS. Hence, a deep and fundamental understanding of AWS KMS can go a long way in understanding the process of encryption on AWS S3.

## AWS SSE-S3 (AWS-managed keys)

This is the default mode of encrypting data objects inside AWS S3. For organizations that need very basic object encryption without wishing to control the lifecycle of the CMK that was used to encrypt the data items, AWS SSE-S3 provides a quick and easy way of introducing encryption on AWS. The biggest advantage of using AWS SSE-S3 is the ease of use and simplicity that it provides to cloud users.

AWS SSE-S3 can be enabled on a per bucket level on the AWS Management Console, as seen in Figure 4-5.

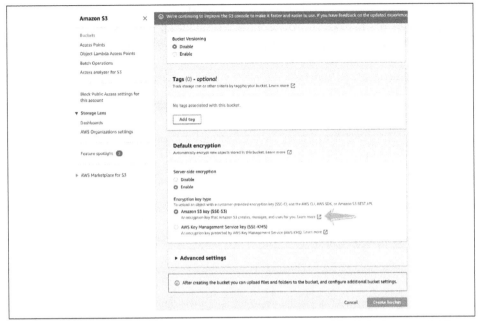

*Figure 4-5. All objects stored inside a bucket can be encrypted by default using AWS SSE-S3 in the "Default encryption" option and selecting "Server-side encryption."*

Once enabled, AWS encrypts all the objects inside this bucket using a data key. This data key is then encrypted using AWS KMS and a CMK that is maintained, protected, and rotated for you by AWS.

 Due to the presence of AWS SSE-S3, the amount of investment required to enable encryption for objects in AWS S3 is now extremely low. Although not ideal (since you completely trust AWS with your key and the encryption process), the ability to enable encryption by the push of a button should nudge all users to encrypt all of their storage objects. I don't know a single reason why objects on AWS S3 shouldn't be encrypted.

Of course, for those interested in more control, there are other ways of encrypting objects that are stored on AWS S3.

## AWS SSE-KMS

Users who prefer a more flexible encryption process than AWS SSE-S3 can use AWS KMS more explicitly for encryption. You can use a KMS key that you control on AWS KMS. This way, you can also be in charge of the lifecycle of the key that is used to encrypt data objects on AWS.

The encryption can be enabled on individual objects or enabled by default for each object in the bucket, similar to how AWS SSE-S3 was enabled in Figure 4-5. Figure 4-6 shows how AWS SSE-KMS can be enabled as the default option for buckets.

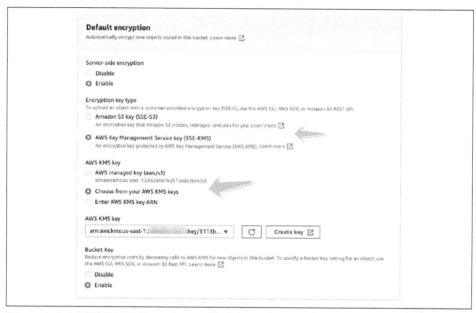

*Figure 4-6. AWS SSE-KMS can be enabled through the management console by providing the ARN of the KMS key that you want your objects to be encrypted with.*

## AWS SSE-C (client-provided key)

The final type of server-side encryption on AWS S3 is the AWS SSE-C. In this encryption process, the control over the encryption process is shifted even more to the end user. Instead of pointing AWS S3 to use an encryption key that is present on AWS KMS, you can include the encryption key within your `PutObject` request and instruct AWS S3 to encrypt the object using the key that you provide. This same key has to be provided during the `GetObject` operation in order to decrypt and retrieve the object. AWS S3 will use the key you provide, encrypt the object, and store it on AWS S3, then delete the key permanently. This way, you can have complete flexibility in controlling access to and securing the decryption key for the objects that are stored on AWS. At the same time, the encryption process takes place entirely on AWS S3 and hence, you need not maintain encryption or decryption code within your services.

AWS SSE-C only encrypts the S3 object but not the metadata associated with the object.

### AWS client-side encryption

AWS provides many different options for encrypting data after it has been uploaded to AWS S3, but you may prefer to encrypt data within your application even before it is transferred to AWS. Client-side encryption is the act of encrypting data before sending it to Amazon S3 and can be used for such use cases. In client-side encryption, you manage the CMK that you want to encrypt the data with. You can then use some of the client-side software development kit (SDK) to encrypt the data within your application and send this data to AWS to store it on the cloud. From the AWS point of view, this client-encrypted data is no different from any other data that it stores. You can then optionally also enable server-side encryption if you desire. This way, client-side encryption can offer an additional layer of protection against potential threats. More information on client-side encryption can be found at Amazon (*https://oreil.ly/C9fWo*).

## Access Control on Amazon S3 Through S3 Bucket Policies

As I discussed in Chapter 2, resource-based policies restrict access to AWS resources and can be applied to certain resources (*https://oreil.ly/fp485*). On AWS S3, these resource-based policies are called *bucket policies*. These policies answer the question, Which principals are allowed to access the objects inside these S3 buckets and under which conditions should this access be permitted or denied? Bucket policies can be added on the AWS Management Console, as seen in Figure 4-7.

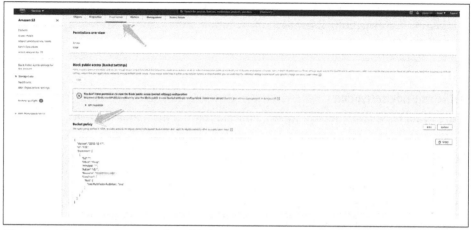

*Figure 4-7. Bucket policies can be added to AWS S3 buckets by going to the Permissions tab on the AWS web console.*

AWS also provides some great documentation (*https://oreil.ly/kOaw4*) on AWS bucket policies. The following two policies are examples of ways you can secure your S3 buckets.

### Example 1: Enforce server-side encryption on all objects

As a security administrator, you can deny unencrypted uploads to your bucket by adding an IAM policy such as recommended by AWS (*https://oreil.ly/5ryzQ*).

```
{
     "Sid": "DenyUnencryptedObjectUploads",
     "Effect": "Deny",
     "Principal": "*",
     "Action": "s3:PutObject",
     "Resource": "arn:aws:s3:::awsexamplebucket1/*",
     "Condition": {
       "Null": {
         "s3:x-amz-server-side-encryption": "true"
       }
     }
}
```

The Condition statement in this block is what makes this policy effective.

### Example 2: Require users to have MFA while interacting with AWS S3

Another commonly used bucket policy is to enforce a multifactor authentication (MFA) requirement for any request that wants to interact with objects in the bucket:

```
{
     "Version": "2012-10-17",
```

```
    "Id": "123",
    "Statement": [
      {
        "Sid": "",
        "Effect": "Deny",
        "Principal": "*",
        "Action": "s3:*",
        "Resource": "arn:aws:s3:::DOC-EXAMPLE-BUCKET/taxdocuments/*",
        "Condition": { "Null": { "aws:MultiFactorAuthAge": true }}
      }
    ]
}
```

Appendix D provides a hands-on tutorial that cloud security professionals can use to apply PoLP to their S3 buckets.

## Amazon GuardDuty

Using Amazon GuardDuty, you can continuously monitor for threats and unauthorized behavior to protect your data stored in Amazon S3. Using machine learning, anomaly detection, and threat intelligence integrated into it, AWS GuardDuty identifies and prioritizes potential threats. AWS CloudTrail and virtual private cloud (VPC) flow logs, as well as DNS logs, are among GuardDuty's data sources. GuardDuty detects threats as well as sends out an automated response, speeding remediation and recovery times.

GuardDuty monitors threats to your Amazon S3 site by looking at CloudTrail S3 management events and CloudTrail management events. Data that GuardDuty customers generate, such as findings, gets encrypted while at rest using AWS KMS with AWS master keys (CMK), which is secured under AWS Shared Responsibility Model (SRM).

## Nonrepudiation Using Glacier Vault Lock

In order to maintain compliance, it is sometimes necessary to have a *system of record (SOR)* that is the authoritative data source for a given piece of information. This SOR is not just for internal consumers but also for external parties such as law enforcement authorities or compliance auditors to inspect in case of discrepancies. As a result, this SOR should be something that external agencies should be able to trust and use as evidence in case of discrepancies where your organization may have a conflict of interest. Thus, a certification of the integrity of the data by a third party may be important in such a situation.

With AWS Glacier Vault Lock, data can be stored in a way that can be certified for regulatory purposes for its integrity and authenticity. At the heart of this integrity process is the Glacier Vault Lock policy that controls how the data is stored and what access controls the organization has over their own data. Vault policies can have controls such as write once read many (WORM), which prevents future changes to the data that is stored. Once the policy has been locked, it cannot be changed.

You can use the AWS S3 Glacier bucket to store the data and lock the bucket to demonstrate to any regulatory body that may decide to audit you that the data has never been altered.

> In contrast to a vault access policy, a vault lock policy may be locked to prevent further changes to your vault, ensuring compliance for the vault.

To initiate a vault lock, you need to perform two steps (*https://oreil.ly/kF6E8*):

1. Attach a vault lock policy to your vault that will set the lock to an in-progress state, returning a lock ID. The lock will expire after 24 hours if the policy has not been validated.

2. If you are not satisfied with the results of the process, you can restart the lock process from scratch during the 24-hour validation period.

> Vault lock policies can help you comply with regulatory frameworks such as SEC Rule 17a-4 and HIPAA.

# Security at Rest for Compute Services

In this section, I will talk about how you can secure the services that are responsible for running your microservices. Before I talk about securing microservices at rest, I will briefly discuss what a typical development process looks like in a typical microservice shop.

Depending on development practices, there may be certain changes in specific steps, but overall, the flow looks something like what is illustrated in Figure 4-8.

1. Developers typically write code in a language of their choice. This may be Java, Python, Go, TypeScript, or any language of choice.

   *Security risk*: attackers may be able to exploit any code-level vulnerabilities or inject insecure libraries at the code level, and thus jeopardize the security posture of your entire application.

2. If you want to run this code on a typical containerized environment such as on a Kubernetes cluster, you compile this code on a continuous integration continuous delivery (CICD) pipeline and perform various steps on it until it turns into a containerized image. This CICD pipeline may use a storage system to hold persistent data such as libraries, configuration files, and more. If it runs on an AWS Elastic Cloud Compute (EC2) instance, an AWS *Elastic Block Store (EBS)* volume will generally hold such data.

*Security risk*: the EBS volumes that are used to build the image may be hijacked and used against your build process to inject vulnerabilities into the application or leak out sensitive code.

3. Once you have a containerized image such as a Docker image, you typically store this image on a Docker repository. You have many options here to store this image. AWS provides you with AWS Elastoc Container Registry (ECR) where you can store a Docker image.

*Security risk*: an unsecured storage of built images may result in allowing malicious actors to tamper with built container images and inject malicious code inside these containers. Alternatively, code can be leaked out of an unsecured container storage.

4. The Docker image from Step 2 can now be promoted to various environments of your choice. This way, you can have the same image running in your production environment as your staging environment. If you use Amazon EKS to run a Kubernetes cluster, and if you have your nodes running on AWS EC2, you may pull the image out of the ECR registry and promote it to the EC2 nodes. Similar to the CICD pipelines in Step 2, these nodes may employ EBS volumes to store persistent data. Security professionals may need to secure these EBS volumes.

*Security risk*: Although the containers run on the Kubernetes nodes, they may use EBS volumes to store persistent data. Very similar to Step 2, malicious actors who gain unauthorized access to these EBS volumes could manipulate the data stored on these volumes or leak out sensitive data to other external entities.

5. Alternatively, if you decide to run your code on AWS Lambda, you may deploy the code directly onto AWS Lambda and not have to worry about Steps 2–3.

*Security risk*: on AWS Lambda, you are not supposed to have long-term storage. However, the environment variables that your functions need may be stored on AWS and may need to be secured.

All microservice shops follow some variant of this flow, as seen in Figure 4-8.

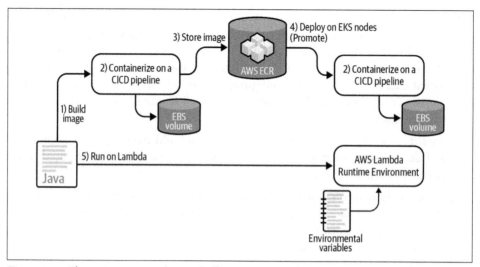

*Figure 4-8. The various steps that code flows through before running on a microservice environment.*

In the following section, I'll discuss the different security tools you have at your disposal to keep this data safe.

## Static Code Analysis Using AWS CodeGuru

Static code analysis is an up-and-coming branch in the field of computer security. Until recently, most static code analysis was difficult to perform, primarily due to the nondeterministic nature of computer languages. However, with the advent of AI and machine learning, security tools that end up identifying security vulnerabilities in code are only getting more accurate over time.

AWS provides users with *AWS CodeGuru*, which uses machine learning and AI to perform various types of analysis on your code. AWS CodeGuru then compares your code with its sample repositories and uses machine learning to identify security-related issues as well as other best practices in code. This analysis includes identifying possible resource leaks, exploits, and vulnerabilities with your code.

Static code analysis ensures that any problems with your codebase are identified early on in their lifecycle before they are shipped to production. Figure 4-9 shows a sample code where AWS CodeGuru recommended code-level changes.

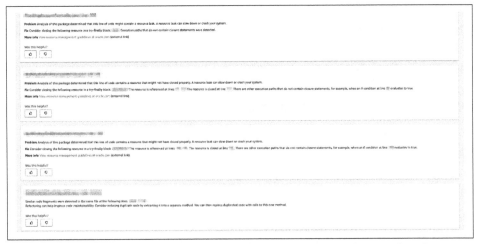

*Figure 4-9. Static code analysis can be enabled on existing repositories to identify Java code-related issues as well as security vulnerabilities.*

# AWS Elastic Container Registry

AWS ECR is the repository that AWS provides you with for storing built containers to house your microservices. This way, you can build microservices using Docker and promote these images to other environments. These images are provided with secure storage throughout their life. Using AWS ECR for storing containers offers multiple advantages, and I will highlight three of the most important reasons why AWS ECR is best suited for the job.

### Access control

AWS allows for the use of IAM policies to control access to the AWS ECR repositories. This way, the various contexts within your organization can be segregated using the PoLP to decide which containers can be accessed by the various entities within your organization. You can use identity-based policies as well as resource-based policies to control access.

AWS maintains a list (*https://oreil.ly/b4LJr*) of various IAM policies that you can apply to your ECR repositories. Here is a sample IAM policy that allows the user to list and manage images in an ECR repository:

```
{
    "Version":"2012-10-17",
    "Statement":[
        {
            "Sid":"ListImagesInRepository",
            "Effect":"Allow",
            "Action":[
                "ecr:ListImages"
```

```
        ],
        "Resource":"arn:aws:ecr:us-east-1:123456789012:repository/my-repo"
      },
      {
        "Sid":"GetAuthorizationToken",
        "Effect":"Allow",
        "Action":[
          "ecr:GetAuthorizationToken"
        ],
        "Resource":"*"
      },
      {
        "Sid":"ManageRepositoryContents",
        "Effect":"Allow",
        "Action":[
            "ecr:BatchCheckLayerAvailability",
            "ecr:GetDownloadUrlForLayer",
            "ecr:GetRepositoryPolicy",
            "ecr:DescribeRepositories",
            "ecr:ListImages",
            "ecr:DescribeImages",
            "ecr:BatchGetImage",
            "ecr:InitiateLayerUpload",
            "ecr:UploadLayerPart",
            "ecr:CompleteLayerUpload",
            "ecr:PutImage"
        ],
        "Resource":"arn:aws:ecr:us-east-1:123456789012:repository/my-repo"
      }
    ]
}
```

Alternatively, if you want to allow users to get read-only access to all images, you can use the managed AWS policies (*https://oreil.ly/sKeIo*) in order to achieve a similar goal.

### Encryption at rest

AWS ECR is backed by AWS S3, which also allows images to be encrypted at rest using very similar techniques to AWS S3. Figure 4-10 illustrates how your containers are protected in AWS ECR using AWS KMS. KMS grants are created each time you need to allow access to the image.

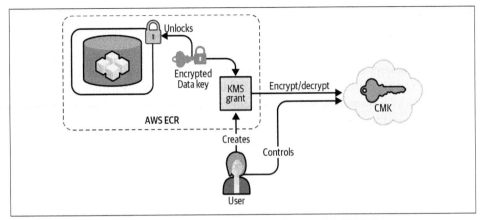

*Figure 4-10. Images within AWS ECR are encrypted using AWS KMS.*

You can enable encryption for container storage in AWS ECR through the AWS Management Console, as seen in Figure 4-11.

*Figure 4-11. KMS encryption can be enabled for AWS ECR by enabling the "Customize encryption settings" box and choosing the KMS CMK you wish to use.*

### Image Common Vulnerability and Exposure scanning

AWS ECR provides the ability to scan containers for common vulnerabilities using the open source clair project (*https://github.com/quay/clair*). This scanning ensures that the containers are protected from malware. You can either enable common vulnerability and exposure (CVE) scanning by default for every container that is uploaded to AWS ECR or manually scan each container image on ECR. Figure 4-12 shows how you can enable CVE for all images.

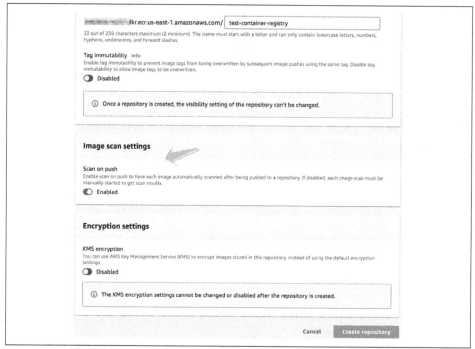

*Figure 4-12. CVE can be enabled by default on every image that is pushed to ECR.*

## AWS Lambda

Although AWS Lambda should not be used for long-term storage, sometimes the input variables that are provided to Lambda functions as *environment variables* may contain sensitive data. Storing this data on the cloud without encrypting may result in a not-so-ideal security situation. Hence, AWS allows you to automatically encrypt the environment variables that are stored for AWS Lambda functions.

There are two ways you can encrypt environment variables:

- Encryption using CMK
- Encryption using external helpers

### Encryption using CMK

Just like AWS S3 and AWS ECR, environment variables can be encrypted on the server side. You can either allow AWS to handle the encryption for you by using the AWS-owned CMK or manage the permissions and the lifecycle around the CMK by providing a reference to an existing CMK. You can then secure this CMK using the PoLP.

### Encryption using helpers

Encryption helpers add an extra layer of protection to your environment variables by encrypting the variables on the command side before adding them to the Lambda. This will ensure that the variables are not visible in their unencrypted form on the AWS console.

## AWS Elastic Block Store

Finally, if you run your services on EC2 (either directly or using Amazon Elastic Kubernetes Service [EKS] with EC2 as the worker nodes), AWS KMS can be used to encrypt the backing EBS volumes that back these EC2 instances. As seen in Figure 4-13, the data key for the EBS volume is cached for the purpose of speed and reliability.

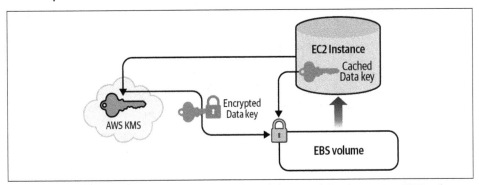

*Figure 4-13. EC2 instances decrypt the data key that is used for decrypting EBS volumes by making requests to AWS KMS. Once decrypted, EC2 instances retain the unencrypted data key in their cache for as long as the instance is running.*

Since the data key is cached inside the EC2 instance, once an instance is attached to the volume, it is able to access the data from the EBS volume without making requests to the KMS-based CMK. Every time the instance is terminated, the instance may need to make a new request to the CMK in order to reattach to the EBS volume.

# Tying It All Together

Now that I've explained why security at rest is important, let's discuss how AWS tools can help protect your microservice code:

1. For code-level vulnerabilities and resource leaks, AWS CodeGuru helps in running through the code and performing static code analysis.

2. AWS KMS can help in encrypting EBS volumes (either using AWS managed/owned keys or customer managed CMKs), resulting in a secure build process.

3. IAM policies can be used to control access to AWS ECR. The containers on ECR can also be encrypted using server-side encryption. Finally, you can use CVE image scanners to scan containers that are stored on AWS ECR for common vulnerabilities.

4. EBS volumes that are used by Kubernetes nodes can also be encrypted on AWS using KMS and thus be protected from unauthorized access.

5. Finally, the environment variables that are provided to AWS Lambdas can also be encrypted using either CMK or encryption helpers.

Figure 4-14 points out the various controls that AWS provides us with in order to increase the security for all the steps outlined in Figure 4-8.

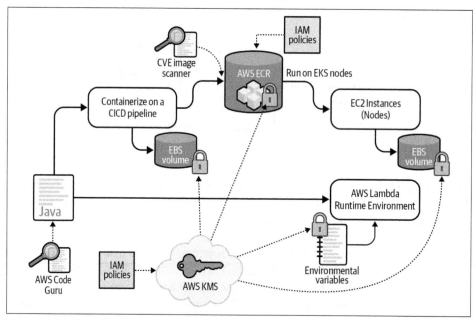

*Figure 4-14. For all the steps I outlined in Figure 4-8, AWS provides us with controls that can help in reducing the exposure to potential threats.*

# Microservice Database Systems

After I've explained the different compute services on AWS, I'll discuss the types of storage options you have for your microservices and how AWS protects your sensitive data.

I have already talked about the possibility of polyglot persistence mechanisms in microservice systems. Figure 4-15 shows a typical microservice-based organization where services are segregated by their functional domains. Each of these domains represents a wider bounded context. Each service talks to a datastore within its bounded context and not to any external datastore. As a result, depending on the needs of the domain, each bounded context may choose to use a different kind of a database.

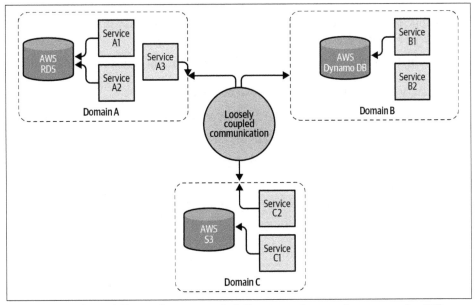

*Figure 4-15. Three different domains with different needs may choose to go for different types of databases. Domain A may need relational data and hence might choose AWS Relational Database Service (RDS) as its datastore. Domain B may prefer to store its data in a NoSQL DynamoDb datastore, while Domain C may store its data in AWS S3 buckets.*

## AWS DynamoDB

AWS DynamoDB is a serverless, fully managed NoSQL database system that can be used for data storage in various applications.

## Access control on AWS DynamoDB

AWS DynamoDB supports IAM policies just like any other resource on AWS. Using AWS DynamoDB, however, gives you control over who can access what part (row or column or both) of the database and when. The conditions section of an IAM policy gives you fine-grained control of permissions. Let me go through an example to illustrate my point.

Consider an organization that stores employee information in a DynamoDB table. Each row contains a variety of information about each employee. This may include their name, state, country, salary, and Social Security number. You might have two types of users that may access this information:

- User: this may be a regular employee who may need to access their own row to change or update their address in the system. However, they may not access their salary or Social Security number for security purposes.

- Admin: this is a more powerful user who may need full access to the entire table.

The primary key for fetching each row can be the Username.

Figure 4-16 shows the employee table that can contain the employee information.

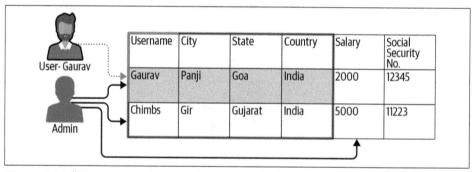

*Figure 4-16. "User - Gaurav" may only access and edit the row that has the username Gaurav and may only access the Username, City, State, and Country columns, as highlighted.*

So for IAM user Gaurav, you want to allow:

- GetItem and UpdateItem access
- Access to specific attributes (Username, City, State, and Country)
- Access for only the rows where the username is Gaurav

The IAM policy you can use for such a situation is shown in Figure 4-17.

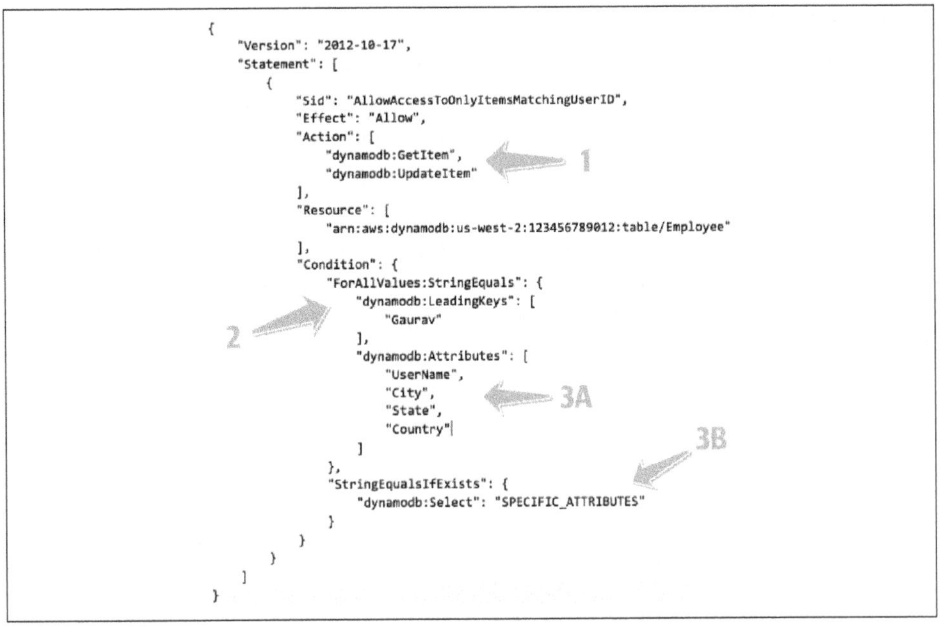

```
{
    "Version": "2012-10-17",
    "Statement": [
        {
            "Sid": "AllowAccessToOnlyItemsMatchingUserID",
            "Effect": "Allow",
            "Action": [
                "dynamodb:GetItem",
                "dynamodb:UpdateItem"
            ],
            "Resource": [
                "arn:aws:dynamodb:us-west-2:123456789012:table/Employee"
            ],
            "Condition": {
                "ForAllValues:StringEquals": {
                    "dynamodb:LeadingKeys": [
                        "Gaurav"
                    ],
                    "dynamodb:Attributes": [
                        "UserName",
                        "City",
                        "State",
                        "Country"
                    ]
                },
                "StringEqualsIfExists": {
                    "dynamodb:Select": "SPECIFIC_ATTRIBUTES"
                }
            }
        }
    ]
}
```

*Figure 4-17. This is the IAM policy that when applied to user Gaurav will result in satisfying our requirement. 1, 2, 3A, and 3B identify the sections of the IAM policy that help in fine-tuning the permission policy.*

As seen in Figure 4-17, you can use certain policy elements to fine-tune the IAM policy:

1. To start, you can apply PoLP to the operations you want to allow.

2. The condition key LeadingKeys can be used to specify the key that should be checked for while applying the policy. In this example, any row that has the key Gaurav will be accessible to the user Gaurav. You can alternatively change the hard-coded name "Gaurav" to ${www.amazon.com:user_id} if you want to direct AWS to allow the currently authenticated user to access a column with their own name, as highlighted in an AWS article (*https://oreil.ly/UBBlb*).

3. 3A and 3B will specify which attributes are accessible. Since I specify SPECIFIC_ATTRIBUTES (3B) in the statement, only the requests that select a specific subset of the attributes specified in 3A will be allowed to proceed, while any privilege escalation will be denied.

AWS maintains a list (*https://oreil.ly/MLK7h*) of various conditions that you can use to fine-tune such access to AWS DynamoDB. With an effective use of key conditions, you can hide data from various users and thus follow the PoLP on DynamoDB.

### Encryption on DynamoDB

DynamoDB offers an easy-to-integrate encryption process to its users in addition to access control. DynamoDB has server-side encryption by default, and it cannot be disabled. DynamoDB uses envelope encryption to encrypt all items that are stored on the table. AWS uses AES-256 symmetric encryption for encrypting all data in DynamoDB.

Each item in a DynamoDB table is encrypted using a *data encryption key (DEK)*. This DEK is then encrypted using a *table key*. There is one table key per table. Each table key can decrypt multiple DEKs. And finally, this table key is encrypted using a CMK. Figure 4-18 illustrates this flow.

*Figure 4-18. AWS DynamoDB uses a three-step envelope encryption process where 1) a CMK is used to encrypt a table key, then 2) the table key is used to encrypt DEKs, and then 3) the keys are used to encrypt items inside DynamoDB.*

Each time a client wishes to read data from the table, the client first has to make a request to KMS and decrypt the table key using KMS. If the client is authorized to decrypt the table key, DynamoDB then decrypts and caches it on behalf of the client. This table key can then be used to decrypt each DEK and thus decrypt individual items out of DynamoDB. This way, the clients don't have to make repeated requests to KMS and thus save on KMS fees.

> The table key in DynamoDb is cached per connection for five minutes. A cached table key avoids repeated calls to AWS KMS and thus results in faster performance and lower costs. To make most use of the caching capability of KMS, using clients that can pool database connections can result in better performance and lower costs.

Now that I have talked about how AWS KMS can be used for encrypting data on DynamoDB, I will introduce you to the three options you have for using KMS. These options are similar to those you had on AWS S3:

- AWS owned CMK
- Customer owned CMK
- Customer managed CMK

As seen in Figure 4-19, the type of CMK can be selected through the AWS Management Console:

*AWS owned CMK*
This is the default option on AWS. An AWS owned CMK is a shared CMK that is used by AWS to encrypt the table key on your account. These keys do not show up on your account. AWS manages and handles all activity related to the CMK. This CMK is not under your control, and you cannot track or audit any access to this CMK. No additional charge is required for encrypting data using an AWS owned CMK.

*KMS–Customer managed CMK*
This is the most flexible option for use with AWS DynamoDB. These keys are completely managed by the customer, and AWS does not control or manage the lifecycle of these keys. While creating a table, you can specify the AWS KMS CMK that you would like to use as the CMK for the table. You can optionally rotate the keys every year.

*KMS–AWS managed CMK*
AWS managed CMKs are keys that are in your account and managed on your behalf by AWS. As a result, you get more control over the keys and you can audit and monitor access to these keys. AWS, on the other hand, handles the security of the infrastructure that backs these keys and rotates these keys periodically. AWS managed keys do, however, incur the routine KMS charges for encryption and decryption.

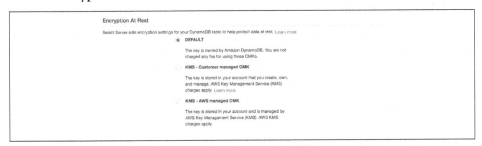

*Figure 4-19. You can select the type of CMK you would like to use for encryption at rest on DynamoDB.*

# Amazon Aurora Relational Data Service

Amazon Aurora is another popular data storage system that is used on AWS. Aurora provides drop-in replacement for popular RDBMS engines such as PostgreSQL and MySQL. Similar to AWS DynamoDB, Aurora databases also can be secured from unauthorized access in two ways:

- Using authentication (*https://oreil.ly/7h0RN*) to prevent unauthorized access. This can be further divided into two categories of authentication:
  - *IAM database authentication*: this uses AWS IAM in order to authorize each request.
  - *Password authentication*: this uses the traditional password-based approach toward authenticating against Aurora.
- Using encryption to protect the data.

As seen in Figure 4-20, you can decide on the type of authentication option you want to use while creating your database.

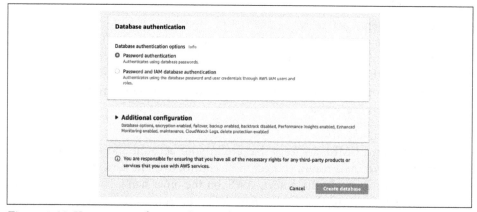

*Figure 4-20. You can specify your choice of authentication during database creation.*

## IAM authentication on Amazon Aurora

In IAM authentication, instead of using a password to authenticate against the database, you create an authentication token that you include with your database request. These tokens can be generated outside the database using AWS Signature Version 4 (SigV4) and can be used in place of regular authentication.

The biggest advantage that IAM authentication provides you with is that your identities within the database are synced with your identities within your AWS account. This stops you from proliferating identities across your resources.

However, IAM authentication has its limitations. There might be a limitation on how many connections a DB cluster can have per second, depending on its DB instance class and your workload. Hence, AWS recommends that IAM authentication be used only for temporary personal access to databases.

### Password authentication

Password authentication is the traditional type of authentication. In this case, every connection to the database has to be initiated with the traditional username and password. Each user and role on the database has to be created by an admin user that exists on the database. The passwords are generally text strings that each calling entity has to remember and enter while establishing the connection. You create users with SQL statements such as CREATE USER for MySQL (*https://oreil.ly/rCYXp*) or PostgreSQL (*https://oreil.ly/aKxk3*).

### Encryption on Amazon Aurora

Similarly to AWS DynamoDB and AWS S3, all data stored on Amazon Aurora can be encrypted using a CMK. Enabling encryption is extremely easy in Aurora, as seen in Figure 4-21.

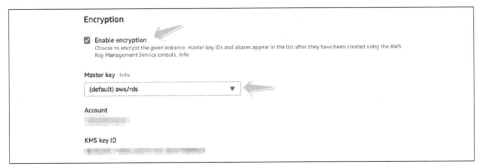

*Figure 4-21. You can enable encryption by simply checking the box titled "Enable encryption" while creating your database. You can also choose the CMK you would like to use for encrypting your database.*

You can either use the AWS managed key to encrypt the database or provide an existing CMK you can control using KMS. The trade-offs of using a customer managed CMK versus using an AWS managed CMK are similar to those when using AWS DynamoDB or using AWS S3.

# Media Sanitization and Data Deletion

Disposal of data is an often overlooked aspect of data protection that security professionals have to account for. In physical data centers, after a server has been decommissioned, IT professionals have to perform certain activities (which I will elaborate later) on this server before it can be reused for any other activities. These activities will depend on the class of data that was originally stored on this server. These may include, but are not limited to, zeroing of all your data, reformatting your data, and so forth.

If your hardware stored top secret data, you may have to securely wipe the data from this hardware before you can use it for storing nonconfidential data. This process is called *media sanitization*. Failure to do so may make the data vulnerable to potentially unauthorized applications that may be able to gain access to these data hashes.

On cloud systems, you may not have complete control over the process of commissioning and decommissioning servers. This problem may be especially more pronounced in microservice architectures where it is common to spin up new projections or take them down.

To begin with, I would like to remind you that any sensitive data in any of your storage volumes must always be encrypted at rest. This at least lessens the probability of a data leak. On its end, AWS assumes the responsibility of sanitizing underlying storage mediums on your behalf, for all of its persistent storage layers, including EBS-backed storage volumes (for example, Amazon Aurora, EC2, and DocumentDB), AWS sanitizes media for you as prescribed by the NIST-800-88 (*https://oreil.ly/4heHR*) standards. AWS guarantees that storage volumes used by you will be sanitized and securely wiped prior to being made available to the next customer. This form of media sanitization makes AWS volumes compliant with most regulatory standards in the industry.

However, if you work in a highly regulated industry where data encryption and the guarantee that AWS provides for media sanitization are not sufficient, you can make use of third-party media sanitization tools to securely wipe your storage volumes before decommissioning them.

## Summary

This chapter has dealt mostly with data storage on AWS. I started off by making a case for security around data storage, access control, and encryption. Most storage mechanisms on AWS can be protected using two ways. First, you can prevent unauthorized access to your sensitive data using AWS IAM policies. Second, you can encrypt the data and secure the encryption key, thus adding an extra layer of security on top of your data protection mechanism.

Since microservice environments generally result in polyglot persistence mechanisms, the onus is on security professionals to ensure that each of these services pay special attention to the security policies around each data storage and apply the PoLP on all the storage mechanisms.

# Networking Security

In Chapter 1, I briefly discussed how some controls are blunt in that they aim to unilaterally block all requests that come their way without attempting to identify the requestor or the context under which the request is made. An example of a blunt security control is a *network control*. This chapter is devoted to discussing the various network controls that you can add on AWS.

A network control is any security control that may be added at the network layer of the infrastructure, as identified by the Open Systems Interconnection (OSI) networking model. For the purposes of this chapter, I will assume that you have a basic understanding of computer networks. You can learn more about computer networks by reading *Computer Networks* by Andrew Tanenbaum and David Wetherall (Pearson).

The network layer security infrastructure does not read or understand application layer semantics. Rather than seeing applications (that run business logic) interacting with one another, the security infrastructure sees *network interfaces* that interact with one another, making it difficult to apply controls that can incorporate business logic. In general, network security is like an axe: solid, powerful, but occasionally blunt and inaccurate. In no way am I discrediting the importance of network security but merely pointing out that it requires refinement to accommodate any nuance in applying security rules.

If you list every service in your application, you can roughly divide these services into two sets. The first are called *edge services*, which allow end users to fetch or change the state of their aggregates. These services are internet facing and hence are exposed to threats from around the world that most internal services may never have to face. The edge services are said to be residing in the *public zone* of your cloud infrastructure. For the purposes of this chapter, I will not be focusing on the services within the public zone. Rest assured, I will go into detail about these public-facing services in Chapter 6.

The second set of services are the ones that communicate *only* with other services or resources within your organization. I will label these as *backend services*. They operate in nonpublic environments, giving them an extra shield of protection against external (public) threats. This chapter focuses mainly on services that live within this private zone.

Figure 5-1 shows how services can be classified into edge and backend services.

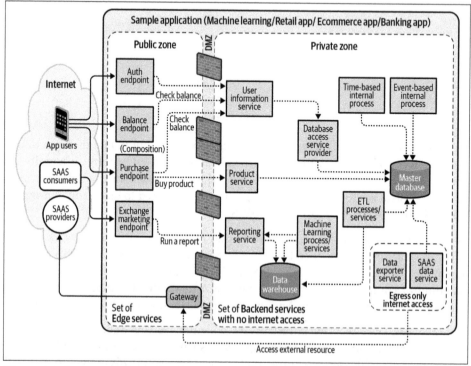

*Figure 5-1. In any sample application, services that are called by external consumers can be classified as edge services. Edge services live in the "public zone" of a cloud environment, while a vast majority of services that either act upon data or are called by other services can exist in isolation in the "private zone," and require different security consideration.*

Almost every application that runs in the cloud will have some edge services and some backend services, whether the application is a mobile app, an ecommerce website, or a data-processing application. If any of your services need access to external Software as a Service (SaaS) providers, you may be able to classify backend services further into a specialized bucket where they can have outgoing internet access in a controlled way, but still cannot be accessed directly from the internet.

In my experience, it is best to keep business logic at the edge (public zone) to a minimum and refactor it as much as possible into the secure private zone. This technique protects the application's core functionality from unknown threats prevalent on the internet, making it much more difficult for outside parties to gain unauthorized access.

Chapter 1 introduced you to the concept of *isolation* and *blast radius* using the analogy of locked doors. In essence, you want your services to be isolated into logical partitions so that any breach of any of these partitions doesn't affect the security of other services. I also made a case for *segmenting* (partitioning) microservice domains based on business logic. At the network layer, this strategy of segmentation based on business logic is called *microsegmentation*.

A microsegmentation strategy where the resulting partitions are too small will result in services making too many calls that span across network segments. This leads to overhead that is costly and complex. A microsegmentation strategy where the resulting partitions are too wide may not enforce the security rules you had hoped to enforce at the network layer. This makes this whole exercise moot. By the end of this chapter, you will know how to make an informed choice on where to draw the line between services and be able to implement the right strategy that fits the security needs of your organization.

A good domain-driven design (DDD) is a prerequisite for a network-level microsegmentation to be cost effective. If microsegmentation is done against a bad domain design where there is a lot of cross-context dependence (coupling), cross-context calls may overwhelm the system, resulting in higher costs and complexity.

# Networking on AWS

Throughout this chapter, segmentation and isolation of services are the guiding theme. Once this segmentation has been achieved, I discuss ways in which legitimate and authorized communication between these isolated partitions can be effectively enabled.

## Controls

A *control* or *countermeasure* is any action that results in reducing the aggregate risk of an application. I want to echo a nuanced but controversial claim that I first came across in the book *Enterprise Security Architecture* by John Sherwood et al. (CRC Press). *Network controls do not provide direct application or data security*. I say controversial because there is so much network layer security software claiming to offer just that (data protection). Network layer controls are unable to read application data, and they cannot understand what is being communicated semantically. Thus, any controls applied to the network need to be blunt. Your ability to use the controls with precision is severely limited. As a result, network restrictions are generally too broad and sometimes obstruct value-adding activities. You may be able to identify and control communication patterns and the channels that facilitate this communication, but you have no visibility into the content of these communication channels. I will now qualify my claim. Although a well-designed network infrastructure does not directly reduce application risk, it can indirectly have a large impact. It allows for a simpler and more secure architecture, thereby indirectly reducing the impact of security incidents through isolation and monitoring.

## Understanding the Monolith and Microservice Models

In the monolithic model, the prevailing approach to security has been to create a security zone by grouping services together in a zone of trust. In such a design, services within a zone trust one another, possibly without authentication in between. This means that the public-facing services may have their own security zone while databases may also have their own security zone. However, in many cases these divisions are not based on business domains but rather technical ones.

In this model, a trusted zone can have a boundary that demarcates what is expendable from the rest of the application. By securing this perimeter, you can protect the parts of your application that host sensitive data, such as the database and application services, from external threats. This protective barrier is sometimes referred to as the *demilitarized zone* (DMZ). Because of the presence of a strong DMZ, the presence of trust within zones can be somewhat justified. This security pattern works well in monolith systems where network communication between services is minimal. On the other hand, if one system gets compromised, the entire network may become compromised and perimeters will become ineffective. Some of the systems can fall victim to attacks by trusted insiders, where employees or contractors can make use of the trust-based advantage they have by being inside the DMZ. To be clear, I am not saying you should take down any perimeter protection. After all, many regulators explicitly require the presence of such a perimeter. I suggest adding extra (in some cases, redundant) protections within the perimeter to protect from a trusted but compromised insider.

With microservices, the work to access database layers and other business logic may be divided up among various isolated services that talk to one another through some form of network-based transport. This isolation allows microservice applications to develop security controls that are more specific to their systems. Now, every communication between every service requires independent access control regardless of whether they are in the same zone or different ones. This setup is called a *zero trust network*. The security aspect of a zero trust network sounds great but comes with an additional overhead. Microservices are supposed to follow the single-responsibility principle (SRP), where they are not supposed to perform any task apart from the one business case that they are designed to be used for. It becomes difficult to justify the presence of extensive network authorization logic inside each and every service provider. This is where we get to an impasse. An ideal microservices architecture should have the benefits of a zero trust network, but without the added complexity.

## Segmentation and Microservices

A good DDD posits that communication between services within the same domain is much more common and likely than communication across domains. Domains even in a good domain-driven system may still require cross-domain communication. This communication, however, will be structured to follow a well-defined contract. Security controls are far more important and easier to implement when using clearly defined API contracts. Thus, it makes more sense to divide the network infrastructure based on domain contexts rather than the technology layer systems in a DDD setup.

DDD applications suggest using a strategy of microsegmentation, where domains or bounded contexts are divided based on their business use case and then secured individually against attacks. In microsegmentation, the traditional network is divided further by compartmentalizing and isolating disparate segments, which have no business justification to talk to one another. A large part of this chapter is devoted toward implementing a successful microsegmentation strategy.

Microsegmentation is not a silver bullet that can solve all security-related concerns at the network layer. It works best by augmenting application-level security, not by replacing it. It also comes with added complexity and costs, which need to be carefully evaluated against the perceived security benefit from such a security measure.

## Software-Defined Network Partitions

In order to achieve microsegmentation, it is important to understand how various networking constructs are structured within AWS. You may be aware that AWS is expanding its infrastructure globally. By dividing the world into different regions, AWS adheres to regulatory restrictions. AWS offers high availability by dividing the cloud landscape into availability zones (AZs) within each region. More information can be found in an AWS article on global regions (*https://oreil.ly/4grdo*). You will ultimately run most of your services in a particular region in a particular availability zone (or zones). However, beyond these divisions, the network infrastructure itself cannot be physically separated. This is especially a problem since you may be sharing an AZ with other AWS customers, possibly your competitors. So instead of physical separation, you are provided with tools for dividing the network infrastructure logically. These tools can be collectively called *software defined networking (SDN)* tools.

These tools provide outcomes similar to the services provided by their physical counterparts in on-premises networks.

Just like any physical network, cloud networks have their own routers for routing requests. AWS provides each network partition with an abstraction in the form of a *route table* to control how traffic flows between the various network partitions on AWS. At a regional level, AWS provides a virtual private cloud (VPC)—Amazon's network virtualization—that isolates your cloud environment into smaller cloud-based partitions. At an AZ level, *subnets* help in grouping and segmenting services using IP address ranges using the Classless Inter-Domain Routing (CIDR) notations. VPCs isolate your networks; hence, I call them hard partitions. Subnets group services together; these I call soft partitions.

The tools shown in Figure 5-2 can be used to isolate each service into its own logical partition to restrict the sphere of influence of each service.

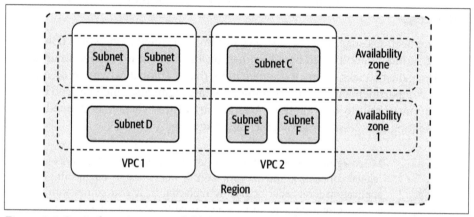

*Figure 5-2. Logical partitions available in the AWS cloud infrastructure (https://oreil.ly/ LV1Le). Each AWS region may have multiple AZs. You can create subnets that restrict your services to a single AZ. Although you can create VPCs that span multiple AZs, each VPC must be tied to a single region.*

I will assume that services within bounded contexts benefit from a level of familiarity with one another. Therefore, communication within bounded contexts has an inherently lower risk and is easier to secure using controls I have discussed. Familiarity, however, cannot be expected across bounded contexts. Therefore, additional controls are required to reduce the risk involved in cross-context communication. Figure 5-3 outlines a microsegmentation strategy that leverages this behavior that is observed around bounded contexts.

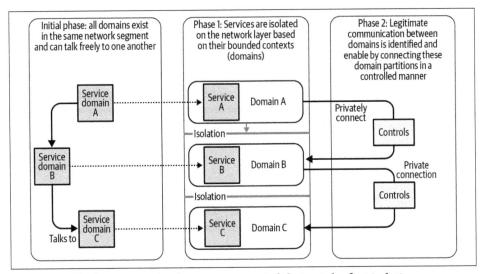

*Figure 5-3. The best way to implement a segregated design is by first isolating your microservice domains using VPCs or subnets, and then connecting the legitimate ones to one another using the tools I will discuss in this chapter.*

As seen in Figure 5-3, you can have a microsegmented network layer that mirrors your domain logic by following the steps outlined in these two phases:

*Phase 1 (Isolate)*
> In this phase, you will divide and isolate your microservices at the network layer based on whether they belong to the same business domain. In the next sections, I will introduce you to the tools you can use to create these network partitions on AWS. The end result of this phase should be that you are in a position to isolate your services according to their business domains and bounded contexts.

*Phase 2 (Connect)*
> With your services isolated based on their domain, you should work on identifying and connecting the services that require legitimate cross-domain communication. This ensures that the network isolation from Phase 1 does not prevent the services from doing their work. It is, of course, communication links that are susceptible to threats. Thus, adding security controls to these internetwork links is a fundamental requirement in this phase.

# Subnetting

Subnets on AWS are not much different from subnets on any traditional networking stack. The IP address space within a cloud can be segmented into smaller building blocks using subnets. Subnets are what I refer to as *soft partitions*. Since they cannot span across AZs, subnets cannot provide the level of isolation that VPCs do.

However, they provide a great way of grouping services together so that you can apply security controls.

On AWS, a subnet is an AZ-level partition. In other words, each subnet must live inside a single AZ. Subnets are declared with the CIDR notation that specifies all the IPs within a particular range that can reside in a particular subnet. Most cloud services will run inside a subnet and will carry an internal IP address that is part of the IP space assigned to this subnet. So a subnet with the CIDR 192.168.0.0/24 includes all IPs from 192.168.0.1 to 192.168.0.254 (the first and last IP address of each block is reserved).

 There are tools available on the internet to help you calculate and create IPv4 subnet CIDR blocks. You can find tools that suit your needs by searching for terms such as "subnet calculator" or "CIDR calculator."

Figure 5-4 shows the process of creating a subnet inside a VPC.

*Figure 5-4. Creating a subnet on AWS requires providing the CIDR block for the IPs that are allowed to exist inside this subnet.*

 An AZ in one account may not map to the same location as an AZ with the same name in a different account. This leads to a lot of confusion, especially while designing endpoint services. Hence, AZs should never be referenced using their names across different accounts.

An AZ may contain one or more subnets. To ensure that services end up in a specific AZ, you should deploy these services to a subnet within that particular AZ. You should consider deploying most of your services to at least two AZs (and in extension, at least two subnets) if you want to maintain high availability. Figure 5-5 shows a typical deployment you may see for most organizations.

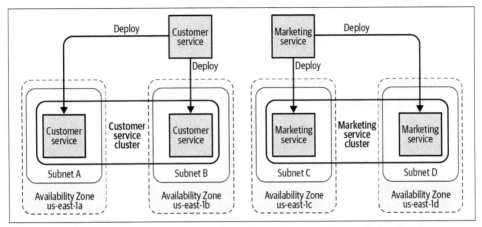

*Figure 5-5. To achieve high availability for a cluster, it is recommended to deploy a service to at least two subnets.*

## Routing in a Subnet

Routing inside the AWS network is governed by a lookup table called the *route table* (*https://oreil.ly/re4UL*), which inspects the network traffic and provides routing details for the next hop for each network packet. Each subnet must be associated with a route table, which controls the routing for the subnet. Route tables are used to orchestrate the controlled cross-partition communication I talked about in "Software-Defined Network Partitions" on page 145. I will be revisiting route tables when I talk about VPCs, the other way of segmenting network partitions.

The entries in a route table are CIDR blocks that encompass a collection of one or more IPs. Apart from individual CIDR blocks, you can also include a named list of CIDRs known as a prefix list. A *prefix list* is either a customer-defined block of IP addresses (also defined using the CIDR notation), in which case it is called a *customer-managed prefix list*, or a managed AWS service, in which case it is called an *AWS-managed prefix list*.

Using route tables, subnets allow you to specify rules on which network partitions can talk to one another and which cannot. Since you get complete control over these rules, subnets can become great tools for setting up the network environment in which your services can run. You can also apply the principle of least privilege (PoLP) at the subnet level by deciding which services can connect to the public internet and isolating services that don't need direct internet access.

Not having internet connectivity will also ensure that sensitive data or information has no direct way of leaving your network without compromising multiple parts of the system.

## Gateways and Subnets

In the networking world, a *gateway* is a node on a network that acts as a forwarding host to another network. On AWS, with respect to subnets, there are three gateways that every cloud network architect should be aware of:

*Internet gateway*
> An internet gateway is the cloud-managed AWS component that acts as the gateway for your private cloud network to the wider public internet. This will enable your private cloud network's services to communicate with the internet and for public services to route to destinations within your private network.

*Network address translation (NAT) gateway*
> A NAT gateway is the cloud-managed AWS component that provides outgoing internet access to your services. A NAT gateway provides one-way stateful access to the internet (through an internet gateway) for services that are otherwise disconnected from the internet.

*Egress-only internet gateway*
> Very similar to a NAT gateway, an egress-only internet gateway also allows one-way stateful access to the internet through an internet gateway. Unlike a NAT gateway, an egress-only internet gateway allows internet access for subnets that use IPv6 addresses and can directly connect with the internet in a stateful manner.

If your network uses IPv4, an internet gateway also provides network address translation (NAT) (*https://oreil.ly/CrKZR*) services for your address space.

## Public Subnet

A *public subnet* is a subnet in which the instances that are present can be routed from the public internet. What makes a subnet *public* is the presence of a route to an internet gateway. An *internet gateway* is a gateway device that gives your subnet a route to or from the public internet. Naturally, this should raise alarms in the minds of security enthusiasts since any remote possibility of having access from the public internet brings with it the possibility of unauthorized access if the administrators are not careful.

When any service is launched on AWS, it receives an IP address. In a public subnet, depending on the settings, your host may get a public IP address from the pool of addresses controlled by AWS. This address is assigned to the instance's elastic network interface (ENI). This address is in addition to a private address that is assigned to the instance.

Just because your service exists in a public subnet does not make it automatically routable from the internet. For that to happen, you need to have a *route* from the internet gateway to your service's host.

## Private Subnet

A *private subnet* is the opposite of a public one. There is no direct route from an internet gateway to this subnet. As a result, for external entities, it is not possible to directly access any resources that are deployed to this subnet without first entering through a public subnet of your network.

Running a service in an isolated network that is logically isolated from the rest of the world ensures that a compromised application can still be contained at a network layer in addition to the controls you may have at the application layer.

If you follow the PoLP, you will want to put all of your code and services in a private subnet except the ones that absolutely need to be routable from the public internet. Making more services private and deploying them in a private subnet may be the single most helpful thing you can do to make your network more secure when dealing with sensitive data.

## Subnets and Availability Zones

When you deploy a microservice on AWS, you will almost always be asked to select a subnet in which this service will run. I call this the *subnetworking problem*. This is true for AWS Lambdas as well as Kubernetes pods. From a security perspective, to decide on which subnet these services will run, you can ask yourself two questions:

- Does this service need to be accessible via the public internet? This will determine whether the service should be deployed to a public subnet or a private subnet.

- Which AZ do you want this service to be deployed in? If you want high availability, you may decide to redundantly deploy multiple services in different AZs.

Overall, you want to choose a subnet that belongs to an AZ where you will get maximum availability.

Figure 5-6 shows an example where I try to answer this question. Let us assume I have a service (Service A) that I want to deploy. Service A is a backend service and should only live in the private zone. Service A already has an instance running in AZ 1B, so I want to specifically deploy it to AZ 1A.

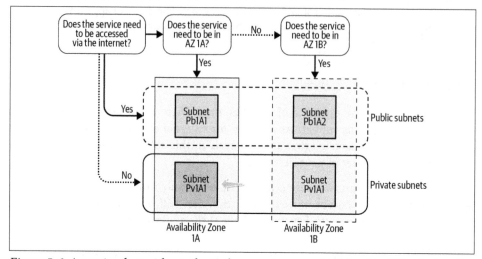

*Figure 5-6. A service that wishes to be in the private zone of AZ 1A should be deployed to Subnet Pv1A1.*

I decide to go with Subnet Pv1A1 because it satisfies both conditions:

- It is a private subnet.
- It belongs to AZ 1A.

While accessibility from the internet is one side of the story, whether or not a device on a private subnet can access the internet by initiating connections from within the private subnet depends on whether there is a gateway associated with this subnet. I cover that use case in the next section when I introduce NAT gateways.

## Internet Access for Subnets

The internet gateway is what makes our services accessible over the internet. In the case of a private subnet, the desire is to not make it routable over the internet. However, many services from within a private subnet may still find the need to access external resources. That may be because they want to call an external rest endpoint or possibly download files from some internet location. The instances in the public subnet can send outbound traffic directly to the internet, whereas the instances in the private subnet cannot. Instead, the instances in the private subnet can access the internet by using a NAT gateway that resides in the public subnet.

 An egress-only internet gateway can be used for almost identical purposes to that of a NAT gateway in subnets that use IPv6 addresses.

A NAT gateway itself lives in a public subnet and routes outgoing requests from a private subnet through the internet gateway to the public internet. Requests that go through the NAT gateway have to be initiated from within the private subnet. Having said that, by default the NAT gateway maintains a stateful connection and therefore, an outgoing request automatically allows an incoming response even if the requestor is inside a private subnet. Thus, it allows for safe outgoing communication even from within the private subnet. Although it does pose the risk that a bad actor from within the private subnet could compromise and send out sensitive data, the compromise ensures that you have a middle ground when it comes to the trade-off between complete isolation and full internet connectivity. Figure 5-7 highlights this flow.

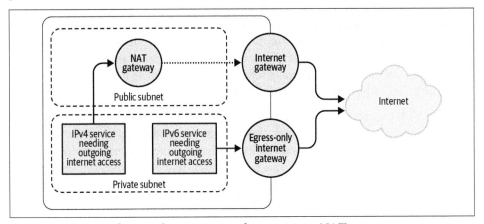

*Figure 5-7. Services from within a private subnet require a NAT gateway or an egress-only internet gateway in order to access the public internet.*

 It is best to follow least privilege and only allow services that absolutely must connect to the internet to be inside such a private subnet, where an outgoing connection to the public internet exists.

Unlike public subnets, private subnets do not need to have a public IP. So by default they are only assigned the private IP that conforms to the CIDR address that the subnet was created with. The NAT gateway can, however, have an elastic IP address if needed. This will ensure that all outgoing microservices from your VPC have the same IP address, which can be used for whitelisting when it comes to certain regulations (such as PCI-DSS).

A NAT gateway is a fully managed service, and hence architects do not have to worry about high availability or bandwidth-related issues. These are handled by AWS under the SRM.

Some regulatory agencies such as the payment card industry (PCI) require the whitelisting of IPs for SaaS providers. In such situations, attaching an elastic IP to a NAT gateway ensures that the same IP will be used whenever a SaaS provider is called by a service from within the private subnet.

# Virtual Private Cloud

Although subnets provide a great way to group together various services, a VPC is another AWS resource that provides complete logical isolation of networks. A VPC can be thought of as a tiny portion of the cloud that has been isolated for your benefit from the rest of the internet. With its own private internet backbone and strong encryption, AWS provides a logically separate environment that gives the same security benefits as your own on-premises data center.

Amazon VPC enables you to launch AWS resources into a virtual network that you've defined. This type of virtual network closely mimics a traditional network that would be operated on your own data center, but with the benefit of utilizing the scalable infrastructure of AWS. This VPC can have its own sets of internal and external IPs. True isolation of bounded contexts as a result can be delegated to the AWS infrastructure by properly isolating each service inside its own VPC.

Amazon VPC supports the processing, storage, and transmission of credit card data by a merchant or service provider and has been validated as being compliant with PCI Data Security Standard (DSS).

# Routing in a VPC

I have already introduced you to route tables and the concept of routing in "Routing in a Subnet" on page 149. In this section, I will expand further and talk about how routing works with VPCs. To begin with, routing within a VPC is entirely private. Whenever a service communicates with another service within the same VPC, AWS ensures that the network traffic generated from these communications does not reach the public internet and that it stays within the AWS private network.

When you create a VPC, it automatically has a main route table. The main route table controls the routing for all subnets that are not explicitly associated with any other route table. Each incoming and outgoing data consults the route table for instructions on where to send it next. Routes can be directed to resources from the same subnet, resources from another subnet, or even resources outside the current VPC. Most of your cloud services will live inside a VPC. Hence, it is important for your VPC route table to control network communication. For communication with services outside the VPC, you may have gateways that live on the VPC. The purpose of a gateway is to accept traffic from within the VPC and then forward it to the right destination address.

## Microsegmentation at the Network Layer

One option for segmentation involves isolating systems based on their environment. Production deployments get their own VPC, as do staging deployments, QA deployments, and any others you may choose to have. This parallels the historic isolation of servers of different environments from one another.

With microsegmentation, only domains and bounded contexts are segmented into network partitions. Multiple services can be located within the same domain and hence within the same network partition.

The overhead of managing too many granular environments is weighted against segmenting further since on-premises systems separated out these environments physically. Figure 5-8 illustrates such a setup where the application runs on a DDD but services are partitioned solely based on their running environment.

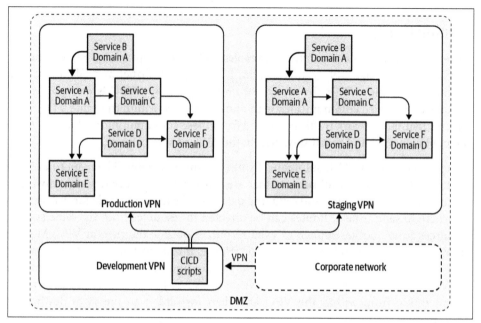

*Figure 5-8. Basic VPC setup for microservices based on environmental isolation.*

Although segmentation is achieved, this is not microsegmentation. This partitioning of networks ignores the business domains that the services belong to. Although the simplicity of putting all services in one network partition can definitely entice some AWS customers, especially ones whose requirements for privacy and security are not too high, for many others it may be possible to isolate systems further based on their bounded contexts.

Given that the overhead of physical partitions is taken away from cloud-based systems, segmentation can be achieved at a much smaller cost. Domain-based segmentation has many benefits from a security perspective since you can put many preventive controls at the network layer that would have been very hard to put in place if the traffic would have been within the same network partition. Figure 5-9 shows an example of a network that is microsegmented based on the business domains that microservices belong to.

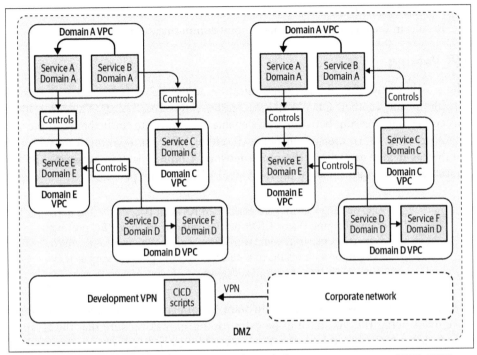

*Figure 5-9. In a microsegmented VPC, each bounded context gets its own VPC. VPCs can communicate with one another, but with controls in between.*

Segmentation using VPC is great for introducing additional levels of isolation and thus adding security controls to the system, but it isn't free. Depending on your segmentation design and communication patterns, there may be costs associated with cross-VPC traffic. Bad domain designs may exacerbate costs due to increased cross-VPC traffic when cross-domain coupling is high.

# Cross-VPC Communication

Even with proper isolation of services within a VPC, there may always be a need for services to communicate with other services from different contexts. AWS provides the necessary tooling to set up, manage, and utilize VPC-based microsegments at scale. There are three main strategies to this:

*VPC peering*
    Results in the creation of a mesh topology

*VPC Transit Gateway*
    Results in the creation of a star topology

Results in the creation of a point-to-point communication

# VPC Peering

The simplest way of enabling communication across VPCs is by connecting them directly to one another. On AWS, *VPC peering (https://oreil.ly/zJMXK)* can achieve this connection. Peering between VPCs enables you to route traffic between the two VPCs privately. Once created, instances in either VPC can communicate with one another as if they are within the same network. Communication between VPCs is controlled by the route tables of the individual VPCs that are peered.

> VPC peering can only be performed between two VPCs that have no overlapping IPs or CIDR blocks. You can create a VPC peering connection between your own VPCs, with a VPC in another AWS account, or with a VPC in a different AWS Region (as long as they do not have overlapping IP addresses).

You first define the two VPCs that you want to connect. Since peered VPCs cannot have overlapping IPs, you have to be extra careful in making sure that the IP space is well defined. Once you have the VPCs set up, you can begin the peering process. Peering can be initiated by either VPC, and the other must accept the peering connection.

Figure 5-10 shows the process of creating a peering connection.

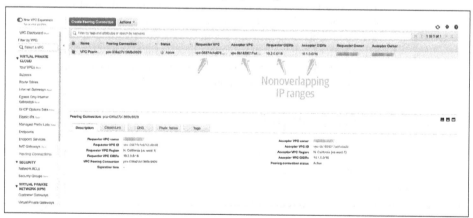

*Figure 5-10. Basic VPC peering between two networks without overlapping IPs.*

VPC peering is not transitive. So if VPC A is peered with VPC B and VPC B is peered with VPC C, services in VPC A cannot automatically communicate with services in VPC C unless VPC A pairs with VPC C independently.

Once you have established the peering connection, you can assume that a link has been established between the two VPCs, which in your case hold different services from different domains. Any data packet sent to the peering connection is automatically forwarded to the peered VPC. This means, for services from one VPC to communicate with services from the other, you simply have to route their data packets to the peering connections. This can be achieved by configuring the route table in the VPC to be aware of IPs that belong to the target VPC.

For example, let's say you have two microservices, Service A and Service B. They both belong to two different bounded contexts—Context A and Context B. As a result, you have microsegemented them into two different VPCs—VPC A and VPC B. It is assumed that you have already configured the route tables in both these VPCs to route traffic properly to local instances within the VPCs. So traffic within VPC B with a destination of Service B will be routed properly to Service B.

Assume that you want to enable cross-VPC communication between Service A and Service B. To do so, first you should create a peering connection between VPC A and VPC B. Within VPC A, you should configure the Route Table A in such a way that, anytime it encounters traffic with a destination IP address belonging to VPC B, it should route this traffic to the peering connection.

As mentioned, the peering connection will then forward this traffic to VPC B. And once the traffic reaches VPC B, as mentioned earlier, it will be routed properly to the right destination—Service B. Figure 5-11 highlights this flow.

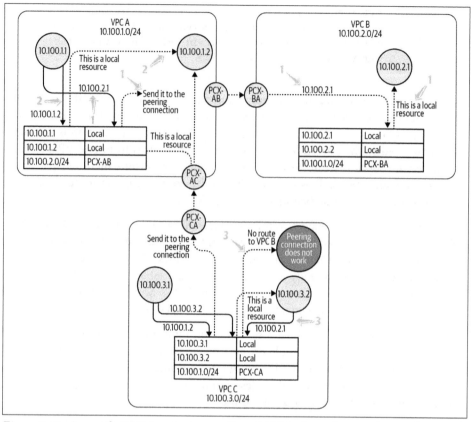

*Figure 5-11. A sample VPC peering connection. (1) This shows how traffic can be routed between two instances on two different VPCs using peering connections, (2) points to how traffic between instances on the same VPC continues to follow the same flow, and (3) shows the limitation of VPC peering when it comes to transitive VPC peerings.*

### Tying it all together with VPC peering

In conclusion, VPC peering allows you to achieve the "connect" phase of the micro-segmentation process as defined in "Software-Defined Network Partitions" on page 145. When you know that you can easily enable cross-VPC communications across services with legitimate use cases, you can be more aggressive during the isolation phase of microsegmentation. In most microsegmented organizations I have seen, there may be multiple peering connections between different VPCs. Figure 5-12 shows just one of the many ways you can partition your organization based on the environment that a service runs in. Since the VPCs are partitioned based on the business use case, the partitioning achieves the reference architecture I was hoping to go toward in Figure 5-7.

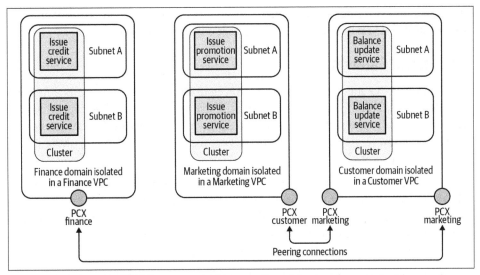

*Figure 5-12. A typical VPC structure with peered working environments. The peering connections connect each domain with one another through a peered connection between PCX customer–PCX marketing.*

The use of VPC peering as the strategy for the connect phase of the microsegmentation process faces two important hurdles:

- Since you cannot have overlapping IPs in VPCs that you wish to connect, you have to be strategic while designing the IP space of your VPCs. When trying to pair your very wide VPC with other VPCs that have overlapping IP ranges, you will likely encounter problems.

- Due to the absence of transitive peering, you may end up creating a lot of peering connections. If you have 5 VPCs, and each of them needs to be paired with every other VPC, you will end up having 10 peering connections. If you have 100 VPCs, you will end up having 4,950 peering connections. As you can imagine, this will lead to complexity in route table designs.

### Cost and complexity trade-off with VPC peering

There is no additional cost for setting up VPC peering connections. Hence, there is no fixed hourly cost vector that is associated with this setup. There is, however, a cost associated with the data that is transferred between peered connections. If you have a lot of cross-domain communication that makes use of peered connections, the cost may be something you need to carefully predict and evaluate when weighing against the security benefit you gain from segregating the networks. If the peering connections are in different regions, the interregion data transfer will also result in an added cost.

On the complexity side, as mentioned, the number of peering connections may get unmanageable if you have a lot of services that talk to one another.

## AWS Transit Gateway

As mentioned, having too many interconnected services that span across multiple bounded contexts can result in an exponential rise in complexity due to peering connections unable to transitively route traffic. In such situations, AWS recommends the use of a different service, AWS Transit Gateway, for the "connect" phase of the microsegmentation process.

AWS Transit Gateway is a fully managed, highly available gateway service provided by AWS that can attach itself to multiple VPCs. The AWS Transit Gateway maintains its own route table. Thus, whenever traffic reaches the Transit Gateway with a destination IP address belonging to a VPC that is attached to this Transit Gateway, the route table is able to route this traffic to the correct VPC attachment.

As an example, if two services, Service A and Service B, in two different VPCs (VPC A and VPC B) need to communicate with one another, they can do so by attaching themselves to the same Transit Gateway. Whenever Service A sends packets to Service B, the route table inside VPC A will route this traffic to the Transit Gateway. The Transit Gateway will receive this traffic, and upon looking up the route table entry in its own route table, it will then route this traffic to VPC B. Multiple services across multiple VPCs can thus communicate with one another by using one Transit Gateway and a well-configured route table. Since one centralized service is now responsible for routing cross-VPC traffic, it becomes easier to add new security-related rules at the Transit Gateway.

 As mentioned, Transit Gateway is a fully managed service. As a result, AWS does not expect you to opt for multiple deployments or any kind of a redundancy mechanism to make the Transit Gateway connection fully available. Transit Gateway is also not a free service and will incur an hourly charge. Deploying multiple Transit Gateways does not make the system faster or more available.

Figure 5-13 demonstrates how traffic is routed in an AWS Transit Gateway by consulting the route table.

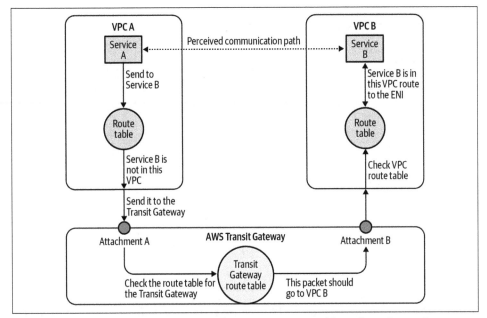

*Figure 5-13. An AWS Transit Gateway has its own route table and can be used to enforce communication rules across VPCs. Segmentation can be achieved by a proper utilization of these route tables.*

Unlike VPC peering, where the connection between peered VPCs is direct, the use of AWS Transit Gateway involves an extra hop, which may be an added delay for some time-sensitive applications.

 AWS Transit Gateway doesn't support routing between Amazon VPCs with overlapping CIDRs. If you attach a new Amazon VPC that has a CIDR that overlaps with an already attached Amazon VPC, AWS Transit Gateway will not propagate the new Amazon VPC route into the AWS Transit Gateway route table.

### Tying it all together using AWS Transit Gateway

In conclusion, similar to VPC peering, AWS Transit Gateway allows you to achieve the "connect" phase of the microsegmentation process. In contrast to VPC peering, where connections are made point-to-point between each VPC, AWS Transit Gateway uses a hub-and-spoke model for connecting different VPCs. In this model, AWS Transit Gateway is the hub, while individual VPC attachments are its spokes.

Using AWS Transit Gateway, you can connect your VPC-based microsegmented domains in a controlled manner. Figure 5-14 shows how the AWS Transit Gateway acts as a centralized routing hub for all your services.

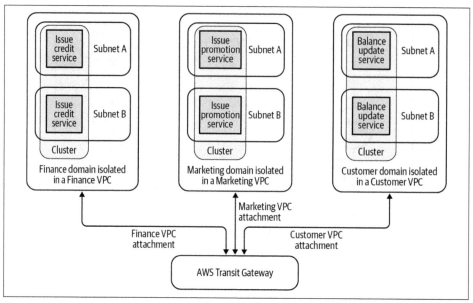

*Figure 5-14. Various accounts and VPCs connected to one another using AWS Transit Gateway. Security controls can be implemented by configuring the routing table at the AWS Transit Gateway to allow only legitimate cross-domain/cross-context communication.*

It is easy to see how the AWS Transit Gateway scales as the number of domains (and, as a result, VPCs) increase within your organization. If you have five domains that are microsegmented into five VPCs, you will need a single AWS Transit Gateway to enable controlled cross-domain communication. Each of these domain-based VPCs can be attached to the same AWS Transit Gateway, and the routes can be configured to enable the right communication patterns while blocking unauthorized communication. If you need to add one more VPC to the mix, you can still use the same Transit Gateway and attach it to the new VPC. Thus, a single Transit Gateway can continue to handle all your connectivity needs, making it much more scalable.

As long as your microservices are isolated within their domain-specific VPC, you get domain-level isolation in such a network topology without sacrificing connectivity for legitimate communication patterns. All of the rules regarding who can talk to one another and under what circumstances can now live on top of the AWS Transit Gateway.

### Cost and complexity trade-off with AWS Transit Gateway

Unlike VPC peering, AWS Transit Gateway is not free to set up. The gateway has a fixed hourly price, regardless of whether it's attached to a VPC or whether it's receiving traffic. In addition to this fixed fee, there is a fee that has to be paid per network attachment. So, if you have a complex network setup with a lot of VPCs talking to one another, each of these attachments will bear an added cost that needs to be evaluated while considering the trade-off. Finally, there is a third dimension to the cost vector, which is proportional to the amount of data that is transferred through the AWS Transit Gateway. Given the two fixed costs associated with the AWS Transit Gateway, the cost equation and economies of scale may follow different paths from that of VPC peering.

From a complexity perspective, AWS Transit Gateway does offer a much simpler setup. By centralizing the rules regarding VPC interconnections at the Transit Gateway instead of dispersing them between the route tables of the VPCs, the complexity benefits of using a Transit Gateway over VPC peering become apparent.

## VPC Endpoints

Although Transit Gateways provide a great way of connecting distinct VPCs into a hub-and-spoke pattern, VPC Endpoints provide an alternative way of allowing cross-VPC communication. VPC endpoints are used in places where you have a clear service provider–service consumer pattern, enabling a service consumer to consume a service that is hosted in another VPC.

A VPC endpoint can act as a secure method of transporting data to and from certain services that exist outside of your VPC. The VPC endpoint can be added to your VPC in two ways:

- For supported services such as AWS DynamoDB or AWS Simple Storage Service (S3), the endpoint can be added as a gateway. These gateways can be added to your route tables using AWS-managed prefix lists.
- The endpoint can be added as an ENI that lives inside your VPC just like any other service. These interfaces can be added to your route tables using their assigned IP addresses or at times using their DNS hostnames.

As soon as the service provider is added to your VPC (as a VPC endpoint), you can treat the provider as if it were part of your network. You can add security groups around this service and include the provider in route tables as you would any other local service within the VPC. This provides you with a nice level of abstraction. The VPC endpoint creates a channel from your VPC all the way to the service provider's VPC. As part of the AWS Shared Responsibility Model (SRM), AWS guarantees secure and encrypted delivery of data from the VPC endpoint all the way to your service provider, which may be in a different VPC (possibly in a different AWS account) without ever exposing these packets to the public internet, thus securing the communication channel for you.

An endpoint (interface or gateway) cannot initiate connection with any service within your VPC, making it possible to be added to any private network without significantly affecting its security posture.

### Gateway VPC endpoint

Gateway VPC endpoints are used to create endpoints for AWS-managed services. As of this writing, two AWS services support gateway endpoints: DynamoDB and AWS S3. These services exist outside VPCs, and accessing them may require the calling services to break out of their own VPC.

Although both AWS S3 as well as AWS DynamoDB allow access using TLS-encrypted endpoints, the fact that this connection has to happen over the public internet is something that makes some organizations a bit uneasy and, therefore, VPC endpoints are preferable.

If any service within the application requires access to these external services, it then loses the ability to run in a closed private environment. This results in a less desirable security design where services are now required to have access to public resources in spite of needing such an access for only one service. If you are to recall our discussion about subnets, such a setup would require the presence of a route to a NAT gateway even if the other services do not need one. Of course, you can individually block access to other services and implement a strong firewall in order to block any malicious outgoing or incoming traffic, but AWS has a better option for this setup in the form of Gateway VPC endpoints. *Gateway VPC endpoints* exist as gateways on the VPC. These gateways can be added as route table entries, making routing very convenient. If you have a service that is running inside the private zone, you can add a gateway VPC endpoint to your network.

If you recall the discussion on route tables, you can reference the destination service (AWS DynamoDB or AWS S3) using its prefix from the managed prefix list for the purposes of route tables. This prefix identifies the service within its region that you wish to reference. Once found, it can now be added to the route table of a VPC as a destination.

The next hop for this prefix can be set to the gateway VPC endpoint that you created for this purpose. Whenever your application tries to send any packets to any of these managed services, the route table looks up the destination using the prefix entry and routes it to the gateway endpoint. AWS then transports this packet privately from the gateway endpoint to the managed service, which was its intended destination.

Figure 5-15 shows how the application can send packets to AWS-managed services using gateway VPC endpoints.

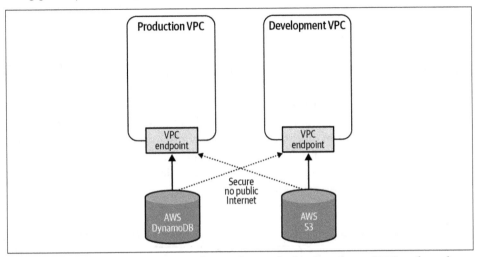

*Figure 5-15. AWS Gateway VPC endpoints live at the border of your VPC and can be added as the next hops on your route tables.*

Once the VPC endpoint receives these packets, AWS assumes the responsibility of transferring the packets to the destination service as part of the SRM. This communication is guaranteed to be on the AWS network and hence can be considered to be secure from the application's perspective. Thus, the services that need access to the managed AWS services can still continue to be inside private networks while maintaining complete connectivity to the managed AWS services.

### Interface VPC endpoints/VPC endpoint services (using PrivateLink)

The benefit of gateway VPC endpoints can be extended to a wider range of services, including user-provided services using interface VPC endpoints. In an interface VPC endpoint, instead of a gateway, an ENI is created inside your network for the service you wish to connect to. If you wish to send packets to a destination service that has an interface endpoint within your VPC, you can add a route to your route table to start directing packets to this interface endpoint. In the route table, the next hop for this route will be this newly added ENI while the destination will be the service you wish to communicate with. The traffic that is directed to this ENI is then transported to the destination service by AWS as part of the SRM. Since the ENI happens to be within the network that hosts your other backend services, the packets do not end up traversing over the public internet to reach their destination. Since an interface endpoint is an ENI that is created for your remote service, you get even more granular control by being able to add a security group to this endpoint for an added layer of protection. I will talk about this in detail in "Security Groups" on page 174.

In containerized developments, it may be a good idea to connect AWS Elastic Container Registry (ECR) to the VPC running your Kubernetes services using an interface VPC endpoint. This is especially useful if your pods run inside a private subnet with no public internet access.

Figure 5-16 shows an example of how a network load balancer (NLB) from the analytics domain is used to create a PrivateLink connection with a VPC by creating interface endpoints inside the marketing domain. In Figure 5-16, NLB from the Analytics domain is projected into the different subnets within the Marketing domain's VPC as if it were a local ENI. From that point onward, your responsibility is to send data only to this local ENI; AWS assumes the responsibility of shipping all of this data from the endpoint to its desired destination within the Analytics VPC, relieving you of the pain of architecting a cross-network connection.

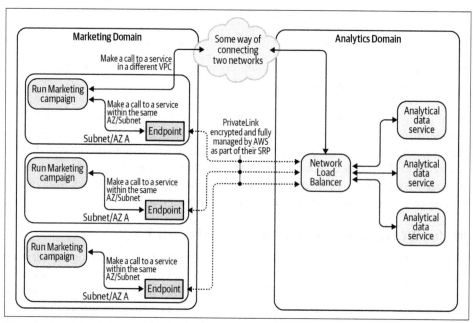

*Figure 5-16. Desired service provider–service consumer setup using VPC endpoints.*

Once the endpoint is created within your VPC, these services can then be treated as full-fledged members of your network, thus taking a considerable amount of overhead off your microservices. Figure 5-17 illustrates the process of creating a VPC endpoint in the AWS Management Console.

*Figure 5-17. Creating a VPC endpoint in the AWS Management Console.*

Under the hood, VPC endpoints are enabled by AWS PrivateLink. PrivateLink allows for the creation of secure tunnels between a provider and service endpoint without exposing your network packets to the public internet, giving you the illusion of having the service endpoint colocated in your VPC.

PrivateLink can also work with Direct Connect or VPN to link your on-premises service with the rest of your cloud infrastructure, allowing you to create an endpoint for any on-premises application. Chapter 9 discusses this option further.

Another common use case for PrivateLink is to connect to any third-party SaaS provider where you don't have to worry about security in transit between your VPC and the SaaS provider's network.

VPC endpoint services can also span across AWS accounts, allowing you the ability to create multiple accounts per organization, based on the bounded context. These accounts can be controlled using service control policies (SCPs):

*On the service provider side*

A VPC interface endpoint can be created using PrivateLink for a variety of services, including AWS Lambdas, AWS Elastic Container Service (ECS) or Amazon Elastic Kubernetes Service (EKS) services behind an NLB, or many other supported third-party or on-premises solutions. These microservices can be running on ECS, EKS, or any other supported architecture as long as the load balancer can isolate the cluster.

*On the service consumer side*

You will have to add the VPC endpoint into the subnet where you want to use it. Best practices dictate using multiple AZs (and hence multiple subnets) to have access to this endpoint. The multiple AZs enable you to have a high availability of this external connection. However, you may want to limit the number of redundant endpoints you create, since every additional VPC endpoint may incur a fee.

 AWS supports transitive routing for VPC endpoints, unlike VPC peering. This is as long as your subnet network access control lists (NACLs) and route tables allow such a route.

Similar to the AWS Transit Gateway, the VPC endpoints allow us to create a microservice network without compromising on control and security. Unlike the AWS Transit Gateway, though, VPC endpoints allow us to create peer-to-peer connections and more granular control over who can talk to which microservice while maintaining complete control.

### Tying it all together using VPC endpoints

You can now start projecting endpoints. To do so, perform the following actions:

- List all the consumer microservices.
- List all the service providers.
- List all the managed services that may need to be accessed by services inside a VPC.

Figure 5-18 illustrates an example of a DDD where the services are laid out and waiting to be connected.

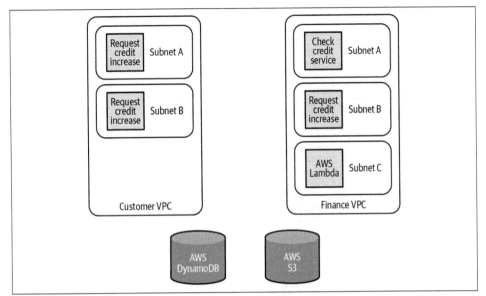

*Figure 5-18. Using AWS PrivateLink and VPC endpoints to implement a point-to-point service provider–service consumer pattern.*

Once these services are listed, you can start the process of connecting them based on allowed communication patterns:

1. Create an NLB to sit on top of the service providers, which are backed by EKS, ECS, or Elastic Cloud Compute (EC2) instances. (AWS Lambdas work directly with VPC endpoints.)

2. Create a cross-account VPC endpoint within the VPC of a consumer microservice that links with the service provider's NLB.

3. Create VPC interface endpoints for the AWS Lambda services, managed AWS services, or any of the services behind an NLB. You may add these endpoints in multiple subnets if you want to maintain high availability.

4. Create gateway endpoints for services that support them, such as AWS S3 and DynamoDB.

5. Update the services and the route tables in the consumer VPC to connect to these endpoints instead of connecting to the destination services.

Figure 5-19 highlights these steps.

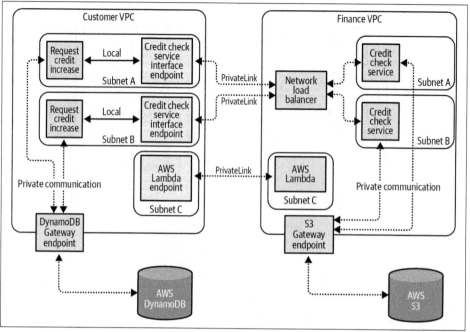

*Figure 5-19. Services from different domains can communicate in a point-to-point way using PrivateLink and VPC endpoints.*

Once all of your service providers have an endpoint in the service consumer's VPC, you can be assured that all communication that happens between services will be secure. The service consumers can isolate their network since it may never need to communicate with any external resource outside of its VPC perimeter, leading to a truly secured infrastructure.

### Cost and complexity trade-off with VPC interface endpoints

Since interface endpoints connect single services across VPCs, the costs associated with them increase as the number of connecting services increases. The pricing structure is a little different in the case of VPC endpoints. For starters, you are charged per endpoint/per subnet. So an endpoint for the same service in multiple subnets will incur multiple fees. You have to pay a fixed cost for each of these endpoints, resulting in possibly higher costs. Apart from the cost of creating an endpoint, you still have to pay per gigabyte for the data that is transferred through the VPC endpoint.

From a complexity perspective, this is probably the easiest to manage if you have fewer services. Since the end result may involve completely containing all services within a VPC, hardening the perimeter becomes easier as a result.

# Wrap-Up of Cross-VPC Communication

After isolating your microservices using VPCs and having a well-partitioned architecture, you can continue to enable controlled communication for legitimate use cases in the three ways I've discussed. Each of these approaches has its own merits and demerits, and which one works best ends up being a choice your organization has to make. Table 5-1 summarizes.

*Table 5-1. A comparison of VPC peering, AWS Transit Gateway, and VPC endpoints/ PrivateLink for cross-VPC communication*

| | **VPC peering** | **AWS Transit Gateway** | **VPC endpoints/PrivateLink** |
|---|---|---|---|
| Network topology | You create a mesh network topology of your contexts where you connect multiple bounded contexts with one another. | You create a hub-and-spoke model of network topology in which you connect multiple bounded contexts with a central router. | You create a point-to-point network topology of microservices in which you granularly make services available across contexts instead of connecting contexts. |
| Cost | Peering connections do not require any additional cost. Data transferred across peering connections is charged. | You are charged for the number of connections you make to the Transit Gateway per hour and the amount of traffic that flows through the Transit Gateway. | You will be billed for each hour that your VPC endpoint remains provisioned in each AZ, irrespective of the state of its association with the service. |
| Independence of microservices | Since your IPs cannot have any overlap, significant coupling and overhead (in terms of invariants) are created that have to be satisfied while designing different networks for different contexts. | This is similar to VPC peering, lacking the ability to connect networks with overlapping CIDR blocks. Transit Gateway does bring in a cross-context invariant when it comes to network design. | Since individual services are exposed independently to their networks, the service provider and service consumer can have overlapping CIDR blocks. |
| Latency | There is no extra latency. | Transit Gateway is an additional hop for communication between VPCs, leading to a slight delay in moving packets around. | There is no extra latency. |
| Use case | This is best used when you have clear rules defined around which service contexts can talk to one another. | Transit Gateway is best used when you have a lot of transitive routing of packets. | This is best used when you have a lot of provider-consumer types of relationships among services. |
| Summary | There is no added cost and it is easy to implement. However, due to its inability to support transitive connections, VPC peering can end up creating a lot of complexity if you have many cross-context calls. | Transit Gateway is not free; however, if your application has a star-like communication pattern, transitive connections make the pattern simpler to implement, but granular security controls may be harder to implement. | Since external services show up as local network interfaces, integration and cross-service communication are simple. However, projecting all endpoints may not be simple in all architectures. |

# Firewall Equivalents on the Cloud

Firewalls are a concept that predate modern cloud computing. They have existed for almost as long as computer networks have. Their use today is still very relevant, mainly because their task is so simple. All a firewall does is decide whether a request is allowed to proceed or is denied.

Roughly speaking, firewalls can be divided into two broad types:

*Default allow*
> This assumes that traffic can be trusted unless explicitly blocked. These rely on explicit deny rules to block traffic but otherwise allow traffic to reach its destination.

*Default deny*
> This assumes that trust needs to be explicitly gained in traffic and as a result, unless a rule is added to explicitly allow a traffic pattern, traffic is automatically and implicitly blocked.

This notion of a firewall can be extended further on the cloud. For starters, although individual operating systems have firewalls, we want to implement a firewall-like effect at the cloud level.

Amazon gives us two main tools to achieve this effect at the network level. One way is to implement host-based firewalls such as iptables on individual machines and continue using the technology. But a better approach is to use the firewalls at the cloud level instead of inside the instance:

*Security groups*
> These are *default deny* firewall rules that act on the network interface.

*NACLs*
> These are *default allow* firewall rules that act on the subnet.

## Security Groups

*Security groups* are similar to firewalls in traditional networking. They are a set of simple rules that can be applied to a network interface. These rules are evaluated against each incoming packet. The rules are evaluated all at once. If any of the rules in the security group apply to the incoming packet, the security group allows the packet to proceed to our instance. Security groups cannot explicitly deny a packet from going further.

Think of security groups as a flexible entity that works at an ENI level. So, if you are to remove the ENI from a cloud instance and apply it to another one, the security groups attached to this ENI get applied to the new cloud instance. Security groups can be added on top of any service that has an ENI. So any AWS Lambdas, load balancers, AWS relational database service (RDS) instances, EC2 instances, or even VPC endpoints can have security groups associated with them.

The simplest forms of security groups involve an incoming or outgoing IP source, a port, and the protocol (TCP or UDP). So we decide for any Lambdas, RDS clusters, EC2 instances, and EKS clusters which IP ranges are allowed to communicate with the service behind this ENI and on which port. Unless a rule exists that allows this communication, by default the security groups don't allow any request (incoming or outgoing) that does not have a rule for it. Figure 5-20 shows a sample security group as created through the AWS Management Console.

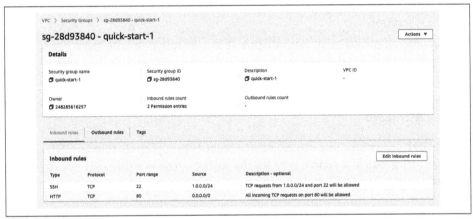

*Figure 5-20. Only TCP requests from 1.0.0.0/24 will be allowed.*

For container-based microservices on EKS, AWS now has the capacity to add security groups to some pods, similar to EC2 instances. It is also possible to use custom networking for EKS if the pods on a particular node would like to use security groups that are different from the node that they are running on.

 For EKS, it is important to allow the use of port 443 and 10250 for minimum inbound and outbound traffic.

## Security Group Referencing (Chaining) and Designs

Security groups also allow other security groups to be a part of the rules instead of using an IP address. It is possible to identify requests based on which security groups their hosts belong to and granularly allow access to resources.

This means you don't have to refer to the IP address of any of your known microservices when trying to allow or deny access to the instance. You can refer to other services in the context of a security group by referring to it by its security group. Since security groups work by only allowing traffic, they fit in well with microservices.

You can design your security groups by following these steps:

1. Create a security group for each of your microservices and come up with an easy-to-use name.

2. Attach these security groups to your containers/instances/Lambdas that run these services.

3. Identify all the other services that need to communicate with these services at a network level and the port at which they need to interact with this service.

4. Attach a policy within the security group that allows the security group from services identified in Step 3 to communicate with this service on the port that is predetermined.

Figure 5-21 shows how you can create one security group, apply it to an ENI, and use that security group as a source item for the rules present in a different security group instead of providing an IP as the source.

*Figure 5-21. Security group inbound rule uses another security group as the source instead of an IP or a CIDR range.*

This way, security group rules can be created without the need to remember hostnames, IP addresses, or any other infrastructure-related information associated with services.

VPCs connected to an AWS Transit Gateway cannot reference security groups in other spokes connected to the same AWS Transit Gateway.

## Properties of Security Groups

Here are some of the properties of security groups:

*They are stateful.*
A request that comes from one direction automatically sets the permissions for a response in the other direction.

*They don't apply to localhost requests.*
They are applied only when traffic enters or leaves an ENI.

*They only allow requests to pass.*
They don't have any mechanism to explicitly deny requests.

In the case of Kubernetes, it is considered to be best practice to set up two different security groups for your infrastructure. Your pods being in the data plane can benefit from one set of rules while your control plane can benefit from another. But it's important to make sure that the security groups involved in communication between the control and the data plane are compatible with one another.

## Network Access Control Lists

NACLs at first glance resemble security groups. For starters, their syntax is very similar to security groups. You can explicitly allow traffic to flow in and out of a subnet using an NACL. And NACLs are another tool that provide us with the ability to firewall malicious traffic. However, the similarity ends there.

As mentioned, NACLs sit at the gateway of the subnet. NACLs inspect the traffic at the gateway and decide whether the traffic can flow through it (in either direction). Unlike security groups, NACLs can have either an ALLOW or a DENY option to them, making them better to use when it comes to enforcing invariants at the subnet level.

As a result, you can think of security groups as a way of enforcing individual security rules, enforcing least privilege, and so on, while NACLs are great at enforcing organizational invariants at an infrastructure level. Figure 5-22 shows a sample NACL being created through the AWS Management Console.

*Figure 5-22. NACLs are present in the Network ACL subsection on the VPC page. Inbound and outbound rules have to be specified separately in the case of NACLs.*

As seen in Figure 5-22, NACLs are evaluated in the ascending order of the value in the column "Rule #." Each packet is matched against a rule in the ascending order, and once a match is established, the evaluation exits. Thus, the order of rules is important since a rule with a higher "Rule #" may never get evaluated if a wider rule with a smaller number matches the packet. Figure 5-23 shows how NACLs and security groups are evaluated during service-service network communication.

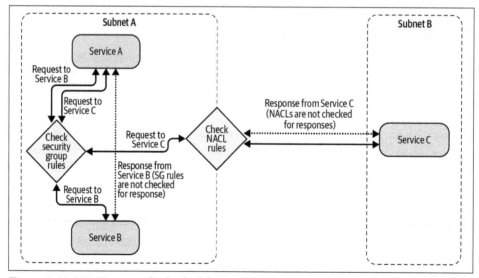

*Figure 5-23. NACLs are only checked for traffic that flows in or out of the subnet. However, they are checked both times whenever the communication extends beyond the subnet.*

As shown in Figure 5-23, unlike security groups, NACLs are stateless. So an outgoing request does not automatically allow an incoming response, and hence NACLs have to be enabled or disabled in both directions for such a request-response pattern of communication to work. NACLs only act at a security gateway. So traffic that flows between hosts in the same subnet may not get evaluated against a NACL, and this is important to note. For requests within the same subnet, security groups are the best way of enforcing firewall rules.

 Due to the added complexity of adding inbound and outbound rules while using NACLs, security groups are more commonly used as firewall measures. In my personal experience, I have only used NACLs as supplemental protection measures but rarely as the primary ways of providing security.

Every default VPC comes with a default NACL that allows all inbound and outbound traffic. In general, NACLs are great at defining subnet-level rules of communication and translating broad business logic into network rules. Each subnet can have only one NACL associated with it. Assigning a new NACL will disassociate the existing one and replace it with the new one.

## Security Groups Versus NACLs

At the surface, security groups and NACLs seem to provide controls for very similar problems. However, there are some subtle differences, which are highlighted in Table 5-2.

*Table 5-2. Comparing security groups and NACLs*

| Security groups | NACLs |
| --- | --- |
| Act at an ENI (and consequently an instance) level | Act at a subnet level |
| Stateful (requests automatically allow responses) | Stateless (requests and responses should be independently specified and allowed) |
| Only allows requests | Allows or denies requests |
| All rules evaluated to find an allow statement | Rules evaluated in an order as prescribed by the "Rule #" column |
| Should be used as a firewall replacement in the cloud | Should be used to make subnet-level rules such as "I never want traffic from this subnet to talk to traffic of this other subnet." |

Figure 5-24 shows how requests between two instances that are in different subnets are evaluated against a waterfall of security rules.

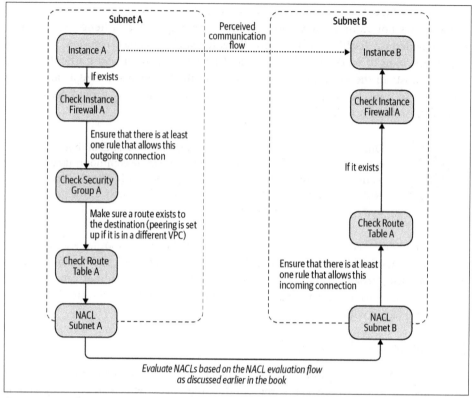

*Figure 5-24. If Service A wants to talk to Service B in a different subnet, security groups and NACLs are evaluated in the order described in the flow.*

The stateliness of security groups is perhaps the most important criteria that network engineers need to be aware of when using NACLs.

Figure 5-25 illustrates how request evaluation differs between NACLs and security groups due to the stateful nature of security groups and the stateless nature of NACLs.

Considering additional complexity associated with NACLs, not to mention the lack of flexibility at an individual service level, individual rules related to individual services are simple to implement using security groups, while security invariants can be best codified and enforced using NACLs.

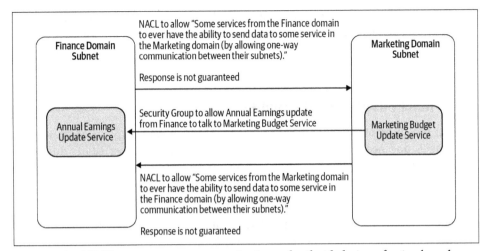

*Figure 5-25. NACLs are one-way communication rules that help in enforcing broader organizational invariants. Security groups give us more granularity in phrasing service-level contracts at the network layer.*

A department-level invariant such as "accounting should never talk to marketing" is best implemented as a NACL. But "customer balance service should not be able to directly communicate with the database" warrants a more granular logic that is best implemented using security groups.

# Containers and Network Security

Until now, I've assumed you set up your container network in a way that follows the same security best practices as your instances and your physical hardware. Although this is generally true in most situations, there are some best practices that can be followed to make your Kubernetes setup more secure from a network perspective.

## Block Instance Metadata Service

Kubernetes pods are abstractions that may be running on actual virtual machines (VMs). The host machines may have roles and permissions that may be different from those intended for your pods. It is important that your pods do not mistake who they are with the roles and identities that are attached to the nodes that they run on. If you have assigned roles to pods using some tool, such as kube2iAM or Kiam, you have to make sure that calls from the pods do not reach the instance metadata service (IMDS) that AWS makes available on each EC2 instance.

An important point worth remembering is, since the IMDS runs locally, you cannot use security groups to block these calls. You can use software tools such as iptables or local firewalls to block this access.

## Try to Run Pods in a Private Subnet

I might be a little opinionated here, but I can't think of too many instances where a Kubernetes pod needs to have direct internet accessibility. Almost all of your access should be streamlined via AWS API Gateway or some sort of an application load balancer. Hence, your Kubernetes data plane should almost always run in a private subnet away from where any attacker can gain access and compromise your pods.

API server endpoints are public by default, and API server access is secured via identity and access management (IAM) and Kubernetes role-based access control (RBAC). You should enable private access to your production cluster endpoints so that all communication between your nodes and the API server stays within your VPC.

## Block Internet Access for Pods Unless Necessary

Generally speaking, it is not too common for pods to connect to the internet. Hence, a default strategy should be to block internet access for pods unless it is absolutely necessary. This can be achieved by running pods inside subnets that do not have NAT routers.

## Use Encrypted Networking Between Pods

This is a new feature that AWS has added in some EC2 Nitro instances. Nearly all container-based applications use only clear text HTTP for traffic and let the load balancers handle transport layer security (TLS). This is an acceptable trade-off. After all, if your pods run in a private subnet in your own VPC, it is generally acceptable to assume your network connections between pods are secure. But with the rise of zero trust networking and the downfall of perimeters, there has been a growing demand for secure networking, especially in the defense and financial sectors.

There are two ways of implementing encryption at the pod networking level. One is to use marketplace solutions such as Cilium, which offers secure networking. However, this comes at a network speed cost since this process is not fast. Another way is to use certain EC2 Nitro instances, which allow AES-encrypted networking when communicating between other instances within the same VPC.

# Lambdas and Network Security

For Lambdas, most of the security aspect of microservices is handed over to AWS as part of the SRM. If you run a Lambda function without configuring it to use your VPC, the function is authorized to get information from the public internet. Since this function lives completely outside your network, it cannot then get any information inside of your VPC and thus cannot interact with any of your VPC-based private resources. Such a Lambda function is useful for performing utility tasks such as error response handling or other tasks that do not require any access to your internal resources. This Lambda function also ensures that there is a clean separation of your resources from the publicly accessible part of your application at a network level.

However, if you decide to use Lambdas for setting up your internal microservices, chances are, for quite a few of your applications, you will need to have access to resources that live on your VPC. In order to provide security, this access needs to happen on the private AWS network so that the communication is not exposed to external threats. To achieve this goal, AWS allows you to configure your Lambdas to run with any of your VPCs. For each function, Lambda will create (*https://oreil.ly/ k1024*) an ENI for any combination of security groups and VPC subnets in your function's VPC configuration. The network interface creation happens when your Lambda function is created or its VPC settings are updated. Invoking a function in the execution environment simply creates a network tunnel and uses the network interface that is created for the execution of this Lambda.

Multiple functions using the same subnets share network interfaces. AWS then performs a cross-account ENI (X-ENI) attachment of this ENI to your VPC, allowing this Lambda to access resources within your private network. Since your function scaling is independent of the number of network interfaces, ENIs can scale to support a large number of concurrent function executions.

Security beyond your network is handled by AWS as part of the SRP. All invocations for functions will be made by the Lambda service API, and no one will have access to the actual execution environment, keeping this Lambda safe in case of a breach of network either on your account or any other tenant. Figure 5-26 illustrates how the ENIs are projected inside VPCs during Lambda execution.

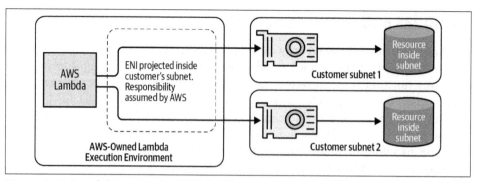

*Figure 5-26. Lambdas projecting ENIs inside customer-owned subnets.*

# Summary

I have described different ways in which you can utilize our sample architecture. Although perimeter security measures have worked well for monoliths and partitioned systems based on an underlying technology, microservices need more network isolation at the service level due to their dispersal across the network. Service-level isolation can be achieved on AWS by properly designing your AWS account and VPC structure. However, this can be difficult if your logic flow requires a lot of cross-service asynchronous communication. I have described three ways of achieving cross-VPC flow through the use of VPC peering, VPC Transit Gateway, and VPC endpoints. I have also talked about the use of various firewall measures to protect your services from unauthorized access. In the next chapter, I will talk about how you can maintain security around services (or resources) that actually need to be accessed by public users who attempt to connect to these services using the public internet.

# Public-Facing Services

In Chapter 5, I discussed the need to divide the network architecture and all your backend services into cleanly segregated pieces through the process of microsegmentation. Microsegmentation is great at having a clean and simple backend process that can be secured thoroughly. Although this process of domain segregation may work well for backend services, the end user–facing systems have to be designed with the requirements and security of the user in mind. These public-facing services are also called *edge servers* because they happen to live at the edge of your application.

Having a clean and separate edge infrastructure helps in decoupling the domain design of your backend services from the ever-evolving requirements of the end user. Figure 6-1 shows an example of a typical application where the edge is cleanly separated from the rest of the backend microservices.

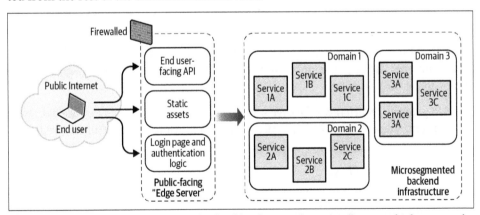

*Figure 6-1. This chapter focuses on the "public-facing edge server" area, which acts as the first point of contact with your application for anyone trying to access your services from the internet.*

Let me begin this chapter by saying that the services on the public-facing edge servers are inherently less secure than the backend services. For any system, potential threats can be classified into three categories: possible, plausible, and probable. A lot of attacks are possible in theory. In the case of backend services, since you may already have controls that prevent attackers from penetrating the perimeter of your system, a significantly smaller subset of threats ends up being plausible and an even smaller subset ends up being probable. As a result, security professionals can focus on the plausible and probable threats to reduce the aggregate risk of the application.

The edge server is connected to the wider internet, making it fair game for malicious actors around the world. Its public visibility increases the likelihood that seemingly unrealistic threats may be realized. Therefore, it is harder to distinguish between possible and probable threats for edge servers. Security professionals are forced to combat every possible threat, making it more difficult to develop controls at the edge of the network.

It is also hard to implicitly trust any incoming requests at the edge since these calls originate beyond the context of your application. This means that each request has to be independently authenticated and checked against an access control policy in order to be allowed. This, as mentioned in previous chapters, is called *zero trust security*. While zero trust security is indeed an important security concept, it adds a significant overhead on microservices that are supposed to be lean and focused on the one issue they are responsible for, the single-responsibility principle (SRP).

The edge application can be divided into services that require the identity of the calling user and those that do not. The security needs for these two sets of services may be quite different, resulting in different designs and the use of different AWS systems in their implementation. Generally, unauthenticated edge services that distribute static assets such as media content, images, and scripts (called content delivery networks or CDNs) may not require the identity of the calling parties.

By definition, a cleanly isolated backend service should never be accessible from the public internet directly. The only two ways to get to the production backend services are by using the following:

*An API gateway (which hosts the edge services)*
   For end users who want to interact with the application in controlled, predefined ways

*Jump boxes or bastion hosts*
   For developers or maintenance use

This chapter shows you how good edge-services design can take advantage of the security architecture that AWS supports. Your application code can focus more on business logic while taking advantage of the AWS Shared Responsibility Model

(SRM) to maintain security for the application's edge service. In particular, this chapter will demonstrate in detail:

- How AWS API Gateway allows you to implement authorization and authentication mechanisms around your resources without violating the single-responsibility principle

- How AWS CloudFront and other edge mechanisms allow you to implement detective and preventive controls around your CDNs

- How you can incorporate encryption processes at the edge to ensure that the remainder of your application does not have to worry about safeguarding data

- How you can identify and prevent some of the most common attacks that edge systems routinely encounter over the internet

- How you can easily deploy approved third-party applications for security processes

# API-First Design and API Gateway

Modularizing and splitting a large application into domains is akin to slicing a pie into smaller pieces. There may be many ways to split a large monolith application. The API-first design methodology is a popular design principle used for exposing microservices to end consumers.

For example, let's say your application is a digital bank that offers cash advances through a credit line. Consider a situation where you have a mobile app that needs to show the user their available balance. Your backend process may be complicated as you identify which balance needs to be shown to the user based on the user's available credit, pending transactions, and so forth. However, the end user should not be affected by this complexity. All a user cares about is their balance.

API-first design works to decouple backend services from frontends. With an API-first approach, the frontend can also start development by substituting a mock response for the backend service. Figure 6-2 illustrates how a mock backend can start the development of frontend applications while the complex microservices backend emerges.

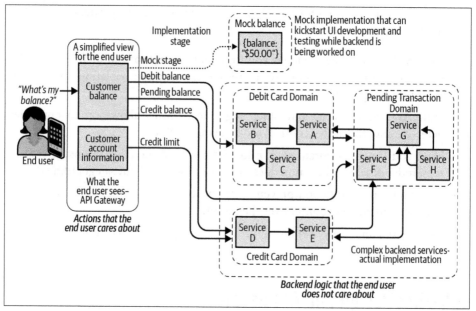

*Figure 6-2. An API gateway does a great job hiding the complexity of your microservice system from the end user.*

The best edge systems do not simply extend an existing business system's architecture but anticipate client needs and then design them accordingly, keeping the client's preferences in mind.

Hiding the complexities of your application and its security architecture from your end consumer is the primary goal of the API-first approach. Using this framework, you can devise security strategies to provide the confidentiality and availability of your application that the end user may expect from your app. More specifically, your API layer can be set up to handle rate limiting, authentication, access control, and firewalls, while your microservices on the backend can handle business logic. Thus, you can expose every service externally with an API designed to hide the internal complexity of your application.

When designing APIs, time is needed to establish contracts. It also often involves more planning and collaboration with the stakeholders who provide feedback on a proposed API design before any code is written. Using mock backend services, API-first design can demonstrate the final application to all stakeholders before the complex backend is designed or deployed. The aim is to make certain the API serves the needs of its end users. Hence, in API-first design, you can start off by drafting the contract first, utilizing the tenets of *test-driven development (TDD)*. For those interested in learning the "art" of TDD, *Test-Driven Development* by Kent Beck (Addison-Wesley) provides a practical step-by-step explanation of the process.

The API-first approach requires API endpoint designers to first mock the backend service behind each API endpoint. In this way, it is possible to write automated tests on the frontend that validate an API's behavior against a predefined contract that consumers can agree upon. The consumer and interface will then agree on the data types and schemas of the request-and-response objects.

By shortening the feedback cycle and introducing automated testing through a mock backend implementation, you enable the use of an iterative approach to API design. End consumers can get quicker feedback on the implementation. Any unintended deviation from the consumer contracts is immediately highlighted in the form of a failing automated test.

In API-first design, edge services are deployed to various stages. It is assumed that your edge service goes through various stages in its development lifecycle and your API's deployment stage determines whether calls to your API reach the microservice application or the mocked backend.

Figure 6-3 shows how your application can have two stages: one for a mock test and another for your production backend. During development and testing phases of the API, the developers can send requests to the mock API that will be designed to respond with responses that will be identical to those in production. Once the testers and stakeholders are sufficiently satisfied by the API design, the API can start using production microservices by simply deploying itself to a new stage.

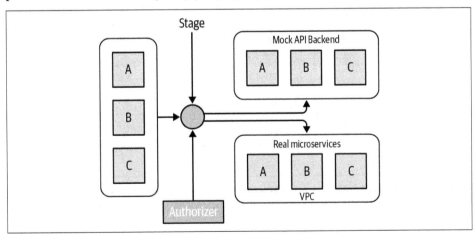

*Figure 6-3. A sample API-first design implementation that routes incoming requests to different backend systems based on the stage that the application is deployed in.*

# AWS API Gateway

AWS API Gateway is a service that AWS provides for implementing client-facing APIs that can be exposed to end users. While a lot can be said about the scalability of API Gateway, from a domain design perspective, AWS API Gateway helps in cleanly decoupling your *backend design perspective* from an *end-user perspective.* This ensures that the backend and the frontend can work independently of each other. This way, you can enforce the SRP on your backend services without compromising on the ease of use for end users.

AWS API Gateway is a fully managed service provided by AWS that allows you to use an API-first approach in a microservice architecture. You can expose either a REST or a WebSocket API to end consumers who can design against it. On the backend, you can easily switch among other AWS services that can handle and process any incoming request.

Figure 6-4, shows how the security components in a traditional monolith can be mapped to an existing prebuilt feature on AWS API Gateway.

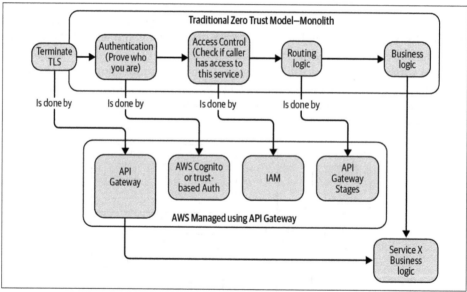

*Figure 6-4. How API Gateway helps you outsource boilerplate activity in zero trust environments onto AWS-managed services so your microservice can focus on business logic.*

To make things better, all these features are provided to you as part of Amazon's SRM, making it easy for you to focus on business logic instead of worrying about the scalability and security of these services.

API Gateway encourages API-first design of code by providing you with the tools required to have different stages for testing and deploying new changes to your API. It also comes with the ability to test your API endpoints to encourage TDD.

AWS API Gateway can call AWS Lambda, AWS load balancers, and a variety of other AWS services. AWS regularly updates the list of services that can service an API Gateway request, and this ever-growing list adds flexibility for an architect to design their application without worrying about the backend implementation at design time.

AWS API Gateway also enables the ability to offload Transport Layer Security (TLS) termination to the edge system and provides a secure perimeter without needing to install certificates on each of your systems. This ensures the simplicity of your infrastructure. So, to create an efficient and secure API design using API Gateway, you can follow these steps:

1. Find all the use cases that the end user needs from your application.

2. Create an API that services all of these use cases.

3. Create automated tests that formalize the contract between the end users and the API.

4. Create a stage where these automated tests can run with mock data from the backend and the tests can be called using an automated testing tool of your choice. (You can use AWS Marketplace tools for this purpose.)

5. Identify the authentication and authorization requirements that need to be satisfied for this API to run properly.

6. Include the authentication and authorization logic inside your tests.

7. Create a second stage that calls the microservice on your backend services using the API Gateway.

8. Ensure that there is no breach of contract using automated tests.

## Types of AWS API Gateway Endpoints

API Gateway exposes multiple services as a collection. These services collectively share the same web hostname and are called API Gateway endpoints. Depending on the needs of your application, AWS provides you with three different types of endpoints for API Gateway:

- Regional API Gateway endpoints
- Edge-optimized API Gateway endpoints
- Private API Gateway endpoints

### Regional API Gateway endpoint

This is the default type of API Gateway interface that is used by many services. It was also the first API Gateway service to come into existence. As the name suggests, this is a regional service. So you do not get the advantage of geo-optimization or caching. You have to choose the region in which this service is deployed. Having said that, the service is open to the internet, and by default you get a global URL generated for you once you deploy this service. This API Gateway is perfect for simple applications or server-to-server calls that may be happening against your web server and where geo-optimization is not really required.

### Edge-optimized API Gateway endpoint

Sometimes you need speed, so you call an API that is at a closer geographic location. Other times, you want a failover, so you call the same API from a bunch of different places. Also, some apps only offer global service, so you use them everywhere. In either of these scenarios, you may want to distribute your edge applications to the location of the end user. Edge-optimized API Gateway helps in achieving geographic distribution of your API Gateway.

Let us say you have a globally distributed user base for your application. All your users need to connect to a centralized backend service. In such a situation, an edge-optimized API Gateway endpoint allows all of your globally distributed users to connect to the closest AWS edge location. AWS then assumes the responsibility of private communication between these edge locations and the rest of your cloud resources as part of its SRM. You can see this in Figure 6-5.

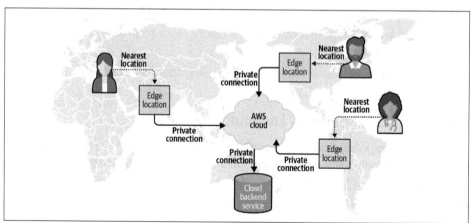

*Figure 6-5. Global users wishing to connect to a centralized cloud resource end up connecting with one of the AWS edge locations. AWS can then assume the responsibility of connecting these edge locations to the rest of your cloud infrastructure.*

An edge-optimized API Gateway endpoint makes use of AWS CloudFront under the hood. AWS's network of edge-optimized servers host an AWS CloudFront distribution across the globe and make sure requests go over AWS's private network instead of the internet before they hit your backend services. This way, you can have a distributed service that is globally available without the need for a distributed backend or a security service that must worry about data traveling across the open internet.

### Private API Gateway endpoint

While a majority of your use cases concerning your API Gateway involve requests that come from the open internet, there are times when you may want to service internal requests. These are requests that are made from a different microservice within your virtual private cloud (VPC) and would like to utilize the advantages that API Gateway provides. A private API Gateway lets you service internal requests using API Gateway.

## Securing the API Gateway

Before I dive into security surrounding the API Gateway, I would like to talk about the high-level architecture that the API Gateway pushes us toward. From a high level, almost all applications will end up having the structure depicted in Figure 6-6.

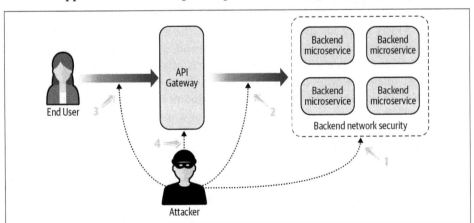

*Figure 6-6. A high-level overview of an application that uses API Gateway along with parts where access control needs to be implemented to secure the application.*

Now that the architecture is laid out, I will talk about four places where security controls may be needed:

- *Backend services:* To start with, the backend services, which do the bulk of the work, need to be clearly and cleanly isolated and secured from any attackers. Since the security controls that are required to secure these backend services are extensively discussed in Chapter 5, I will not go into the details here.

- *API Gateway integration:* Communication between an API Gateway server and the backend services needs to be secure and private. This will be covered in the next section.

- *API Gateway authorizers:* It is also important to make sure that only authenticated and authorized users have access to the endpoints exposed to the end user. On AWS API Gateway, this piece is handled by *authorizers*, and will be covered in "Access Control on API Gateway" on page 198.

- *Infrastructure security:* Finally, the infrastructure that supports this architecture setup needs to be properly secured. This will involve limiting frequent accesses and ensuring proper end-to-end encryption between the various components of your infrastructure. I will talk briefly about the tools available to you in "Infrastructure Security on API Gateway" on page 205

## API Gateway Integration

Once the API is ready for use by the consumer, the architects have to think about how the edge services can start consuming backend microservices. This process of linking a backend service with the API Gateway is called an *integration process.* The service that integrates with the API Gateway as part of the integration process is called an *integration endpoint.* An integration endpoint can be an AWS Lambda function, an HTTP webpage, another AWS service, or a mock response that is used for testing. There are two elements in each API integration: an integration request and an integration response. Integration requests are encapsulations of request data sent to the backend service as requests. AWS allows you to map incoming data into a request body that is expected by the backend microservice that services this request. It might be different from the method request submitted by the client. Likewise, an integration response receives output from a backend application and can then be repackaged and sent to the client. Figure 6-7 highlights this setup.

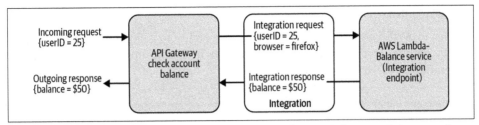

Figure 6-7. A sample flow of requests and responses when API Gateway is integrated with an AWS Lambda integration endpoint.

### AWS Lambda integrations

AWS Lambda is a common backend microservice used in microservice applications to provide a serverless backend. If your microservices are mainly written using AWS Lambda, integrating them with API Gateway is a fairly straightforward task. You simply need the name of the Lambda function that your edge API endpoint needs to call as part of the integration, and then add it to the integration.

You may also specify the mappings between the request data and the integration request and the integration response data resulting from the integration. Figure 6-8 shows how a Lambda integration can be specified using the AWS console.

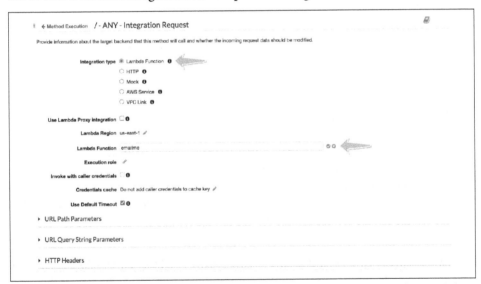

Figure 6-8. Choosing Lambda Function as integration type and specifying the Lambda function's name will ensure the right function is called.

## HTTP integration

Similar to AWS Lambda, API Gateway has the ability to call any public HTTP endpoints. Setting up HTTP integration is similar to setting up AWS Lambda—based integrations, as seen in Figure 6-9.

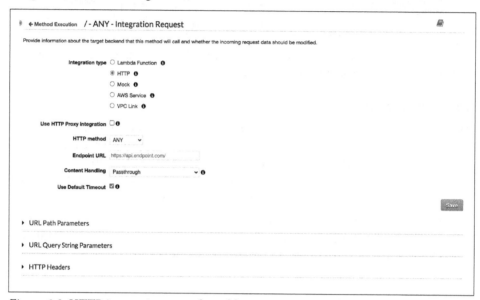

*Figure 6-9. HTTP integrations can also add or remove custom headers from the integration request if needed.*

## VPC links

While HTTP integrations work well in calling public HTTP endpoints, from a security perspective, you may not want to expose your entire microservice backend infrastructure to the public internet just for it to be accessible via the API Gateway. This is where VPC links come into the picture. VPC links connect resources in a VPC to edge endpoints that can be accessed via HTTP API routes. If your setup uses Amazon Elastic Kubernetes Service (EKS) or any other Kubernetes setup, you can add a network load balancer (NLB) that can then route incoming requests to the right destination pod.

The NLB can be a private NLB that lives entirely within your private VPC. This way, API Gateway can allow controlled access to your private backend environment. A VPC link also uses security groups to restrict unauthorized access.

For application load balancers (ALBs), you can use a VPC link for HTTP APIs. A VPC link is created within each specified subnet, allowing your customers to access the HTTP endpoints inside their private VPCs. Figure 6-10 shows how you can add a VPC link to your account.

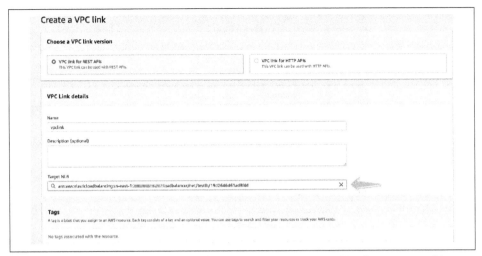

*Figure 6-10. VPC links can be created to connect to a private NLB that exists within your VPC. For ALB and other HTTP support, you can use a VPC link for HTTP API and add VPC links to subnets.*

VPC links are immutable. Once created, you cannot change their subnets or security groups.

### Kubernetes microservices and API Gateway

With VPC links, API Gateway can now be extended to call all of your REST backend services that run on private Kubernetes environments. These services can be running inside your private VPC.

To connect these services to your API Gateway, you can create an NLB and have your Kubernetes cluster as a target group for this load balancer. This setup is really no different than any other Kubernetes setup. For further information on setting up Kubernetes on AWS, AWS provides great documentation (*https://oreil.ly/UqqUk*).

This setup is highlighted in Figure 6-11.

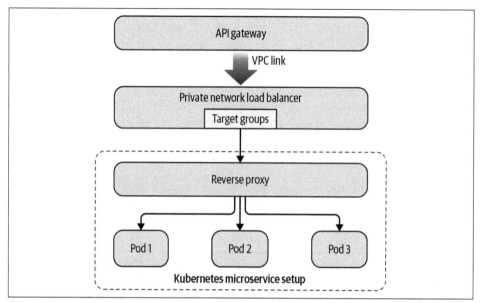

*Figure 6-11. A VPC link can be used to connect the customer-facing API Gateway with your private NLB that can then connect to your Kubernetes setup.*

## Access Control on API Gateway

By definition, API Gateway is open to all requests that seek access to your cloud resources. This means that an API Gateway is at the heart of securing your entire infrastructure. While your backend services enjoy a clean isolation and a strong moat, your edge services need to be prepared to handle an array of threats from the outside world. Because perimeter protection is weak when it comes to edge security, it is more important than ever to use a zero trust model in edge networks. It means all edge services will not trust incoming requests until they've established trust in the system through some approved methods.

To implement the zero trust model in systems, every request needs to be authenticated and validated against your permission policy. Logic such as this must be repeated, either by distributing across numerous services or by allocating it to a centralized service. Although still possible, several security requirements would have been harder to incorporate into your design without AWS API Gateway. For this reason, AWS API Gateway provides users with predefined frameworks that in turn, simplify the setup process significantly.

From the end user's perspective, API Gateway supports a zero trust policy through a set of authorizers. Authorizers can be considered as interceptors that check each incoming request and enforce zero trust on each request. Only the requests that satisfy the demands of these preconfigured authorizers are allowed to proceed.

This also indicates that every request must be able to identify itself, ensuring our application against the many different types of phishing attacks. Figure 6-12 shows how an interceptor manages each request made to the API Gateway endpoint. For software developers who have worked with design patterns, API Gateway imitates the facade design pattern that is commonly used in software development. The actual implementation of the access control logic can be abstracted away using this facade.

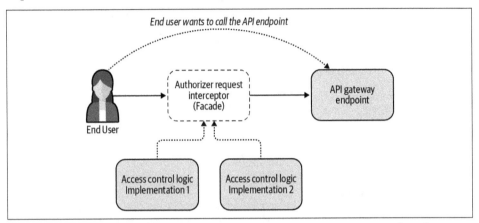

*Figure 6-12. The API Gateway authorizer intercepts incoming requests and applies access control logic to each request based on the type of authorizer used.*

There are three types of authorizers that AWS supports natively, and each of them has a different use case:

- API-based identity and access management (IAM) authorizer
- Cognito-based authorizer
- Lambda-based authorizer

### IAM authorizer (API-based authorizer)

The simplest way of extending access control to AWS API Gateway is to map the identity of the calling entity to a principal (an AWS user or an AWS role) that can be identified by AWS. Once the caller finds a way to tie its own identity to that of an AWS principal, access control becomes easy using IAM policies that are covered extensively in Chapter 2.

So to implement IAM authorization on API Gateway, you will need to perform the following steps:

1. Identify a principal that the calling application is going to use to make this request.

2. First ensure that the calling application is allowed to assume the identity that you wish to use for authorization at the API Gateway.

3. Create and attach an IAM policy that defines how and in what context this principal is allowed or denied calling this method.

4. Enable IAM authorization on the API Gateway with this policy.

Figure 6-13 explains how IAM authorizer can be used on the AWS API Gateway.

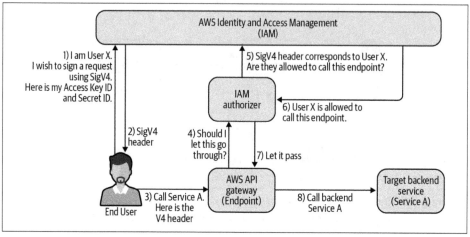

*Figure 6-13. The flow of an API Gateway request that uses an IAM authorizer.*

If an AWS user (say, User X) decides to access a service (say, Service A):

1. User X first downloads their credentials (AWS account ID and AWS secret key).

2. To validate the API request against the IAM policy, the API Gateway must ask the principals to identify themselves. This can be achieved by signing the request (*https://oreil.ly/eWKu5*) using approved request signing methods such as AWS Sinature Version 4 (SigV4).

3. The user then includes this signature in its request to the API Gateway endpoint.

4. The API Gateway endpoint delegates the authentication to the IAM authorizer.

5. The IAM authorizer has the capacity to read the access policy for the user who has signed this request by querying the AWS IAM service.

6. It then evaluates the access policy against the request in a manner similar to the way that any incoming request is evaluated (see Chapter 2).

7. Depending on the result of this policy evaluation, the IAM authorizer decides whether the signed incoming request should be allowed to pass or should be denied.

Since every request has to be separately signed, API Gateway does indeed support zero trust in this instance. However, since this means each calling entity has to be able to sign requests using a principal from your AWS account, it is not a scalable solution for the customer or end user–facing API Gateways.

To set up IAM authorization, follow these steps:

1. In the API Gateway console, choose the name of your API.

2. In the Resources pane, choose a method (such as GET or POST) for which you want to enable IAM authentication.

3. In the Method Execution pane, choose Method Request.

4. Under Settings, for authorization choose the pencil icon (Edit), choose AWS_IAM from the drop-down menu, and then choose the checkmark icon (Update).

You can then deploy this API to a stage. To make a request, you will have to use SigV4 to make requests:

```
curl --location --request GET https://iam.amazonaws.com/?Action=ListUsers&Version
=2010-05-08 HTTP/1.1
Authorization: AWS4-HMAC-SHA256 Credential=AKIDEXAMPLE/20150830/
us-east-1/iam/aws4_request,
SignedHeaders=content-type;host;x-amz-date,
Signature=5d672d79c15b13162d9279b0855cfba6789a8edb4c82c400e06b5924a6f2b5d7
content-type: application/x-www-form-urlencoded; charset=utf-8
host: iam.amazonaws.com
x-amz-date: 20150830T123600Z'
```

Any request made using the AWS Command Line Interface (CLI) is automatically signed, and hence it can be executed as long as the calling user has the right IAM access.

### AWS Cognito authorizer

AWS Cognito can also provide end-user authentication, to be used against an API Gateway. In order to use AWS Cognito, I will assume you have the initial user-pool setup ready. Let's also assume you maintain a user pool of all of your users in Cognito. This means every legitimate incoming request can be traced back to a valid user that exists in this user pool.

To use an Amazon Cognito user pool with your API, you must first create an authorizer of type Cognito User Pools. You can then configure an API method to use this authorizer. Figure 6-14 shows how you can add a Cognito authorizer to an existing API endpoint.

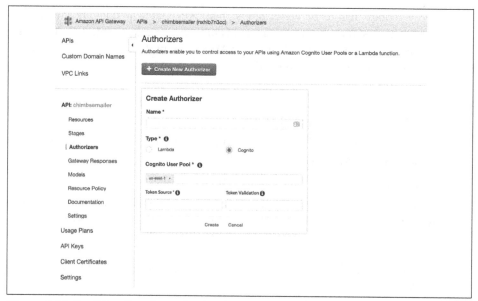

*Figure 6-14. Enabling Cognito authorization on your API Gateway endpoint using the AWS Management Console.*

As highlighted in Figure 6-15, once enabled, your API Gateway will delegate the request authorization to AWS Cognito and track user permissions based on its user pool.

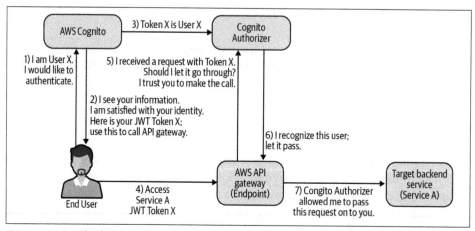

*Figure 6-15. A high-level view of a request authorization with AWS Cognito enabled.*

Here's how it works if a user (say, User X) decides to access a service (say, Service A):

1. User X will first make a request to AWS Cognito. User X can use any of the authentication methods supported by AWS Cognito to establish their identity.

2. Once the identity of the caller is established, AWS Cognito responds with a JSON Web Token (JWT).

3. At the same time, AWS Cognito will synchronize its JWTs with the Cognito authorizer.

4. User X makes a request to the API Gateway with the JWT.

5. API Gateway delegates the authorization process with the Cognito authorizer. As mentioned in Step 3, the Cognito authorizer should already have been informed by AWS Cognito of this JWT.

6. As a result, the Cognito authorizer is able to map the incoming request to an authorized user.

7. The Cognito authorizer gives the go-ahead for this incoming request, allowing it to access the target backend service—Service A.

Since every call always contains the token, you still achieve zero trust access. The JWT also can be configured to expire, allowing an injection of more security into the system.

The disadvantage of using a Cognito authorizer is that each and every end user needs to be in the Cognito user pool. This may be straightforward for greenfield installations. For established applications, though, it may not be the case since they may already use their own authentication and authorization mechanisms.

### Lambda authorizer

The Cognito authorizer gives a scalable but elegant way of achieving zero trust security at the API Gateway level. But it comes with the overhead of maintaining a Cognito user pool, which may or may not agree with the security infrastructure of your organization. Although Cognito is secure, it may be out of the scope of your security project. Moreover, Cognito does not offer an easy way to add custom authentication logic that can be applied to an existing application.

It is likely that an organization has already implemented mechanisms for user validation, authentication, and storage that they do not want to eliminate. The good news is that AWS lets you plug in your own authorization code to replace the one that was managed for you.

In order to implement this custom authorization logic, each API Gateway request is given the ability to call an AWS Lambda function to evaluate its access and privileges. AWS Lambda functions are extremely customizable and can end up calling any other resource or service of your choice. If your organization already has custom access control logic, this authorizing Lambda can delegate access control to your organization's custom authorization logic. Lambda authorizers require incoming requests to have information that can help them perform their tasks.

This information can be present in the form of the following:

- A JWT that can be present and passed along with the request
- A combination of headers/request parameters that are passed along with the incoming request

 WebSocket-based Lambdas only support the parameter-based Lambda authorizers.

Figure 6-16 shows how you can implement a Lambda authorizer, if a user (User X) decides to access a service (Service A), while Service B provides the authorization service.

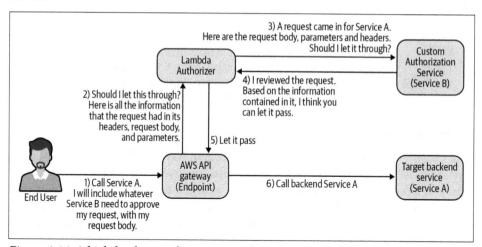

*Figure 6-16. A high-level view of a request authorization using an AWS Lambda authorizer.*

To explain each step further:

1. User X in this case can call the API Gateway endpoint directly by including whatever information it needs to satisfy the existing custom authentication logic.

2. The API Gateway then delegates the authorization to an AWS Lambda function in the form of a Lambda authorizer.

3. This function calls the existing backend service to get a response.

4. This backend service evaluates the incoming request and responds with either an ALLOW or a DENY response.

5. The response from Step 4 will then decide whether the incoming request needs to be blocked or can proceed.

The request should carry all required items for access control within itself. For example, this could mean a bearer authorization token in the header or in the request's parameters.

Given the customizable nature of this authorization method, as long as the API and authorization service can agree on the authorization methods, it is fairly straightforward to implement the end-to-end flow of the request.

## Infrastructure Security on API Gateway

In this section, I will talk about a few infrastructure-level controls that AWS offers to you in order to safeguard the API Gateway infrastructure.

### Rate limiting

API Gateway has limits on the number of requests it can process. Although authorizers can be great at blocking unauthenticated traffic, given that the API Gateway is the first line of defense in many attacks, a sudden burst of requests to the endpoints may be indicative of a wider DoS attack that the API Gateway may be required to prevent. It would be disappointing if the only option that the API Gateway had was to pass the buck to the underlying microservices. Hence, AWS allows API Gateway to rate limit incoming requests. There are two types of rates that are considered while enforcing this rate limit: the *sustained request rate* and the *burst request rate*. The sustained request rate is the average rate at which your application gets requests over a long period of time. Online traffic tends to exhibit sudden spikes and seasonality, which is accounted for by this long window of averaging. A sustained request rate is the rate that most developers will consider while designing their systems. This rate is shared across all API Gateway endpoints in an account in any particular region.

The burst request rate is a buffer rate that helps in accounting for a sudden and temporary spike in requests that may push the rate of incoming requests beyond the threshold for a very small period of time (usually less than a second).

For those interested in the algorithm behind this calculation, the burst rate is calculated using a token bucket algorithm. For example, if the burst limit is 5,000 requests per second, the following will occur:

- When a caller sends 10,000 requests evenly in a second (10 requests per millisecond), API Gateway processes all of them without dropping any.
- If the caller sends 10,000 requests in the first millisecond, API Gateway serves 5,000 of those requests and throttles the rest in the one-second period following this instant.
- If the caller submits 5,000 requests in the first millisecond and then evenly spreads another 5,000 requests through the remaining 999 milliseconds, API Gateway processes all 10,000 requests in the one-second period without any throttling.

API Gateway sets a throughput limit on the sustained request rates as well as the burst request rates against your APIs, per region. The burst represents the maximum bucket size in the token bucket algorithm. When there are too many requests in a short period of time and the burst-limit threshold is reached, API Gateway throws back 429 Too Many Requests errors. The client can back off and resubmit the failed requests when it can do it within the throttling limits.

While these limits are generally high (as of this writing, it is at 10,000 requests per second, per account, per region), if they do become a sticking point, as an API developer you can restrict client requests to specific limits for individual API stages or methods. Additionally, you can limit client requests for all APIs in your account by limiting them to individual API stages or methods. This limits the overall number of requests to ensure they don't exceed account-level throttling limits in a particular region.

In addition to account-level throttling, a per client throttling limit can be placed on each endpoint as part of the usage plan. Since this involves identifying the calling client, the usage plan uses API keys to identify API clients and meters access to the associated API stages for each key.

## Mutual TLS

Mutual TLS (mTLS) is a slightly newer standard that is rapidly gaining popularity among secure systems everywhere. TLS is discussed in detail in Chapter 7, but as an overview, TLS helps validate the server using a standardized handshake and digital certificates signed by trusted certificate authorities for each domain.

With traditional TLS, security measures are performed only by the server; mTLS takes things a step further by asking the client to authenticate every request for each HTTP request that is sent, thus increasing the security of the protocol.

To set up mTLS, you first need to create the private certificate authority and the client certificates. For API Gateway to authenticate certificates using mTLS, you need the public keys of the root certificate authority and any intermediate certificate authorities. These need to be uploaded to API Gateway. Figure 6-17 shows the steps required to enable mTLS for any custom domain endpoint that is served using API Gateway.

*Figure 6-17. mTLS can be enabled on any custom domain on the API Gateway by entering the Amazon Simple Storage Service (S3) URI of your truststore bundle file.*

mTLS is commonly used for business-to-business (B2B) applications. It is also used in standards such as *open banking*.

# Cost Considerations While Using AWS API Gateway

API Gateway allows edge services to provide a decoupled and modularized backend microservice application that is not bound by the whims of end users. However, it has certain costs associated with it, and knowing how costs pile up can help architects in making informed decisions on whether API Gateway is the right tool for them.

The pricing model for the basic API Gateway service is quite straightforward; you are charged for each independent request that is serviced. To make things simpler and fairer, many invalid requests made to the API Gateway may not be charged under this model. Authentication failures, for example, are not charged. This includes requests made without access keys to endpoints that require keys. Furthermore, throttled requests are also charged. Charges will be assessed based on the number of messages transferred as well as the duration of the connection for WebSocket endpoints.

Most additional services, however, incur an additional charge on the AWS API Gateway beyond the basic services. If caching is enabled on the API Gateway, you will be charged an hourly rate for each hour that the cache is stored on the AWS servers. This charge will be applied without any long-term commitment.

If the API Gateway makes cross-region calls to microservices in a different region, cross-region data-transfer rates may apply. Similarly, if the API Gateway calls other AWS Lambda functions—either for authorization or as an underlying service—the calls to these AWS resources will be evaluated separately.

# Bastion Host

Consider an organization that has completely and securely isolated all of its microservices and separated them from the customer-facing edge requests. However, isolation also comes at a cost. Sometimes, legitimate maintenance has to be carried out on the infrastructure that hosts these services. Alternatively, at times debugging, tracing, and other database-related development require authorized developers to have access to these isolated services.

## Solution

Bastion hosts are used by your internal developers, administrators, and other users to perform maintenance tasks directly on your private infrastructure. Bastion hosts are generally used for ad hoc access, performing maintenance actions around internal services that cannot be accessed from the public internet.

A public internet—routed instance of the AWS Elastic Cloud Compute (EC2) can be setup for use as a bastion host. This instance is highly hardened and secured to a point that any unintended service or user cannot penetrate through the security barrier. Security groups and network access control lists (NACLs) can be used for ensuring this setup. You also need to ensure that tampering with any settings of the bastion host requires elevated permissions. After you harden this server, you can make sure that your backend services can be accessed only from the jump box. NACLs can be used to ensure compliance at the subnet level, while security groups can ensure the same at the elastic network interface/container network interface (ENI/CNI) level.

A bastion host may reside in a separate account where only certain users from within your main account can assume roles that can tamper with the settings on the bastion host. This ensures complete isolation of services.

Bastion hosts are deployed within the public subnets of a VPC. A bastion host ensures that packets are never exchanged directly between your private network and your corporate network.

It is critical to block any internet access from the jump box, and possibly, any port that is not a pure SSH (Secure Shell) access port. It is also a good idea to put the host on a VPC that requires VPN tunneling. An auto scaling group can be used to make sure that an instance pool always matches the number of instances you specified during launch.

 Bastion hosts can be deployed in their own subnets, and NACLs can be used to restrict access. The advantage of isolating bastion hosts into their own subnets is that if a bastion host ever gets compromised, the administrators can immediately use NACLs to secure the perimeter without much delay.

When you add new instances to the VPC to require administrative access from the bastion host, make sure to associate a security group ingress rule to grant this access from the bastion security group (using security group chaining, as discussed earlier). Further, limit this access to only the required ports.

 The jump box should be updated and patched regularly to protect the operating system from intrusions that would compromise your backend system.

# Static Asset Distribution (Content Distribution Network)

This part of the network requires special consideration from a security point of view. Attacks that happen on content distribution networks may try to mask the malicious nature of their traffic by mimicking regular production traffic. Because of this, it is extremely hard to discern a malicious user when it comes to users who are not authenticated.

In many situations, the general strategy toward mitigating attacks on content distribution is to have a business continuity plan that will try to make sure that the underlying system can scale. This will accommodate the increase in requests so that the availability of the application does not suffer while an attack is in progress.

Before I get into how to protect your unauthenticated network, I will describe exactly what I am trying to achieve by security in this network.

# AWS CloudFront

The AWS-recommended way of serving static files is by using an AWS CloudFront distribution. AWS CloudFront is the Amazon CDN asset management system that helps in caching content at the edge for distribution. Each CloudFront distribution uses an *origin*, which is a storage location where the static content is stored. Cloud-Front is a highly available and scalable system. It enables the users to ensure constant uptime and performance without being affected in case of attacks.

CloudFront works by caching your static content across various edge locations throughout the world. A request for a resource will be connected to an edge location that is best suited to handle it based on the end user's location and current traffic. Often known as *global traffic management* (GTM), this process can lead to improved app performance. A requested static resource is first checked against the cache of the edge location, and only if it does not exist in its edge cache will a request be made to your origin. This entire operation is abstracted away from the developer as well as the end user, making it easy to implement and deploy.

CloudFront also conforms to the SRM of AWS; you do not have to worry about the infrastructure security of the edge locations, cache, or the communication between the edge locations and your origins. This is handled securely and privately by AWS using its own internet backbone. In this manner, you will be able to focus on your application code without worrying about achieving compliance with distribution of your content. Figure 6-18 shows how different users can connect with a local edge connection in order to access the static content of your application. The edge-optimized API Gateway works in a similar way, and for good reason. Under the hood, edge-optimized API Gateway makes use of AWS CloudFront to distribute content to regions around the globe.

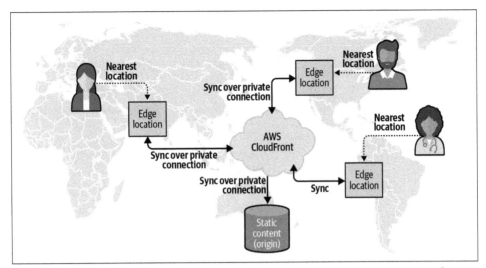

*Figure 6-18. AWS CloudFront distributes cached static resources across various edge locations and connects users to locations closest to the user's geographic region.*

### CloudFront origins

The data repository backing a CloudFront distribution is called an *origin*. The origin is where content is stored for CloudFront to pick up and cache across all its edge locations.

> While CloudFront is optimized to work with S3, it is by no means the only origin that CloudFront works with. CloudFront supports any of the following origins, and the list keeps growing, making it a versatile CDN service that can be easily customized based on your use case:

- Amazon S3 bucket that is configured with static website hosting
- AWS Elastic Load Balancing load balancer
- AWS Elemental MediaPackage endpoint
- AWS Elemental MediaStore container
- Any other HTTP server, running on an Amazon EC2 instance or any other kind of host

Using CloudFront distributions, you can access your content in any country using a globally accessible domain name. You can also use a custom domain name with CloudFront distributions. Figure 6-19 shows how you can add a custom domain name while creating a CloudFront distribution.

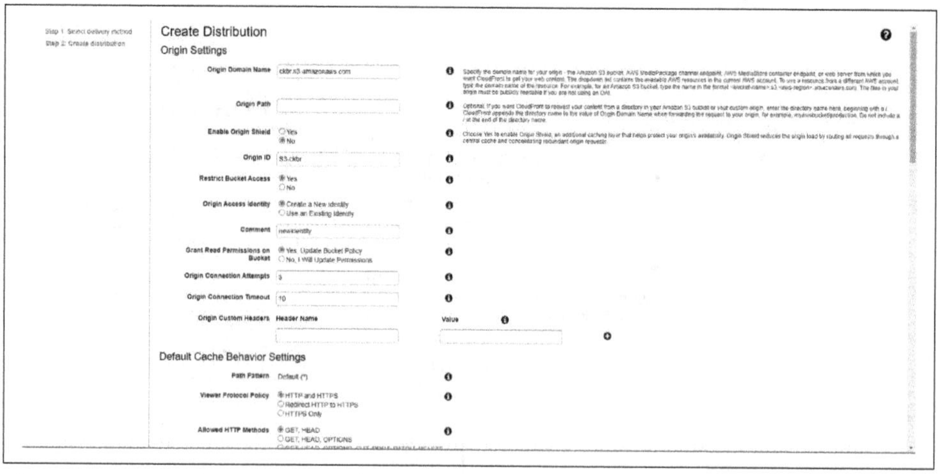

*Figure 6-19. Specifying a custom domain name while creating a CloudFront distribution*

AWS CloudFront only allows secure HTTPS access to its content. So, if you use a custom domain, you will have to add your TLS certificate to the CloudFront distribution for TLS termination. TLS is covered in detail in Chapter 7, but for the purposes of this chapter, it is important to know that a valid TLS certificate must be added to every CloudFront distribution. Figure 6-20 shows the steps required to add a TLS certificate to CloudFront.

*Figure 6-20. Specifying the CloudFront certificate while creating the CloudFront distribution.*

### Origin Access Identity

Say you're using an AWS S3 bucket as the origin for your CloudFront distribution. To ensure protection from attacks and escalating costs, it is important to ensure that access to the static content is locked from every other location except from AWS CloudFront. An important (though not the only) reason for using CloudFront is to safeguard against attacks and escalating costs. However, this is not possible if attackers find a way to directly access the S3 buckets by circumventing CloudFront. This is why you want to make sure that the only resource authorized to access your bucket is your CloudFront distribution, and this access is allowed exclusively for serving static content.

AWS gives you the choice of creating a new identity to be used by your CloudFront distribution. This identity is called the *Origin Access Identity* (OAI). The OAI is what your CloudFront distribution uses to access resources from the origin. It is important that your service use this identity and disable any other access to your S3 buckets once your CloudFront identity is created. Doing so will render the previously accessible backdoor to your S3 buckets unusable, making them less vulnerable to attacks. Figure 6-21 shows how you can add an origin for your CloudFront distribution.

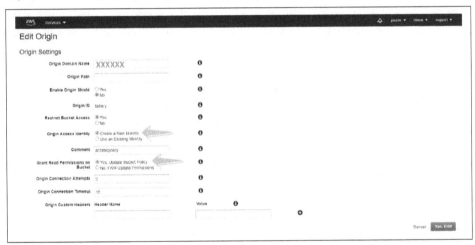

*Figure 6-21. Specifying the creation of an OAI while creating a CloudFront distribution.*

# Signed URLs or Cookies

With the rise of the digital economy, a lot of content providers have realized the need to provide premium content. A lot of times, companies like to charge a premium and provide this content to only certain users. Online newspapers and magazines are examples that come to mind when it comes to such a *freemium* model. In these situations, generally the end user needs access to certain static objects but can be granted this access only after having gone through a basic authentication mechanism. I have already talked about authentication and authorization for services, but remember that static content may also have the requirement to be protected at times.

### Business problem

You want to include a set of digital media content that you would like to serve to end users through your e-commerce website. These videos and graphics are available only to paid customers and can be accessed only once the user has paid for a premium service. You would like to make sure the content is available for a fixed duration of time after the login, but once a certain time duration has elapsed, access to this content is revoked. You would like to maintain this content isolated away from the back-end services.

### Solution

In addition to the use of a trusted service that handles access control on behalf of users, AWS also allows the creation of signed URLs from content-providing object repositories like S3 or CloudFront directly.

The private object repository (S3 or CloudFront) delegates access control to a signing service that acts as an access arbitrator. AWS calls this service a *trusted signer*. AWS makes use of the digital signatures and asymmetric encryption (discussed in Chapter 3) to verify the identity of users and control access.

In order for third parties to gain access to the object repository, the trusted signer shares an exclusive URL signed by its own private key. This signature can be verified by the object repository. When the object repository sees a request with a valid signature, it allows the request to bypass certain authorization requirements.

Using a signed URL, you can distribute access to private objects for only as long as the requester desires—possibly for several minutes. This sort of access is beneficial when used to distribute content-on-demand to a user, for instance, to provide movie rentals or music downloads. The access arbitration service in a media rental company could possibly be a system that has access to subscription and billing information about individual subscribers and can determine whether the users can access premium static content based on their subscription status.

As long as the end users use the secret, signed URL to access the private objects behind the paywall, these objects can be made accessible to legitimate subscribers.

 AWS also enables you to generate longer-term signed URLs for business situations where you may want to share sensitive information with a timestamp on them. An example could be when you share a business plan with investors. You may also share training materials with employees that you would rather redact upon their departure.

I will assume you have the origin and a CloudFront distribution set up along with a trusted signer (say, Signer A). Imagine a situation where an end user (User X) wants to access a private object (Object A). Figure 6-22 highlights the flow of such a request.

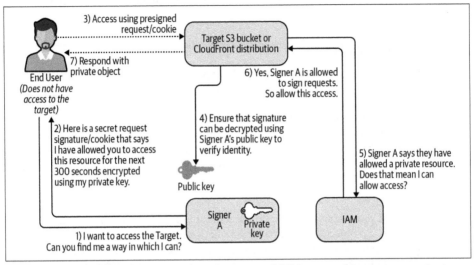

*Figure 6-22. The flow of requests when using signed URLs or cookies to access private content from CloudFront or S3.*

To elaborate on each step:

1. User X knows that Signer A is the trusted signer. So, it makes a request to Signer A asking Signer A to digitally sign this request.

2. Signer A signs this request using its private key.

3. User X uses this signed request to now access Object A from AWS CloudFront or S3.

4. S3 or CloudFront checks the request's signature and makes sure the signer is a trusted signer by decrypting this request using Signer A's public key.

5. S3 or CloudFront checks IAM to make sure that Signer A is allowed to access this resource.

6. If Signer A is allowed to access this object, IAM allows the operation to move forward.

7. S3 or CloudFront returns the private object back to the end-user.

As you might have guessed, what makes a signed URL special is the presence of a signature token in the URL. This signature informs the object repository that some other preassigned service is willing to assume the responsibility of this access, and hence the object repository allows such an access to the end client.

Although both AWS S3 and AWS CloudFront support signed URLs, a signed link can be accessed by anyone with access to the public internet. So, from a security point of view, it might be advisable to use AWS CloudFront whenever you intend to share objects with signed URLs.

### Signed URLs versus signed cookies

Aside from pre-signed URLs, users can also employ HTTP cookies. AWS checks a cookie on the calling host to verify the token instead of checking the URL signature.

Both services provide the same level of security from the perspective of AWS. In both cases, access control is delegated to the trusted signer service, rather than being assessed within the object repository. Thus, either of these methods is acceptable for providing access to your private objects, and architects can choose either of these methods.

 If your application likes to use standard REST formats for accessing static objects, using pre-signed URLs may affect their format. In a similar fashion, since pre-signed URLs need to be created on a per-object basis, if your application simply has two tiers (free and premium) or if you want to provide access to multiple files at the same time, signed cookies are a better fit for your use case. Signed cookies are also handy when you have an existing application that does not want to change its existing URLs. On the other hand, you may prefer granular access control to files. Or if you have multiple tiers of membership, pre-signed URLs may be better suited for your application.

### AWS CloudFront and signed URLs

To use the design of signed URLs securely to distribute private content, here are the steps to follow:

1. Store your private objects in a private bucket.

2. Restrict or control access to content in your Amazon S3 bucket so that users can access it by means of CloudFront but not directly using an Amazon S3 URL. Doing so prevents unauthorized users from bypassing CloudFront and acquiring content by using S3 URLs. You can do this using the OAI.

3. Create a CloudFront *signer*. This can be either a trusted key group that you've created that lets CloudFront know the keys are trusted or an AWS account that contains a CloudFront key pair.

4. When a signed URL or cookie is created, it's signed with the private key of the owner's key pair. Upon reaching CloudFront, a restricted file will be verified

based on the signature included in the URL or the cookie, to confirm that it has not been tampered with.

5. Viewers require signed URLs or cookies to access your files when you add the signer to your distribution.

If signed URLs are used to determine that the viewer has been allowed to request a file and the viewer has this same restriction via signed cookies, CloudFront uses only the signed URLs.

### Signing a URL using AWS CloudFront

Though AWS provides many libraries for different programming languages to sign URLs, here is an example from their reference docs that uses the AWS client to sign a URL:

```
aws cloudfront sign \
    --url https://d111111abcdef8.cloudfront.net/
                private-content/private-file.html \
    --key-pair-id APKAEIBAERJR2EXAMPLE \
    --private-key file://cf-signer-priv-key.pem \
    --date-less-than 2020-01-01
Output:
https://d111111abcdef8.cloudfront.net/private-content/private-
file.html?Expires=1577836800&Signature=nEXK7Kby47XKeZQKVc6pwkif6oZc-
JWSpDkH0UH7EBGGqvgurkecCbgL5VfUAXyLQuJxFwRQWscz-
owcq9KpmewCXrXQbPaJZNi9XSNwf4YKurPDQYaRQawKoeenH0GFteRf9ELK-Bs3nljTLjtbgzIUt
7QJNKXcWr8AuUYikzGdJ4
-qzx6WnxXfH~fxg4-
GGl6l2kgCpXUB6Jx6K~Y3kpVOdzUPOIqFLHAnJojbhxqrVejomZZ2XrquDvNUCCIbePGnR3d
24UPaLXG4FKOqNEaWDIBXu7jUUPwOyQCv
pt-GNvjRJxqWf93uMobeMOiVYahb-e0KItiQewGcm0eLZQ__&
Key-Pair-Id=APKAEIBAERJR2EXAMPLE
```

 CloudFront verifies the expiration date and time embedded in a signed URL when an HTTP request is received. If a client begins downloading a large file right before the expiration period ends, the download should be allowed to continue even if the expiration period elapses as the transfer is taking place. If the TCP connection gets dropped and the client attempts to restart the download after the download expiration time passes, the download will fail.

# AWS Lambda@Edge

One of the most powerful applications of microservices for a security purpose is the ability to run AWS Lambda—based microservices at the edge locations where AWS CloudFront distributions are distributed. This affords you the flexibility to run custom security logic at the edge. With Lambda@Edge, you don't have to provision or manage infrastructure in multiple locations around the world. Although this has a lot of positive benefits in terms of scalability, speed, and efficiency, I would like to discuss some of the security-related benefits it provides. Two common security-related use cases where Lambda@Edge is useful are:

- Inspecting dynamic security headers before passing requests to the origin
- Bot mitigation at the edge

AWS Lambdas can be made to run at each edge location in response to four different types of events:

*Viewer request*
> A request arrives at an AWS Lambda location, and the event is triggered (regardless of whether the request is going to be serviced purely out of the cached data at the edge location or if it has to go to the origin to fetch new content).

*Origin request*
> This event is triggered when the edge location is about to make a request back to the origin, due to the fact that the requested object is not cached at the edge location.

*Origin response*
> This event is triggered after the origin returns a response to a request. It has access to the response from the origin.

*Viewer response*
> This event is triggered before the edge location returns a response to the viewer. It has access to the response.

AWS Lambda@Edge allows you to add new headers to the response object to make the site more secure to end users even if it has only static content and is distributed from the edge.

X-XSS-Protection, Content-Security-Policy, and X-Content-Type-Options are some of the headers you can add to your response headers to ensure security. Lambdas can also be used to perform some basic validation at the edge location to protect the rest of your edge services.

## Protecting Against Common Attacks on Edge Networks

Although AWS CloudFront and AWS API Gateway provide you with a great way of protecting your static assets and your microservices from threats on the internet, you may still want to add additional controls around the entry points to your application's infrastructure. In this section, I will discuss two of the most commonly used controls at the edge of your infrastructure: AWS Web Application Firewall (AWS WAF) and AWS Shield.

## AWS Web Application Firewall

AWS WAF protects against known attacks at the edge of your network, and AWS CloudFront, AWS API Gateway REST API, and AWS ALB support AWS WAF as an added layer of security.

The AWS WAF enables you to define certain configurable rules you can apply to your edge services to shield your services from any malicious traffic. This allows the service to focus on business logic and not have to worry about an attack.

WAF is composed of five parts:

*Rules:*
Each rule includes a statement of what it will inspect and what action to take if the inspection criteria are met. You can perform one of three actions whenever these criteria are met:
- Count: counts the request but doesn't determine whether to allow it or block it, allowing any other rule to make the decision
- Allow: allows the request to be forwarded to the AWS resource for processing
- Block: blocks the request and the AWS resource responds with an HTTP 403 (Forbidden) status code.

*Rule sets:*
It is possible to group some of the commonly used rules together into a collection called a *rule set*. This way, you have the option of associating multiple rules with an access control list (ACL) as part of the rule set.

*IP sets:*
This is a set of IPs that you can define together to be provided to the rule sets so that the rule sets can be applied on a per IP basis. These IPs can act as whitelists, blacklists, or just values to look at depending on the rules you associate them with.

*Regex pattern sets:*
Similar to IPs, AWS allows you to identify requests based on regex patterns. These regex patterns can also be used to augment existing rules by making it easier to block or accept requests.

*Web ACLs:*
A web ACL protects the website by defining its protection strategy with the help of rules or rule sets.

## Setting up basic rules using regex and IPs

The steps to add AWS WAF to your system are as follows:

1. Set up AWS WAF in your account.

2. Create a web ACL for your edge services account.

3. Attach the web ACL to your edge service. This could include either the AWS API Gateway for your external-facing API or the CloudFront distributions for your CDNs and static content.

4. Create a set of rule sets or rules that you feel are associated with common exploits and attacks that your application may face.

5. Attach these rules or rule sets to your web ACL to limit exposure to common web attacks.

## Other rules for protecting your application

Apart from matching on IPs and regex, where rules are applied at an individual request level, AWS WAF allows some advanced aggregate-level filtering:

*Common vulnerability matching*

AWS WAF allows you to protect your application from common vulnerabilities like SQL injection attacks, cross-site scripting attacks, and more. These attacks are designed to mimic usual traffic; hence, the use of rules designed specially for such traffic helps in reducing the overhead required to protect your application. Although in no way am I suggesting that using this rule will completely eliminate the threat of such an attack on your edge systems, enabling them is definitely a step in the right direction.

*Rate-based rules*

Instead of having a rule applied to individual requests, AWS WAF allows you to apply a rule on an aggregated set of requests that are grouped by an IP address. A rate-based rule triggers an action based on the traffic rate of IP addresses that immediately precede it in the request stream. You can use a rule like this to stop requests from an IP address that is sending out excessive requests. You can configure AWS WAF to aggregate requests based on the IP address of the web request's origin, such as X-Forwarded-For, but it is enabled by default to aggregate based on the IP address.

## Managed and Marketplace rule sets

Amazon also gives you some preconfigured, fully managed rule sets for common attacks that you can use in your applications. This makes it easy for you to hit the ground running when it comes to protecting your application from common attacks. Managed rule sets are maintained by AWS, and new rules are added from time to time to add even better levels of security and block malicious attacks from compromising your edge applications.

However, for systems that want to take it a step further, AWS WAF has extended its WAF offering by allowing for third parties to offer premium protection services through WAF by providing you with possibly more up-to-date or targeted rules. These rules may be purchased at a premium price that is added on top of your usual AWS WAF charges. The Marketplace can be accessed by going to the AWS Marketplace tab, as shown in Figure 6-23.

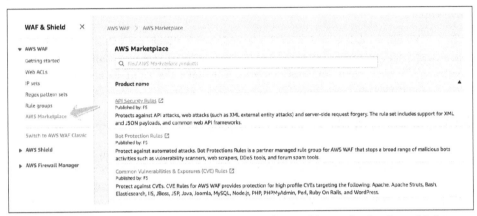

*Figure 6-23. AWS Marketplace allows you to purchase additional rules from third-party security providers.*

## AWS Shield and AWS Shield Advanced

AWS helps defend against most network and transport layer distributed denial of service (DDoS) attacks against your applications. You get the added benefit of comprehensive site protection if you use Amazon CloudFront and Amazon Route 53. DDoS attacks can be sent by individual systems (zombie computers or bots) or by botnets, to flood the bandwidth or storage space of a target.

AWS Shield provides always-on detection and *automatic inline mitigations* that minimize application downtime and latency, so there is no need to engage AWS Support to benefit from DDoS protection. It is also included in your AWS service arrangement and hence comes at no added cost.

AWS Shield Advanced works in conjunction with AWS WAF to provide additional protection from DDoS attacks but is activated separately. AWS Shield Advanced works with multiple edge services to add the extra protection.

Shield Advanced can temporarily promote your network ACLs to the AWS border to process traffic during a DDoS attack. This means traffic that was supposed to get inside your network and get blocked either way inside your VPC (due to a well-configured NACL) will now be blocked right at the border of the AWS network, thus keeping your application away from any malicious traffic. With the network ACLs at the network's border, Shield Advanced can handle larger DDoS events. This also protects the internal perimeter and ensures that the DDoS traffic is stopped from entering your VPC. AWS Shield Advanced customers can access real-time metrics and reports and contact the 24x7 AWS DDoS Response Team for assistance during a DDoS attack.

When AWS Shield Advanced detects a large Layer 7 attack against one of your applications, the data retrieval tool (DRT) contacts you to let you know about it. The DRT creates AWS WAF rules and notifies you. You have the right to either accept new security measures or reject them.

## Microservices and AWS Shield Advanced

Since microservices work as clusters, sometimes the unavailability of one service may not be evidence of an attack. AWS Shield Advanced customizes the scope of its protection by resource groups (called *protection groups*) so that multiple protected resources are protected as one whole cluster unit. Protection groups are especially useful for protecting against false positives during events such as deployments and swaps.

Due to their nature, microservices generally facilitate horizontal scaling during times of intense load. This is a huge advantage that microservices present and should be part of every architecture design.

During security incidents, if the attack somehow manages to penetrate through your perimeter protection, this scalability can turn out to be a liability since your scaling costs will only be used to fight a malicious attack. So, not only will you be spending extra to garrison your resources against an attack, but you would actually be paying for the added scale that your infrastructure has to support until you can successfully block this attack at the perimeter.

As part of AWS Shield Advanced, AWS provides cost protection in case your AWS resources scale up in response to a DDoS attack. If your protected AWS resources scale up, you can request credits through regular AWS Support channels.

## Cost Considerations for Edge Protection

Protecting the system from external attacks is something that every organization should consider, but the additional costs that come along with this protection could be unaffordable for some organizations, and hence a *risk-benefit analysis (RBA)* is required in some cases. In this section, I have mentioned three AWS-provided edge protection systems (AWS WAF, AWS Shield Standard, and AWS Shield Advanced). Each has its own cost structure. Additionally, I have shown you the AWS Marketplace, which has additional systems that may be able to add extra protection that may not be available in AWS systems.

With AWS WAF, you can incur a cost in one of three ways. Each web ACL you create incurs an hourly charge. Each rule you create for your web ACL is charged on an hourly basis. Apart from this, you also pay per million requests that your application receives regardless of whether they are blocked or allowed. AWS provides a great calculator (*https://aws.amazon.com/waf/pricing*) for calculating your estimated charges.

AWS Shield Standard is available free of cost for all AWS users. AWS Shield Advanced, though, incurs a monthly fee that is charged for every organization. For multiple accounts under the same organization, this monthly fee remains the same.

In addition, AWS Shield Advanced provides a business continuity plan for all its users in the event they are under attack; this can be an attractive investment in case your application cannot afford any downtime, even during an attack. This is like an insurance policy for your infrastructure against malicious users.

A good way of performing an RBA is to weigh the cost of protection measures against a probability-weighted cost of a security incident. Any business continuity measures you may put in place for such an incident should also be factored into this cost calculation. Ironically, your organization could end up spending a lot of money for servicing requests from malicious users if you don't prevent an attack.

# Summary

This chapter discussed the need for separate consideration when it comes to the edge systems of your application. Edge systems for microservices should be designed to accommodate the use cases that end clients of our applications encounter. They should never be designed to suit the structure of our backend system. As a result, edge systems benefit from an API-first design methodology that I discussed in this chapter.

AWS API Gateway provides a framework to organize our code in a manner that fulfills the SRP using authorizers to adhere to the principle of zero trust. I also talked about the protections you can place on networks where the end user does not need to be authenticated. These involve the use of CloudFront and signed URLs for individual object access or using AWS WAF and AWS Shield to protect an application from known vulnerabilities and DDoS attacks.

Finally, for services that are not provided by AWS, the chapter gave an overview of what users can use from the AWS Marketplace to add protection at the edge.

In general, the edge system is the most vulnerable of all the systems. It is critical to isolate and safeguard it as much as you can.

# Security in Transit

If two modules in a monolith are to communicate with each other, it is generally a simple in-memory method call. Microservices, unlike monoliths, rely on an external transport (such as a network) to communicate with each other (since modules are decomposed into independent services possibly running on different machines).

External communication channels are more likely to be vulnerable to potential threats from malicious actors compared to in-memory calls. Thus, by definition, external communication channels run with a higher *aggregate risk.*

To illustrate this point, I will use an example of an ecommerce application's checkout process, as outlined in Figure 7-1. Imagine that the checkout process involves the application calculating the item's price and charging the customer by looking it up in a repository. Upon checking out, the company then decrements this item's available inventory.

Since an external communication channel inherently increases the aggregate risk of the application, security professionals need to add *controls* to ensure that potential threats are minimized. *Encryption in transit* is the most commonly used control that reduces the potential threat of messages being intercepted, tampered with, or spoofed. (Encryption is covered in detail in Chapter 3).

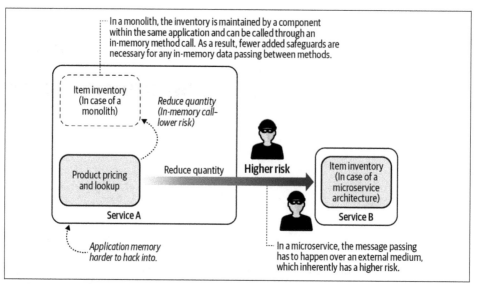

*Figure 7-1. In the case of microservices, calls to external services happen over an external medium as opposed to the in-memory calls that monoliths afford.*

You can achieve interservice communication between microservices in many ways. Here are some common communication patterns. This list is not exhaustive and not mutually exclusive:

- Using asynchronous representational state transfer (REST)
- Using messaging queues such as AWS Simple Queue Service (SQS) or message brokers such as Apache Kafka
- Using wrappers on top of HTTP or HTTP/2 such as Google Remote Procedure Call (gRPC).
- Using a *service mesh* such as Istio or the AWS-managed AWS App Mesh

Transport Layer Security (TLS) is by far the most commonly used method of encrypting data in transit. This chapter discusses the various systems that AWS has in place for ensuring easy and simple end-to-end security of your applications using TLS and AWS ACM. I will also briefly introduce you to AWS App Mesh, a managed service mesh (*https://oreil.ly/WjFiv*) that helps microservices deal with boilerplate code that goes into securing and maintaining the additional complexity that external communication channels bring with it.

My focus in this chapter will be on the security aspects of these external communication channels. However, architects may also need to consider scalability, latency, and which ones dictate a lot of trade-offs in microservice architectures. For these issues, I will refer you to other reading materials since that is outside of the focus of this book.

In the book *Fundamentals of Software Architecture* (O'Reilly) (*https://oreil.ly/W6ZKa*), authors Mark Richards and Neal Ford go over a lot of the trade-offs associated with microservices. *Building Microservices* (O'Reilly) (*https://oreil.ly/H865s*) by Sam Newman is a great resource for designing microservices to address all of these scalability and throughput issues.

 AWS Key Management Service (KMS) plays an important role in implementing TLS under the hood on AWS. A conceptual understanding of KMS (described in Chapter 3) will go a long way toward understanding the workings of TLS.

# Basics of Transport Layer Security

When it comes to HTTP communication, there are two very common ways in which malicious actors can gain unauthorized access to the data that is being communicated or is *in transit*. Figure 7-2 shows a standard communication between a service (Service A) and a credit card processor service (CCPS).

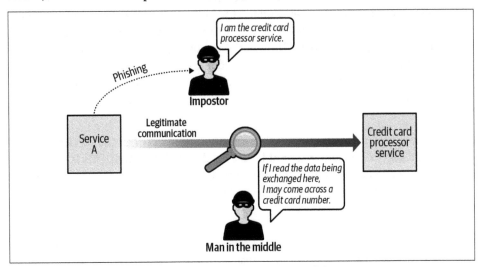

*Figure 7-2. "Phishing" and "man in the middle" are two of the most common ways in which malicious actors steal user data while in transit.*

Let's assume Service A needs to send sensitive information to the CCPS. There are two ways in which malicious actors may try to steal this sensitive information:

*Phishing*

An imposter could pretend to be the CCPS. If Service A has no way of identifying the real CCPS, it may end up sending sensitive information to the imposter.

*Man in the middle*

Another service could start snooping and recording all the data that is being exchanged legitimately between Service A and CCPS and thus come across sensitive information.

TLS reduces the risk of these potential threats by helping you implement authentication and encryption controls on the communication channels.

In the following section, I will explain in detail how authentication and encryption work to reduce this risk:

*Authentication*

The purpose of authentication is to identify and validate the identity of a server in a communication channel. Under TLS, both parties, the client and the server, agree to entrust the authentication task to a trusted party called a trusted certificate authority (trusted CA). Through the use of digital certificates and public key encryption, a trusted CA can verify the identity of the server to a client that has trusted the CA. Server validation can help to prevent impersonation and phishing attacks.

*Encryption*

Encryption aims to ensure that any communication between the service provider and the service consumer cannot be accessed by a third party. This is done using end-to-end encryption that TLS provides after a secure line has been established. Through encryption, TLS can help prevent man-in-the-middle or communication channel hijacking attacks.

We live today in a world where encryption in transit is expected in almost every application that is designed. However, this wasn't always the case. During the 1990s, most internet communications happened over unencrypted channels (see YouTube video on TLS (*https://oreil.ly/XlbTD*)), resulting in significant losses to the companies who used such insecure channels. Today, the lack of TLS may cause you to violate compliance requirements in most regulatory compliance standards. So, it is best to have TLS in addition to any other security controls you may have in place.

# Digital Signing

As you might remember from Chapter 3, in computing, the integrity of your data can be ensured mathematically through a process known as *digital signing*. Security in transit applies this process of digital signing to ensure the integrity of the communication in flight. Digital signing is the process of encrypting a document using a private key so that other parties can verify its authenticity using asymmetric encryption. To refresh your memory:

- In an asymmetric key encryption, data encrypted by a private key can only be decrypted by a public key.
- If a service (say, Service A) encrypts a document using its private key, we can assume that anyone with the public key of this service will be able to decrypt it.

A signed document implies that the signer had access to the private key. And conversely, a service that has access to the private key is able to sign any document using the private key, thus guaranteeing the integrity of the signed document.

## Certificates, Certificate Authority, and Identity Verification

TLS achieves authentication using public-key cryptography in the form of digital certificates. *Digital certificates* are electronic documents that prove ownership of private keys based on digital signatures. The certificate includes the public key of the server (called the *subject*), which is digitally signed by a trusted third party. If this signature of the third party is valid, then the client can trust the authenticity of the server's public key and encrypt data using this public key.

Consider a scenario where you have two services talking to each other, Service A and Service B. Service A is the client that initiates the connection, and Service B is the server that provides the service. The purpose of TLS authentication is for Service B to prove its identity to Service A.

Service B knows that Service A trusts Trusted CA—CA1. Hence, Service B can entrust CA1 to help identify itself. Figure 7-3 shows how Service B can use CA1 to gain the trust of Service A.

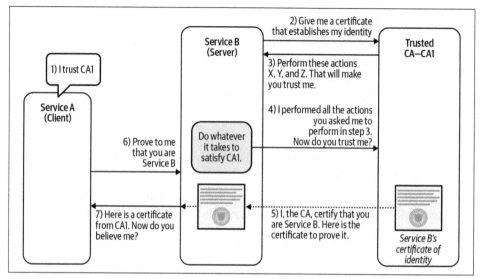

*Figure 7-3. An overview of how a trusted CA can help establish a trusted connection.*

Here is how the process plays out:

1. Service A decides to trust any certificate signed by CA1 (that's everything that can be decrypted using the public key of the CA1).

2. Service B decides to entrust the CA1 with proving its own identity.

3. CA1 asks Service B to perform certain "actions" that it thinks can be performed only by Service B. (This will ensure that Service B is able to identify itself to CA1's satisfaction. I talk more about these actions later in this chapter.)

4. Service B performs these actions and waits for CA1 to confirm its identity.

5. If CA1 is satisfied with the actions that Service B performed, CA1 then sends over a digital certificate to Service B establishing its identity.

Using these steps, now TLS authentication between Service A and Service B is possible. If Service A asks for authentication from Service B, Service B can respond with the TLS certificate from Step 5.

A few things stand out in the exchange between Service A and Service B from Figure 7-3:

- Because there is a trusted third party (trusted CA) willing to take on the responsibility of authenticating Service B and digitally signing its certificate, Service A can verify Service B's certificate.

- The trusted CA allows Service B to prove its identity. In other words, Service B knows what it needs to do to satisfy the trusted CA.

- The trusted CA can securely share a private key with Service B that is paired with the public key that is present in the certificate. If an intruder managed to get their hands on this private key, they could use the certificate and impersonate Service B.

- A certificate is only valid if the private key of the server (Service B) is indeed private. If this private key had been compromised or leaked, it is important to invalidate the digital certificate immediately since it no longer identifies Service B as the sole owner of the private key. The process of invalidating such certificates is called *TLS certificate revocation*.

The steps outlined in Figure 7-4 show how TLS is made secure, and the absence of any of them would compromise the design. AWS provides various services, as seen in Figure 7-4, that ensure all of these steps are properly followed while you issue certificates to all your services. I will describe how each of these services helps in securing the TLS setup later in this chapter.

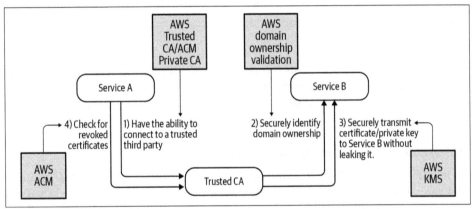

*Figure 7-4. For each step involved in making TLS secure, AWS provides users with a service that can be leveraged for the purpose of security.*

### Certificate agility and the need for certificate agility

Digital certificates play an important role in any microservice system that uses HTTP communication. If the underlying private key that backs the certificate is compromised, an attacker can take over the identity of a service and exploit the trust that a service consumer places in the security of your system. Hence, digital certificates, just like any other security asset, require maintenance and management (*https://oreil.ly/q3Ndj*). Mismanagement of TLS certificates is a routine cause of service outages. Some examples include the outage caused at Microsoft due to their delay in renewing a certificate (*https://oreil.ly/Anjnq*) or the outage caused at Spotify (*https://oreil.ly/P4t3A*) due to an expired TLS certificate.

Hence, it is important to realize that the security benefits that come with secure communication come at an operational cost. In the next section, I will introduce you to an AWS service, AWS ACM, which aims at simplifying the process of certificate management for you.

## AWS Certificate Manager

At its heart, AWS provides a service, AWS ACM, for dealing with digital certificates. ACM certificates are X.509 TLS certificates (*https://oreil.ly/gTkLh*) that bind a service (URL) to the public key that is contained in the certificate. Think of a certificate as a driver's license for the URL that identifies the server. Using ACM, customers can do the following:

- Create digitally signed certificates for services that need TLS encryption
- Manage private keys and public keys for all of the services
- Automatically renew certificates for each of these services
- Either use AWS's publicly used shared trusted CA or set up a trusted private CA for internal services

On AWS ACM, a certificate exists independently of a server and is bound to the URL. The purpose of this certificate installation is to allow the new service to identify itself. AWS assumes the responsibility of installing and managing the certificate on an ACM-supported service once you configure it to do so.

### Publicly trusted certificate authority—Amazon Trust Services

As mentioned, one of the cornerstones of TLS is the presence of a trusted authority that can verify the identity of the server (to the satisfaction of the client). It is the server's responsibility to ensure that any certificate of authenticity that it presents to the client is digitally signed by a CA that the client trusts.

This is where a *public CA* comes into the picture. AWS maintains a public CA under the name Amazon Trust Services, which is trusted by billions of browsers and systems throughout the world, almost making it a universally trusted CA. A certificate that is signed by this public CA can therefore be used in most client-server communication.

If you are a server, the steps for using this CA are simple. First, you need to create a certificate for the domain that you wish to get TLS-certified. You should then convince AWS Trust Services of your identity (using steps that I will discuss later in "Validating domain ownership" on page 235). Once that is done, you will receive the certificate from AWS. Most modern web browsers will be able to identify and trust any communication they have with your server. Figure 7-5 shows an example of such a certificate being issued to a server.

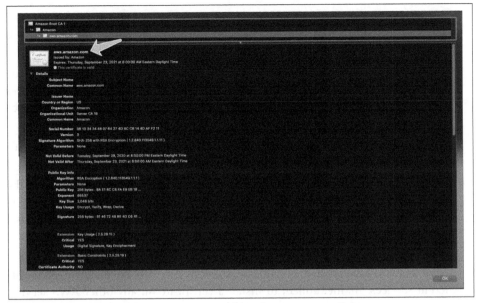

*Figure 7-5. Sample certificate that is signed by the AWS trusted CA.*

You might be wondering about two important questions:

- Once a certificate is issued with a public key on it, what process does AWS use to transmit the corresponding private keys to your server without any intruder receiving them? After all, any possible leak of private keys can seriously compromise the entire TLS chain.

- How do you convince the AWS trusted CA that you own the domain listed on the certificate? If everyone could get a certificate for any domain without much oversight into whether they really controlled the domain, it would be pointless.

I'll answer these questions in the following two sections.

### Inner workings of AWS ACM

An ACM certificate verifies that the public key in the certificate belongs to the domain listed in the certificate. Essentially, it is stating, *Trust that anything that can be decrypted by this public key belongs to the domain listed on the certificate.*

The private key is encrypted and stored securely by ACM and can be accessed by multiple services. Once this private key is in the hands of a service, it will be able to use TLS to authenticate itself. The security of TLS rests on the ability of the certificate authority to transmit protected private keys. In this section, I'll explain how this is achieved in practice and at scale:

1. The first time you request a certificate, ACM CA will perform any trust-related activities to ensure that you actually own the domain name the certificate is issued for. (See "Validating domain ownership" on page 235.)

2. ACM will then create a plaintext certificate on the CA and a public key–private key pair in memory. The public key becomes part of the certificate. ACM stores the certificate and its corresponding private key and uses AWS KMS to help protect it.

3. ACM will create a customer master key (CMK) in KMS to encrypt this certificate. This AWS managed CMK will have a key alias *aws/acm*.

4. ACM does not store the private key in plaintext form. Instead, it will use the CMK from Step 3 to encrypt the private key, storing only its encrypted ciphertext. This encrypted ciphertext can only be decrypted using KMS, which, as I pointed out in Chapter 3, has good access control mechanisms built into it. So it is safe to say the private key has been secured and never exposed.

Now that you have created a certificate, think of how this can be deployed to different services. As mentioned, to install a certificate on any other AWS service, you have to transmit the private key of the certificate so that the service can start identifying itself. ACM uses KMS grants to distribute the private key across AWS.

Figure 7-6 illustrates how AWS uses AWS KMS to create digital certificates at scale for your organization.

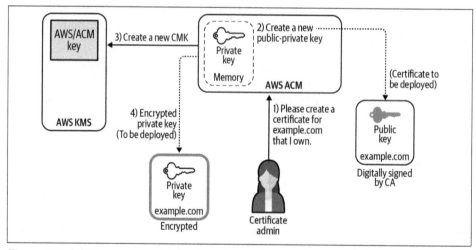

*Figure 7-6. ACM creates a public-private key and stores the encrypted certificate securely in order to be distributed to other supported services.*

Figure 7-7 illustrates the process of distributing a certificate securely to different services without ever exposing the unencrypted private key to any third party.

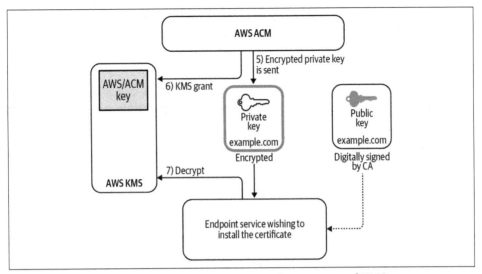

*Figure 7-7. Certificate setup using AWS ACM. With proper use of KMS, you can ensure that the unencrypted certificate as well as the unencrypted private key are never transmitted on the network, even during the setup phase.*

5. Recall the ciphertext private key that was encrypted back in Step 4. When you associate the certificate with a service that is integrated with AWS ACM, ACM sends the certificate and the encrypted private key to the service. The fact that this private key is encrypted makes it impossible for a malicious user to decode this key, and thus makes it impossible to falsely prove ownership of the domain.

6. ACM also creates a KMS grant that only allows the identity and access management (IAM) principal of the receiving service to decrypt this certificate.

7. Once it decrypts this certificate, the end service can then post this certificate in its memory to terminate TLS and identify itself anytime someone makes a request.

Every certificate owner should be careful to make sure that the private key backing the certificate is never exposed. If exposed, the certificate should be immediately revoked and a new certificate should be issued in its place.

For every new service that needs to get the certificate installed, ACM creates KMS grants that allow the new server to encrypt or decrypt using the private key, thus making this system extremely scalable in a microservice environment.

### Validating domain ownership

I have explained how a certificate is created for a particular domain. Additionally, I have discussed how you can distribute this certificate to multiple servers that host your microservices, thereby making it simple to manage secure communication in otherwise complex environments. This still leaves one important puzzle piece unanswered, though: how does ACM confirm that you own the domain that you specify on the certificate?

As mentioned earlier, browsers and clients around the world put their trust in the ability of this CA to check evidence of domain ownership quickly and accurately.

ACM provides two ways to prove domain ownership, as shown in Figure 7-8. You can select the validation method while issuing your certificate.

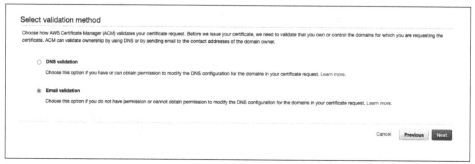

*Figure 7-8. AWS provides you with two ways of validating your domain ownership.*

**Email validation for domain ownership.**   When you choose "Email validation" to generate a certificate, AWS sends an email to the registered owner of each domain listed on the certificate. To validate control of the domain, the owner of the domain or an authorized representative must go to the Amazon certificate approval website and approve the request. Further instructions are provided in the body of the email, as seen in Figure 7-9.

*Figure 7-9. A sample AWS email for domain ownership verification.*

**DNS validation.** ACM uses CNAME records to validate that you own or control a domain. When you choose DNS validation, ACM provides you one or more CNAME records to insert into your DNS database. You are required to insert these records in your DNS hosted zone and AWS will verify the domain once it can see that you were indeed able to create these records.

If you own the domain through Amazon Route 53, it becomes even easier because ACM will automatically generate the CNAME record for you.

## ACM Private CA

As I mentioned in the previous section, the purpose of a public CA is to use a globally recognized and trusted certification authority to certify the fact that the domain you claim to own is yours using the verification methods mentioned before. This is important in public-facing services where the server does not know who the end consumer is. In using a CA that is widely trusted, the server becomes more likely to be recognized by more clients.

However, not all communication happens to be public facing or with unknown clients. This fact is especially relevant for microservice applications where the communication might take place mainly within the application. In such a situation, the only parties that need to trust the CA are internal, and so using a widely accepted public CA is overkill.

This is where private CA comes in handy. Private CA gives you a few great advantages:

- In a public CA, the CA certifies each domain for ownership as part of the process of issuing certificates. In contrast, a private CA eliminates this external check. Thus, internal communication continues between two internal services without having to go to any public authority, even for certificate validation, helping you maintain compliance.

- You are not required to provide any proof of domain ownership. This means you can use internal domains for referencing your microservices that do not have to be registered with a top-level domain authority.

- Services such as AWS App Mesh integrate seamlessly with ACM Private CA (ACM-PCA), which leads to a simpler setup.

Since the private CA is set up by an internal administrator, a client can trust the communication with the server based on certificates issued by this CA. The fact that both the provider and the consumer put a high degree of trust in this third-party certificate-issuing authority makes this communication secure.

ACM can set you up with a fully managed private CA that will issue certificates without domain ownership validation. This CA works closely with other AWS services without the need to communicate with any external CA.

The implicit assumption here is that the private CA should have high security and should never be breached. AWS ACM gives you a fully managed private CA where its security is handled under AWS Shared Responsibility Model (SRM), so that you do not have to worry. ACM-PCA uses the same security mechanism as public CAs to sign and distribute certificates on integrated services.

AWS ACM-PCA provides a lot of flexibility. Using a private CA, you can do all of the following:

- Use any subject name (server domain URL)
- Use any private-key algorithm supported by ACM-PCA
- Use any signing algorithm supported by ACM-PCA
- Specify any validity period of your choice

AWS Private CA can also be shared using AWS Resource Access Manager, as seen in Figure 7-10.

*Figure 7-10. Sharing a private CA in AWS Resource Access Manager.*

Since your private CA will be the key to any trust you have in communication across domains in your organization, keeping your private CA locked out of domain-specific accounts in a centralized location may help minimize the blast radius in case any of your domain accounts get hijacked.

In this setup, you can create a separate AWS account where all of your private CAs will live. Only the users with elevated trust privileges will be able to assume roles within this account to perform routine maintenance and modify the CA. This CA can then be shared with the rest of your domain accounts. This keeps a nice taxonomy of domains and avoids coupling your private CA with any of the domains within your organization, which maintains a totally autonomous entity with your organization.

 ACM-PCA can create a complete CA hierarchy, including a root CA and subordinate CAs, with no need for external CAs. The CA hierarchy provides strong security and granular control of certificates for the most-trusted root CA, while allowing bulk issuance and less-restrictive access for subordinate CAs in the chain. Microservices can use the subordinate CAs for most of their known communication patterns while services such as service discovery, logging, and other centrally managed services can make use of the root CA. This flexibility is beneficial if you must identify a subject by a specific name or if you cannot rotate certificates easily.

# Encryption Using TLS

The second important role that TLS plays in any given system is to provide end-to-end encryption of data that is in transit.

Contrary to popular belief, TLS in itself is not an encryption algorithm. TLS instead defines certain steps that both the client and the server need to take in order to mutually decide which cipher works best for communication between them.

In fact, one of the first steps of any TLS connection is a *negotiation* process where the client and the server mutually agree on which cipher works best for both of them.

This information exchange happens during the phase of communication known as *TLS Handshake*. TLS Handshake is also used to exchange encryption keys for end-to-end encryption. This makes TLS Handshake one of the most crucial, yet often overlooked, aspects of communication between any two processes.

## TLS Handshake

As mentioned, encryption using TLS is done using a symmetric key algorithm. This means that both the server and the client use the same encryption key as well as an encryption algorithm that they agree upon to encrypt the communication channel with.

Various AWS services support a vast variety of ciphers, and the strongest cipher is chosen based on a *waterfall* process of selection. A waterfall process is where the server creates a list of ciphers that it supports in the descending order of strength. The client agrees to use the strongest cipher that it can support within that list. Thus, the server and the client mutually decide on what they believe is the best common algorithm that is supported by both parties.

AWS regularly updates the list of supported ciphers in its documentation; using a strong and secure cipher is vital to the security of your application. It is also important to note that some of the early implementation of TLS had considerable issues when it came to safety and security. Historic attacks such as the POODLE or the Heartbleed seemed to affect many early implementations of TLS and Secret Socket Layer (SSL). Hence, there may be a requirement from a compliance point of view to use TLS V1.1 or higher (*https:// oreil.ly/S7BYP*).

When an algorithm is selected, the client and the server have to agree on an encryption key. They use a *key exchange mechanism* (such as the *Diffie–Hellman key exchange*), to exchange encryption keys that can then be used to encrypt all the data that needs to be sent over the channel.

### Perfect forward secrecy

A key weakness of any security system is the key becoming compromised. And based on what we have discussed so far, TLS should be no exception.

Consider a scenario where some malicious actor happens to be snooping on all of the encrypted traffic that flows between two secure services engaged in a secure communication channel that is storing every single exchanged message in its encrypted form. Until this malicious actor has the server key to decrypt these messages, all is good. But what happens if this key somehow ends up in the actor's hands? Will the actor be able to decrypt every single piece of historic communication that took place?

We can use perfect forward secrecy (PFS) in our TLS configuration on the server side to ensure that compromising the server key does not compromise the entire session data. In order to have PFS, you need to use a cipher that supports it, such as the elliptical curve Diffie–Hellman or any of the other popular ciphers that support PFS, to protect your application from such attacks.

AWS supports a wide range of ciphers that support PFS as outlined in this document (*https://oreil.ly/uyccW*).

## TLS Termination and Trade-offs with Microservices

As you may have noticed, TLS does involve a fair number of steps when it comes to establishing and maintaining communication. TLS Handshakes, version negotiation, cipher negotiation, key exchange, and others are in no way simple operations. Furthermore, the upkeep of certificates may be an added responsibility that is thrusted on all containers that may hold microservices within them.

ACM allows the creation of certificates that are tied to a URL, and with the certificate distribution mechanism, allows you to deploy ACM certificates to multiple servers across the AWS infrastructure. Therefore, it may be possible for an architect to be more strategic in deciding who performs these responsibilities.

In any system, the point where all of these TLS-related activities are handled is often called the *point of TLS termination*. So the natural question in a microservice environment is: what should be your point of TLS termination? Should it be individual pods? At the load balancer? Does it make sense to assume that a private microservice operating on its own subnet does not require TLS? These are all questions that your security plan should aim to answer.

One way of making TLS efficient is to terminate TLS at the edge system. This may work in cases where the private network that exists beyond the edge is completely private. This does compromise on some elements of security in favor of convenience. On the other hand, you could also terminate your TLS at a load balancer instead of the microservice pod.

Figure 7-11 shows a typical organization that decides to terminate TLS at the edge (public-facing endpoints) of the system. This means that internal backend services such as Service A, Service C, and Service D are not required to perform the TLS Handshakes when they communicate with one another, thus increasing the simplicity and efficiency of internal communication.

Any request from the end user is still secure since TLS is indeed enforced between the end user and the public endpoints (see 1 in Figure 7-11); intruders on the public internet are unable to intercept any such communication. However, such a setup assumes that all internal communication among services A, C, and D can be trusted. As mentioned in Chapter 5, this may not always be the case. A compromised insider such as (2) can still intercept the communication between endpoint C and Service D, thus compromising the security of this communication. Similarly, due to the lack of strong authentication that TLS would have otherwise provided, an impersonator could possibly masquerade as a legitimate microservice, as seen in (3).

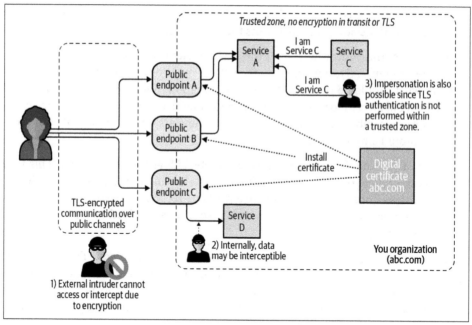

*Figure 7-11. Terminating TLS at the edge of the infrastructure relieves internal microservices from performing TLS-related computation, thus increasing efficiency. However, it also decreases the security posture of the organization since the application is still at a risk from internal threats.*

To sum up, what Figure 7-11 tells us is that TLS termination is a trade-off, and where it should be performed depends on the confidence you have in the trust zone of your application. Having your application's termination point as close as possible to your application will make it slightly more secure from insider attacks. However, it also means the TLS termination logic is more redundantly dispersed throughout your infrastructure since each service that you own will need its own TLS termination mechanism.

 A security architect should find out which part of the communication chain can be trusted enough to engage in unencrypted communication, and beyond which point every communication channel has to be encrypted. In my experience, TLS is often terminated at load balancers. If you use AWS load balancers, terminating TLS at the Elastic Load Balancing is a fairly common practice.

Given this complexity, a philosophical question to ask is: should the microservice (that was designed to handle a business use case) be expected to handle the heavy lifting related to TLS termination and end-to-end encryption?

In some applications, end-to-end encryption may be a compliance requirement; therefore, microservices have no choice but to terminate TLS on containers or at the application endpoints, instead of load balancers.

## TLS Offloading and Termination

In "TLS Termination and Trade-offs with Microservices" on page 240, I introduced the trade-off that security architects have to make in order to decide where TLS termination logic lives. I presented two alternatives, the first of which is terminating TLS at a load balancer or content delivery network (CDN), while the second is to allow applications or microservice containers to terminate TLS. In this section, I will assume you have decided to allow TLS termination to be performed at the load balancer. This process is also called *TLS offloading*. In order for an AWS service to support TLS termination, you need to use ACM and install the TLS certificate on top of the service that is responsible for TLS offloading. ACM allows you to renew your certificates automatically once they expire, so you won't have to remember to do it manually.

### AWS Application Load Balancer

An application load balancer (ALB) supports TLS termination. The load balancer requires X.509 certificates (SSL/TLS server certificates) that are signed by a CA (either private or public).

Since ALB always looks at requests at the application layer, it has to terminate all TLS connections in order to analyze application-level details. In other words, end-to-end encryption is not possible on services that use ALB. You can, however, install any of your ACM certificates or import any of your existing certificates to install on the ALB. This way, your application code is not affected by any TLS logic. However, if your regulatory compliance requirements require end-to-end encryption, you may have to re-encrypt data at the load balancer in order to send it back to the cluster nodes or the microservice that is the final recipient of this data. Figure 7-12 shows how you can add an HTTPS listener on an ALB using the AWS Management Console.

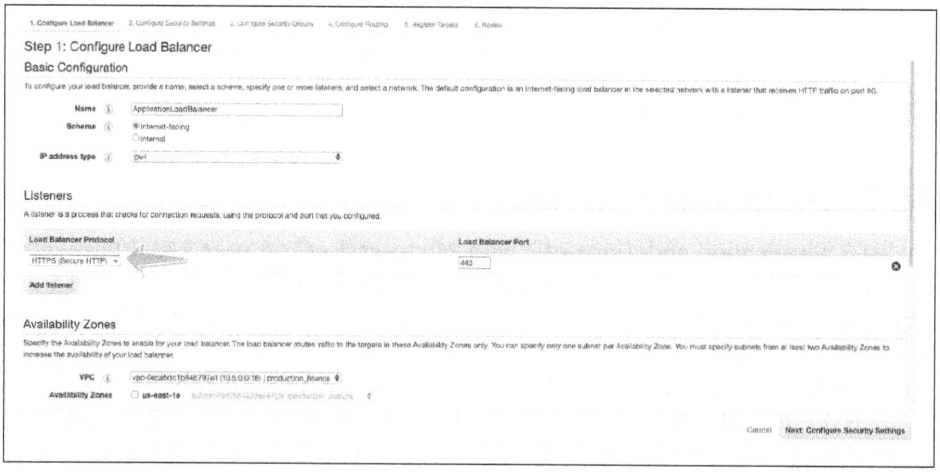

*Figure 7-12. Adding an HTTPS listener to an ALB.*

To install the certificate:

1. Navigate to the Load Balancer screen using the AWS Console and add a listener.

2. For the protocol port, choose HTTPS and keep the default port or enter a different port.

Figure 7-13 illustrates these steps.

*Figure 7-13. Adding an SSL certificate to an AWS ALB to offload TLS.*

## Network load balancers

A network load balancer (NLB) operates at the network layer of the OSI model and therefore, does not need to access application layer data. This means an NLB has the option of not terminating TLS and can allow end-to-end encryption if needed using TLS passthrough.

However, if you don't need end-to-end encryption, you can always terminate the TLS at the NLB by adding your ACM certificate to the NLB, as seen in Figure 7-14.

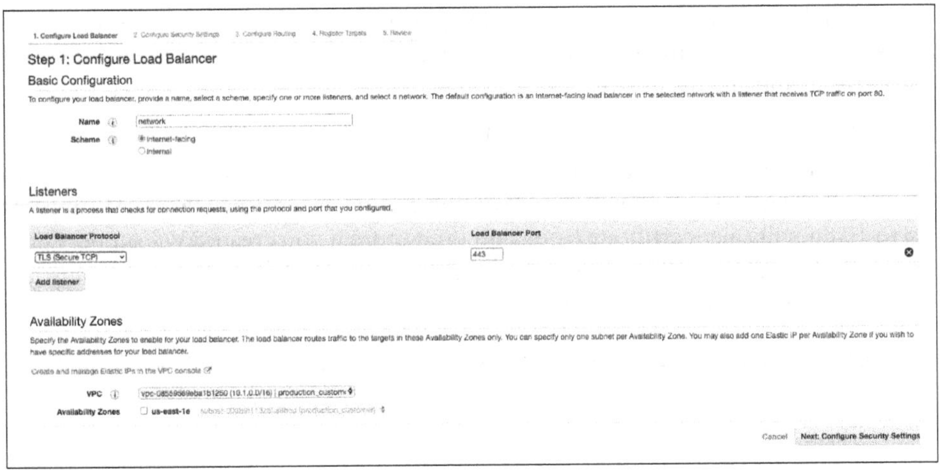

*Figure 7-14. Adding a TCP listener to port 443 for HTTPS connections on an NLB on AWS.*

Figure 7-15 shows how you can add an ACM certificate to your NLB.

*Figure 7-15. Adding an ACM certificate to the NLB to offload the TLS termination.*

### CloudFront TLS termination and caching

Just as microservices calling one another can use the load balancer to terminate TLS, CloudFront can also terminate end-to-end encryption for services. As you know from Chapter 6, CloudFront provides a caching layer for content on the various edge locations that AWS provides throughout the world.

However, caching provides a challenge when it comes to encryption, since the cache check requires your distribution to terminate TLS in order to view the contents of the request and check for their presence in the globally cached origin. Hence, similar to the ALBs, you are required to install your ACM public certificate on the CloudFront distribution and end TLS there.

Figure 7-16 describes how you can add the ACM certificate to a CloudFront distribution and enable it to terminate TLS connection. When using CloudFront, you need to specify all the domains you wish to use on the certificate. Fortunately, ACM supports up to 10 domains per certificate by default (and more if you create AWS support tickets). The CloudFront distribution also supports wildcard domains, increasing the number of domains it can support.

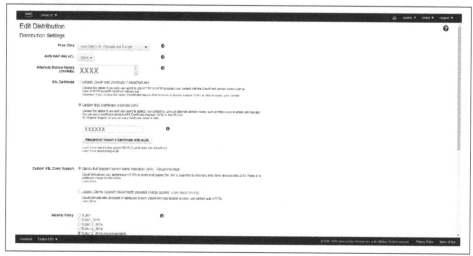

*Figure 7-16. Adding an ACM certificate, which includes the domain of your CloudFront distribution.*

## Server Name Indication

Since CloudFront uses fully managed, shared edge servers to serve content, no single terminal server is responsible for content distribution. Furthermore, AWS hosts multiple websites at each edge location, and multiple websites may share the same IP address. So it becomes difficult for CloudFront to serve the right certificate if a request is made to one single IP address. CloudFront handles this by using a technique called Server Name Indication (SNI), which makes it possible to use a single IP address for multiple SSL-supported sites. Amazon CloudFront delivers content from its edge locations using the same level of SSL security used in its dedicated IP service.

SNI is like sending mail addressed to a multi-unit building rather than a house. When mail is addressed to any specific unit, in addition to the street address, an apartment number is also needed.

However, this extension may not be supported by all legacy browsers and hence, if you want to add support for legacy browsers, you have the option of using dedicated IP addresses for an extra fee.

# Cost and Complexity Considerations with Encryption in Transit

Encryption in transit is an important security requirement for most compliance frameworks. HIPAA, Payment Card Industry Data Security Standard (PCI DSS), and many other standards explicitly require data to be encrypted while it is in flight, and Amazon Trust Services provides a globally recognized and accepted certificate authority to help users meet these compliance requirements. With AWS Private CA, organizations can add new services at scale and still expect end-to-end encryption for microservices.

It is not uncommon for the number of certificates in microservice environments to be quite high. Thus, internal services that need to expose APIs across domains are advised to carefully analyze their security benefits and the complexity involved. There is also a monetary charge associated with using encryption in transit.

Public ACM certificates themselves are free. So you can create as many certificates as you please for any of your public domains. Private ACM certificates generally incur a one-time fee. A few exceptions to this rule are private certificates installed on AWS services such as AWS Elastic Load Balancing, where the private key is never disclosed to the end user. Private certificates that do not have access to the private key are free on AWS.

ACM-PCA also has a monthly fee (*https://oreil.ly/Le3yc*) associated with it. At the time of writing, ACM-PCA costs $400 per month and is billed monthly, until it is deleted.

# Application of TLS in Microservices

Now that a solid foundation for TLS has been laid, let's look at how TLS can be used in the various communication patterns. As a reminder, microservices can talk to one another in these forms:

- Using asynchronous REST
- Using messaging queues such as AWS SQS or message brokers such as Apache Kafka

- Using wrappers on top of HTTP/2 such as gRPC (which is a thin application layer wrapper on top of HTTP/2)

- Using a service mesh such as Istio or the AWS-managed AWS App Mesh

I have already talked about how REST-based communication that happens using plain HTTP can benefit from TLS. In the next sections, I will move to the other options that are available.

## Security in Transit While Using Message Queues (AWS SQS)

Message brokers or queuing systems are commonly used for cross-domain communication in microservices. Queuing systems help in reducing *coupling* (cross-domain interdependence) between two domains by allowing the two microservices to scale independently of each other.

Consider the communication between two services (say, Service A and Service B). By using a queuing service instead of sending a message directly to the other service, the messages will pass through an intermediary. This queuing service acts as a buffer between two services. Service A will place any message that it wants to send to Service B on this queue. Service B will listen to messages on this queue and process them at its own pace.

Once processed, Service B will place the response back on a different queue that Service A will listen to. Figure 7-17 illustrates this example.

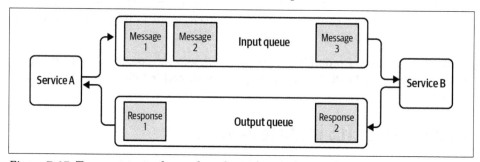

*Figure 7-17. Two queues can be used in place of a regular synchronous communication pattern to decouple two services from each other.*

This form of a decoupled, queue-based communication pattern has two advantages:

- If due to a sudden spike in throughput, Service A starts sending more messages per second than Service B can handle, the input queue can simply expand until Service B can either scale up capacity or wait until the throughput reduces.

- If Service B temporarily goes down for a few seconds, the input queue can still retain the messages for Service B to process after it comes back up again.

Communication through message queues occurs asynchronously, which means the endpoints that publish and consume messages interact with the queue, rather than with each other. Producers can add messages to the queue once they are ready, and consumers can handle messages only if they have enough capacity. No component in the system is ever stalled waiting for another. Most microservice architects are aware of these benefits, so queuing systems have become somewhat synonymous with microservice communication.

Since AWS SQS is the easiest to integrate with the rest of the microservice application, I will use it here as an example of a message queue. In SQS, AWS provides a simple queuing system while assuming the responsibility of the infrastructure, its resiliency, and scalability as part of the SRM. However, the principles apply to any other queuing application.

Going back to Figure 7-17, message queues aim to replace the direct, synchronous, encrypted connection between Service A and Service B. From a security perspective, this means communication between Service A and Service B should continue to be encrypted after the use of a message queue. In order to ensure that encryption is maintained while a message is in transit, I will break its journey into two parts:

- After it has been placed on a message queue
- While it's in flight between the service producer and the queue

Every message that is placed on the SQS queue can be encrypted at rest using AWS KMS. So, in order to obtain a true replacement for TLS-based synchronous encryption, the first step is to ensure that all of the AWS SQS queues involved in this communication encrypt their content at rest.

The second time to enforce encryption is when clients (Service A and Service B) connect with SQS. Even though the queue itself is encrypted, a man-in-the-middle attack could intercept messages before or after they have been taken out of the queue.

The solution to this problem is to enforce a TLS connection any time a client connects to an SQS queue. This is made possible with the use of a resource-based IAM policy, as discussed in Chapter 2. The constraint `aws:SecureTransport` ensures that any client that connects to an SQS queue does so using TLS:

```
{
  "Version": "2012-10-17",
  "Id": "arn:aws:sqs:region:aws-account-id:queue-name/DenyNonTLS",
  "Statement": [
    {
      "Effect": "Deny",
```

```
        "Principal": "*",
        "Action": "*",
        "Resource": "arn:aws:sqs:region:aws-account-id:queue-name",
        "Condition": {
          "Bool": {
            "aws:SecureTransport":"false"
          }
        }
      }
    ]
  }
```

This policy will deny access to the queue to anyone who does not connect using TLS.

## gRPC and Application Load Balancer

gRPC (*https://grpc.io*) is a popular protocol that is increasingly used by microservices to communicate with one another. gRPC is an open source remote procedure call (RPC). For transport, it uses HTTP/2 and protocol buffers as interface descriptors. A number of features are available, such as authentication, bidirectional streaming and flow control, bindings for blocking and nonblocking traffic, cancellation, and timeouts.

gRPC has the benefit of being built on trusted, tested infrastructure. HTTP/2 is a relatively new protocol, but HTTP has existed for quite some time as a transport protocol, and it is for this reason that many of its security considerations have been examined by experts throughout the world. gRPC has been widely embraced by microservices for many of its benefits, including scalability and customizability, among others. I will, however, focus on how AWS can help when it comes to securing an in-transit connection using gRPC.

If your microservices want to use gRPC to communicate with one another, AWS ALB allows you to configure gRPC as a target. gRPC can be enabled on any targets in an ALB, as highlighted in Figure 7-18.

Figure 7-18 area at top:

**Step 4: Configure Routing**
Target group

| | |
|---|---|
| Target group | New target group |
| Name | gRPC |
| Target type | ● Instance<br>○ IP<br>○ Lambda function |
| Protocol | HTTP |
| Port | 80 |
| Protocol version | ○ HTTP1<br>Send requests to targets using HTTP/1.1. Supported when the request protocol is HTTP/1.1 or HTTP/2.<br>○ HTTP2<br>Send requests to targets using HTTP/2. Supported when the request protocol is HTTP/2 or gRPC, but gRPC-specific features are not available.<br>◉ gRPC<br>Send requests to targets using gRPC. Supported when the request protocol is gRPC. |

Health checks

| | |
|---|---|
| Protocol | HTTP |
| Path | /AWS.ALB/healthcheck |

▶ Advanced health check settings

Cancel   Previous   Next: Register Targets

*Figure 7-18. Just like HTTP targets, gRPC can be used as the target protocol for incoming requests.*

As mentioned, gRPC still uses HTTP/2 as its transport, so encryption on gRPC can still be achieved using TLS as for most of the other HTTP connections. The TLS certificate is installed on the ALB when the load balancer is chosen. Doing so will ensure encrypted gRPC communication between the pods and the ALB.

TLS for gRPC can also be implemented using a service mesh, discussed later in the chapter.

## Mutual TLS

Chapter 6 introduced Mutual TLS (mTLS). Let's now revisit the concept of mTLS and I'll explain how it makes communication more secure. The TLS protocol uses X.509 certificates to prove the identity of the server, but the application layer is responsible for verifying the identity of the client to the server. mTLS attempts to make TLS more secure by adding client validation as part of the TLS process.

> To paraphrase the Financial Services Technology Consortium (*https://oreil.ly/yjUsC*): Better institution-to-customer authentication would prevent attackers from successfully impersonating financial institutions to steal customers' account credentials; and better customer-to-institution authentication would prevent attackers from successfully impersonating customers to financial institutions in order to perpetrate fraud.

As discussed in "TLS Handshake" on page 239, a client trusts a CA while the server presents a certificate that is signed by the CA. Upon successful establishment of the connection, both parties can communicate in an encrypted format. mTLS requires that both the client and server establish their identities as part of the TLS Handshake. This additional step ensures that the identities of both parties involved in a communication process are established and confirmed. Certificate verification is an integral part of the TLS Handshake. With the requirement for client validation, mTLS essentially mandates that clients are required to maintain a signed certificate that trusted CAs vouch for, thus making client verification possible.

This would mean installing a signed certificate on each of the microservice clients that wants to make any outgoing request, unlike a load balancer that could be used to terminate TLS on the servers. An operation of this magnitude requires significant investment in infrastructure and security in order to implement such a setup.

As a result of this added complexity and the amount of work required to implement mTLS, it is rarely seen in setups that use traditional servers or container systems. However, mTLS is significantly easier to implement when two AWS-managed services talk to each other. This is why API Gateway and AWS Lambda can easily communicate with each other using mTLS.

The downside of mTLS is that it is complicated. However, the next sections introduce an AWS service called AWS App Mesh, which can make implementing mTLS more straightforward and thus practical.

# A (Very Brief) Introduction to Service Meshes: A Security Perspective

The most complex part of a microservice architecture is often communication between services, rather than the actual services themselves. Many of the mechanisms (such as TLS termination, mTLS, etc.) used to secure the communication channels add complexity to the application. This added complexity may lead to more work on the application side. This is especially true if your services run on pod-based environments such as Amazon Elastic Kubernetes Service (EKS), AWS Elastic Container Service (ECS), or plain AWS Elastic Cloud Compute (EC2).

Although my focus is on TLS and the security of cross-pod communication, there are other cross-pod communication concerns. Communication complexities like *observability*, *logging*, *distributed tracing*, and *traffic monitoring* need to be addressed by microservices.

It goes without saying that microservices, when introduced for applications that are not at scale, may end up adding complexity to the working environment of every application. Although I have always been an optimist on microservices, they do have downsides. Many of these shortcomings are related to the increased complexity and, as a result, additional work required on the infrastructure level to support the microservice approach. This additional work is repetitive and has little to do with business logic. Service meshes are an additional layer that can be implemented in a microservice architecture entirely dedicated to such repetitive tasks. By encapsulating infrastructure logic into a service mesh, services can continue to concentrate on business logic.

## Proxies and Sidecars

Before service meshes were introduced, the logic related to TLS termination, observability, and trace logging was embedded inside application code, resulting in it being bloated. What made matters worse was that since this logic crossed pods, this application had to be kept in sync with other pods. One solution was to introduce a proxy application that would run alongside existing containers. Any aspect related to communication with other pods could be outsourced to this proxy service that ran alongside the original pod. This would include network management, request logging, and most importantly from our point of view, TLS.

These proxies would intercept every request that takes place between multiple applications. In order to reduce latency, these proxies run right next to the original service as *sidecar (https://oreil.ly/DNaev)* containers. I will discuss a proxy application called *Envoy* to implement a service mesh. Envoy (*https://www.envoyproxy.io*) is an open source proxy implementation designed specifically for cloud applications, and it works well with AWS services.

Figure 7-19 shows how a traditional communication between Service A and Service B can be transformed into a proxy-based communication by introducing a sidecar proxy to outsource network-related activities.

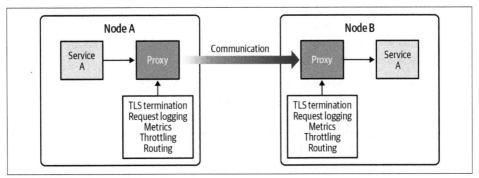

*Figure 7-19. Proxy containers run as "sidecar" processes alongside the original pod and handle the repetitive logic related to the communication. Services, on the other hand, can communicate through these proxies.*

You can imagine a new network where, instead of services connecting to one another, each service is connected to a proxy to form what is called a *virtual service* that represents the original service. All of the proxies are then connected to one another, creating a *mesh*. This is exactly what a service mesh aims to create. When a mesh of proxies communicates with one another, the plane of microservices (known as the *data plane*) is transformed into a virtual service plane. A mesh is illustrated in Figure 7-20.

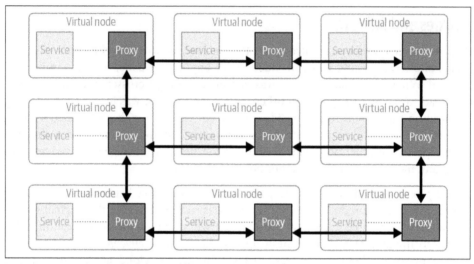

*Figure 7-20. Instead of connecting services with one another, services are connected to proxies and proxies form a network of their own (data plane of the application).*

Services in this picture can be as lean as possible, focusing solely on business logic, while the proxies can create a mesh of TLS endpoints that can now handle end-to-end encryption for all processes. This still leaves one issue unsolved. There needs to be a centralized service responsible for keeping all of these services in sync with one another. This way, any change of communication protocol between endpoints can be propagated seamlessly to all of the working proxies.

Service meshes are neither new nor an invention of AWS. They borrow from service-oriented architecture and have been around in some form for at least a decade. Despite this, their adoption has been limited due to the fact that managing a service mesh within an already complex microservice architecture can be a daunting task. You can see that Figure 7-20 shows nine proxies and all of these have to be kept in sync with one another for communication to be effective.

Proxies require a lot of maintenance, so how do they get synchronized? As an example, if you outsource the management of TLS to these proxies, you need some mechanism of keeping the TLS certificates up to date and renewed. If you had to do this individually on each proxy, the overhead would have been as bad as it would be without a service mesh.

This is where a centralized control plane comes into the picture. A *control plane* is a mechanism that controls all the proxies by sending them instructions from a centralized location.

AWS provides a fully managed service that manages the control plane for this mesh of envoy proxies in the form of *AWS App Mesh*. AWS App Mesh (*https://oreil.ly/ZdTwm*) lets you communicate across multiple applications, infrastructures, and cloud services using application-level networking. App Mesh gives end-to-end visibility and high availability for your applications. Figure 7-21 illustrates how a managed proxy controller can help keep proxies in sync.

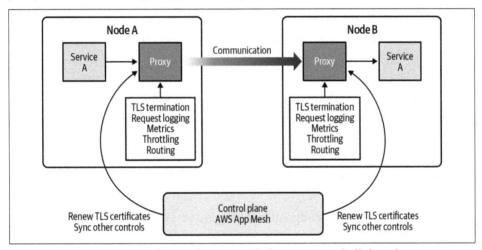

*Figure 7-21. AWS App Mesh provides a control plane to control all the sidecar proxies.*

AWS App Mesh provides diverse integration options for microservice containers of every size and complexity, as it connects only at the application level. The focus here is on the use of AWS App Mesh with Kubernetes, but this is not the only application that works with AWS App Mesh. It can be used with microservice containers managed by Amazon ECS, Amazon EKS, AWS Fargate, Kubernetes running on AWS, and services running on Amazon EC2.

## App Mesh Components and Terminology

As mentioned, App Mesh is made up of individual components:

*Mesh*

This is the representation of your entire microservice network on AWS App Mesh.

*Virtual service*

A virtual service is an abstraction for a real service microservice.

*Virtual gateway*

A virtual gateway works like a network gateway, allowing remote resources to communicate with resources inside your mesh. A virtual gateway has its own routes that identify individual virtual services.

*Virtual node*

A virtual node identifies specific task groups, such as Kubernetes deployments. Any inbound traffic that your virtual node expects is specified as a listener. Any virtual service that a virtual node sends outbound traffic to is specified as a backend.

*Mesh endpoint*

A virtual gateway and a virtual node together can sometimes be referred to as a mesh endpoint.

*Virtual router*

A virtual router provides a virtual service with the ability to route services to particular nodes. You can perform advanced HTTP, HTTP/2, and gRPC routing.

*Listener*

A listener for any mesh endpoint is the ingress part of the endpoint that listens to incoming requests.

*Backend*

A backend for any mesh endpoint is the egress part that sends outgoing requests to other components within the infrastructure.

Say you have a mesh of microservices for displaying the account information of a customer, and you get a request to find the balance of the following user:

```
http://balanceservice.local/getBalance/{id}
```

The flow is as follows:

1. The virtual gateway is the first service that gets the request since it is on the edges of the mesh and is the place where the incoming TLS is terminated.

2. The virtual gateway route identifies that this request belongs to the balance service based on the routes that it has, and it forwards it to the right virtual service.

3. The virtual service forwards it to the virtual router.

4. The virtual router looks at its existing targets and decides which node should process this request.

5. The virtual nodes then work with their containers to come up with a response.

Figure 7-22 illustrates this flow.

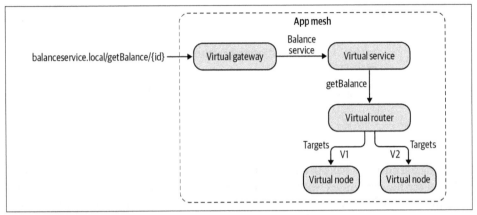

*Figure 7-22. How a request flows through AWS App Mesh.*

## TLS and App Mesh

Now let's discuss some of App Mesh's security aspects. As described in the introduction, the idea is to outsource the handling of TLS validation and termination to the Envoy proxy so it can perform the Handshakes, TLS validation, and end-to-end encryption of communication channels at mesh endpoints.

The first step toward TLS validation is the certificate check that requires a trusted CA. AWS App Mesh works seamlessly with AWS ACM-PCA. Using ACM-PCA simplifies the process of certificate installation and renewal.

> AWS App Mesh provides you with three options: AWS ACM-PCA, Envoy Secret Discovery Service (SDS), and a local hosted certificate for TLS validation. Since ACM-PCA integrates easily with AWS and simplifies the renewal process for certificates using auto-renewal, it is the tool that I recommend.

TLS validation through certificate checks can be enforced at the virtual gateway as well as at each virtual node. In App Mesh, TLS encrypts communication between the Envoy proxies (which are represented in App Mesh by mesh endpoints, such as virtual nodes and virtual gateways). AWS App Mesh ensures that each running Envoy proxy has the latest renewed certificate within 35 minutes of renewal, thus taking away the added complexity of renewing Envoy certificates. In order to use Envoy proxies, the `StreamAggregatedResources` action must be allowed for the mesh end-point that runs the Envoy proxy.

This can be added by applying the following policy:

```
{
    "Version": "2012-10-17",
    "Statement": [
        {
            "Effect": "Allow",
            "Action": "appmesh:StreamAggregatedResources",
            "Resource": [
              "arn:aws:appmesh:us-east-1:234562343322:mesh/
                <appName>/virtualNode/<>"
            ]
        }
    ]
}
```

Once the permissions have been set, you can specify the CA that App Mesh can use to validate certificates while creating a virtual gateway or a virtual node. You can enable TLS validation for any outgoing requests to the backends as well as perform TLS termination for any incoming requests. Figures 7-23 and 7-24 show how you can enable TLS validation for a virtual gateway.

*Figure 7-23. ACM-PCA can be used for enforcing and assisting with TLS termination for each Envoy proxy.*

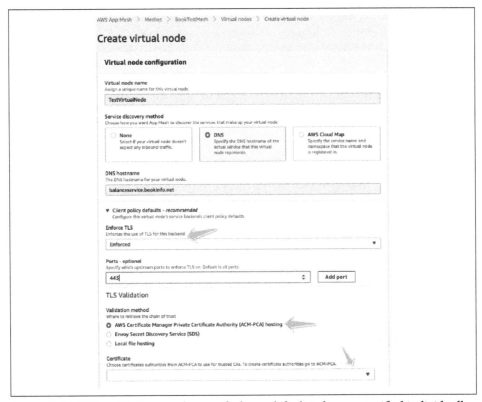

*Figure 7-24. TLS validation can be specified as a default policy or specified individually for each backend client.*

From a security perspective, it is a good idea to enable "strict mode," as seen in Figure 7-25.

*Figure 7-25. Enabling TLS termination in strict mode will ensure that any external service calling the listener will be required to use TLS for communicating with services that are backed by this gateway.*

## mTLS Revisited

Let's now revisit a security construct that I introduced briefly and disregarded: mTLS. If you recall, the reason why mTLS proved to be impractical was mainly due to the added complexity of managing TLS certificates for all the clients that communicate with one another. But AWS App Mesh, as described, helps install certificates on all of the Envoy proxies. It also helps keep these certificates up to date. So the added effort of maintaining certificates no longer exists on services that use AWS App Mesh. As a result, it is now no longer impractical or unfeasible to use mTLS. In fact, mTLS is supported fully by AWS App Mesh and at times recommended for applications that need client validation for additional security purposes.

mTLS can be enabled for virtual gateways by enabling the "Require client certificate" option for TLS validation on mesh endpoints.

### Trust inside a mesh

TLS can be enabled for trust inside a mesh by configuring server-side TLS certificates on the listeners and client-side TLS certificates on backends of virtual nodes.

## Trust outside a mesh

TLS can be enabled for communication outside a mesh by enabling specified server-side TLS certificates on the listeners and client-side certificates on the external services that end up connecting to a virtual gateway. The same CA should be used to derive the certificate by both the client and server for mTLS to work.

 App Mesh does not store certificates or private keys in any persistent storage. Instead, Envoy stores them in memory.

You can use Envoy's SDS or host the certificate locally to enable the chain of trust and configure mTLS, as seen in Figure 7-26.

*Figure 7-26. mTLS can be enabled for client validation either by using Envoy SDS or by hosting the certificate chain of trust locally.*

 Although App Mesh enables mTLS authentication and encryption between Envoy proxies and services, communications between your applications and Envoy proxies remain unencrypted.

## AWS App Mesh: Wrap-Up

Unlike other microservice communication patterns, in my opinion service meshes fundamentally change the way apps interact with one another. Although it is true that once implemented, a service mesh can reduce the complexity of commonly used security infrastructure, the initial implementation is a fairly involved task in itself. A service mesh requires buy-in from every team that decides to use it.

Though I have focused on AWS App Mesh, it is not the only service mesh solution available for microservice users. Istio, Consul, and Linkerd are just some of the many popular service mesh solutions available in the market today, and each has great features to offer. However, AWS App Mesh does simplify the implementation of a service mesh by integrating easily with the rest of the AWS infrastructure.

Integrating a service mesh into a microservice architecture is not a simple task. It is more common for greenfield projects to use a service mesh than for projects that have an established microservice structure. Of course, it would be impossible to cover everything related to service meshes in a short section. If you believe service mesh provides value, AWS has great documentation (*https://oreil.ly/XRCli*) for AWS App Mesh.

From a cost perspective, there is no additional charge for using AWS App Mesh. You pay only for the AWS resources consumed by the Envoy proxy that is deployed alongside your containers.

# Serverless Microservices and Encryption in Transit

This section talks about how TLS can be enabled and enforced when using serverless microservice technologies—specifically, AWS Lambda.

## AWS API Gateway and AWS Lambda

As mentioned, API Gateway mainly works at the edge of your network to provide you with the ability to accept incoming requests. Clients need to support TLS 1.0 and ciphers with PFS, like ephemeral Diffie–Hellman (DHE) and Elliptic-Curve–Diffie-Hellman Ephemeral (ECDHE).

Your API Gateway custom domain can enforce a minimum TLS protocol version for greater security.

If you use API Gateway to call any internal service, you have two choices. If you call the Lambdas or any other serverless service, you can use the private AWS network to pass all your data, thus ensuring proper security in transit.

HTTP APIs now give developers access to Amazon resources secured in an Amazon Virtual Private Cloud (VPC). When using technologies like containers via ECS or

EKS, the underlying Amazon EC2 clusters must live in a VPC. Although it is possible to make these services available through Elastic Load Balancing, developers can also take advantage of HTTP APIs to front their applications as shown in Figure 7-27.

*Figure 7-27. Creating an API Gateway for your serverless services.*

If you want to integrate privately, you need to have a VPC link. By using this technology, multiple HTTP APIs can share a single VPC link. HTTP APIs on the API Gateway can connect with an ALB or an NLB or with AWS Cloud Map, as seen in Figure 7-28.

*Figure 7-28. Using API Gateway to call private microservices.*

Alternatively, in places where you cannot enable VPC link to communicate with backend services, you can force certificate checks for backend services by generating a client certificate on the API Gateway, as shown in Figure 7-29.

*Figure 7-29. Creating a secure connection between your API Gateway and backend services.*

## Caching, API Gateway, and Encryption in Transit

AWS API Gateway enables you to cache your endpoints' responses, which makes it faster and reduces the number of calls your endpoints get. AWS allows you to encrypt all of the cached storage on AWS API Gateway, thus protecting your data from unauthorized access.

Another common attack on network systems is a cache invalidation attack where an attacker may try to maliciously invalidate your cache. You can either allow all clients to invalidate the cache or use the IAM policy to decide who gets to invalidate your cache by attaching this policy to authorized clients:

```
"Action": [
    "execute-api:InvalidateCache"
],
```

Encryption can be enabled for API Gateway cache through the AWS Management Console, as seen in Figure 7-30.

*Figure 7-30. Enabling a cache and cache invalidation policy in API Gateway.*

# Field-Level Encryption

Given the single-responsibility principle, there are times when only certain secure microservices are permitted to read certain sensitive data. For example, if the data that your application needs includes a user password or medical records, only servers that operate inside a very secure perimeter may be allowed to read this information in plaintext.

AWS allows the encryption of sensitive data fields at the edge locations. This way, data is encrypted as close to the end user as possible and sent only in an encrypted format over the wire. Until this data reaches the right service that has the secure authorized access to this data, the plaintext of this sensitive information is kept hidden from the rest of the microservices. Figure 7-31 shows a typical microservice setup where a request passes hands between various services before reaching its intended destination (service d).

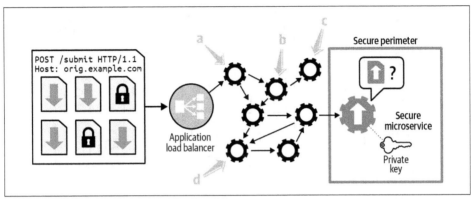

*Figure 7-31. Field-level resolution overview.*

As an example, even if the data is sent through a variety of microservices (a, b, c, d), the services are not able to decipher this data until it hits the secure microservice.

Field-level encryption makes use of an asymmetric key encryption by using the private key that only the secure microservice inside the perimeter has access to. Ensuring that sensitive data is never passed unencrypted through the rest of the network also means that our external and edge-level microservices do not have to face strict security controls:

- The microservice that is ultimately able to decrypt this sensitive data shares its public key with the CloudFront distribution, which distributes it to the edge locations.

- Sensitive data is encrypted using this public key.

- This data can only be read by decrypting it with the private key.

- Since the private key is secret and only known to the secure microservice, no other service is able to decrypt this data.

- While services can forward encrypted data and work on functions, such as validation of the request or cleaning of it or on any other parameters present in this request, they do not ever get to read this sensitive data.

This process is illustrated in Figure 7-32.

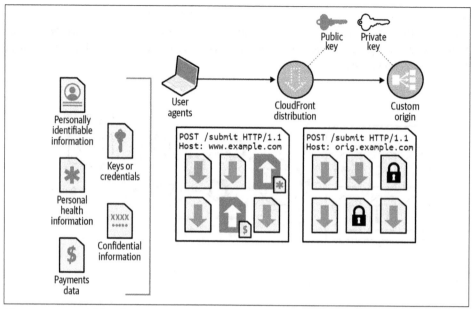

*Figure 7-32. Field-level encryption in practice.*

Follow these steps to use field-level encryption:

1. Go to the CloudFront management page in the AWS Management Console.
2. Choose "Add your public key" to the distribution.
3. Create a profile that tells CloudFront which fields to encrypt.
4. To use field-level encryption, link a configuration to a cache behavior for a distribution by adding the configuration ID as a value for your distribution.

Here are the advantages of field-level encryption:

- Since everything happens at the edge, it reduces the blast radius for sensitive data. Also, since the encryption is handled as part of the AWS SRM, it reduces operational overhead.
- Other microservices do not have to comply with strict sensitive data protection protocols since they never have to deal with unencrypted sensitive data.
- It is easier to meet various regulatory standards such as PCI-DSS since unencrypted data is never sent over the wire, not even on a private AWS network.

# Summary

This chapter considered an often-overlooked aspect of any application: cross-service communication, especially the security of information while it is in transit. In a microservice environment, communication among services is relatively common. This communication may take place over mediums that are not necessarily secure, and as a result, your application security can be undermined.

In general, you want to separate infrastructure concerns and security issues from application logic. This means that your application microservices focus more on business logic while the infrastructure takes care of the security needed to communicate with other microservices. This is the only way you can ensure and enforce the single-responsibility principle in microservices. Having said that, simplicity should never be an excuse for a compromise on security.

I started the chapter by looking at ways in which you can simplify the setup of your microservices without losing the security associated with traditional systems. You can achieve this by having a DNS architecture that helps in canonical naming and referencing of services by their names instead of their hosts. This helps decouple microservices from their deployments, thus making applications infrastructure (and stage) agnostic. I discussed how to ensure that security extends not just at the data stored in various systems, but also as it moves between two services. TLS is the crux of this encryption in transit, and we looked into the details of how AWS implements TLS at various stages of your application. Finally, I ended the chapter by discussing how TLS offloading helps you maintain leaner applications.

# CHAPTER 8

# Security Design for Organizational Complexity

Until now, the focus of this book has been on the architecture of the organization without regard for how teams are structured. This chapter talks about how security architects can construct security measures that are compatible with the organizational structure of a microservice-based organization and how they can focus on the human aspect of security design.

It's our job as security professionals to make sure that every employee within our organization has a smooth experience with the security mechanisms in place. A company's security team should empower employees by equipping them with the right protection that keeps them safe from threats both external and internal, while ensuring that individuals don't need to deal with systems in which they are not trained. At the same time, employees should be able to carry on with their work without the fear of running into a state where employees experience friction while performing their day-to-day job, also known as "security hell."

It is often said that *the road to "security hell" is paved with good intentions.* Many individuals with good intentions believe their actions are beneficial for the organization at large. As a result, a blunt increase in security practices may negatively impact developers and result in less efficiency. Many organizations go overboard with security measures that make it harder for legitimate employees to do their work. Often, there is a trade-off between security and autonomy. In this chapter, I aim to provide employees and teams with as much autonomy and flexibility as possible without compromising on security.

In large organizations, the teams closest to the action are best equipped to grasp the security parameters and identify any potential threats. Hence, instead of concentrating security policy and control in a centralized security team, it will be important to delegate as much control as possible to the individual teams. The delegation will include checks and balances that need to be put in place to ensure that rogue teams or disgruntled employees do not turn into malicious actors who pose a threat.

This chapter will first talk about the different types of organizational structures (org structures) that exist across companies. I will then talk about the different roles that employees play in these organizations and how these roles can benefit from various AWS tools. The general idea will be to grant teams as much autonomy as possible so they can perform their job without overhead, enabling them to innovate for the company. At the same time, there will be security controls to ensure that autonomous teams, disgruntled employees, or compromised actors are not allowed to breach the security of the application.

# Organizational Structure and Microservices

When organizations are small, operations may rely on informal procedures to add security controls while adding value. Teams working on different subdomains may work closely with one another in a synergistic way to create software. A team that needs to use shared resources approaches their software administrator, who grants them elevated permissions. There is trust, a shared understanding, and mutual respect among teams when it comes to using shared resources—formal guidelines seem unnecessary. When there is a security incident, you can pull together a team of developers, administrators, and stakeholders who are all committed to mitigating the incident since they all share a common goal of adding value to the process. However, such a tribal approach toward software development does not scale well.

As soon as an organization scales, clearly defined processes need to be put in place to guide development and communication around subdomains in microservice architectures. These processes need to govern resource sharing and permissions and help make teams autonomous while still imposing checks and balances. They need to account for processes during regular development as well as incident-response processes. In this section, I will talk about the various organizational structures that exist within companies today, and then briefly introduce you to tools that can help you design a permissions structure that uses cloud resources to gain the controlled autonomy you desire.

## Conway's Law

In 1967, when computer science was still in its infancy, a software programmer, Melvin Conway, came up with an amusing yet interesting adage that became known as Conway's law: *Any company that designs a system will produce a design whose structure is a copy of the company's organizational structure.*

This statement highlights the tendency for companies to build software that reflects their own org structures, which results in software that is more complex than necessary. For example, as Eric S. Raymond once said, "If you have four groups working on a compiler, you'll get a 4-pass compiler." Conway's law has sparked many debates about the efficacy and the rationale behind this observation.

A research paper (*https://oreil.ly/L8aB2*) published in *Harvard Business Review* in 2008 supports the notion that the product lines of most organizations mirror their departmental structure, calling it the "mirroring hypothesis." And I vouch for the same from my own professional experience. I have seen most organizations begin product development by identifying the development team, thus assuming that there is a one-to-one mapping between the product and the development team.

One of the biggest criticisms of such organizations that embody Conway's law is the lack of alignment between application design and consumer needs. Domain-driven design (DDD) attempts to bridge this gap by developing systems whose designs are based on functional and consumer domains instead of the organizational team structure.

## Single Team Oriented Service Architecture

In his book *Architecting for Scale* (O'Reilly) (*https://oreil.ly/MaaZw*), Lee Atchison introduces a concept called *Single Team Oriented Service Architecture (STOSA)*. In a STOSA-based application, teams have clear ownership of the services and domains they are responsible for. Conversely, there are no overlapping claims of ownership for any services (and more broadly, domains) that exist within a STOSA application, thus providing a good 1:1 mapping between services and teams in an organization. STOSA-based architectures help businesses develop software that aligns well with their org structures.

Now, going back to a domain-driven organization, the application is generally divided into bounded contexts. Organizations that follow the STOSA architecture can assign clear ownership to various bounded contexts. Together with Conway's law, one can imagine that the org structure reflects the application's contextual boundaries. In my experience, such alignment is common in most high-performing companies.

Figure 8-1 shows a typical engineering organization that is trying to implement a microservice application. STOSA-based organizations typically split and align their teams around various business functions.

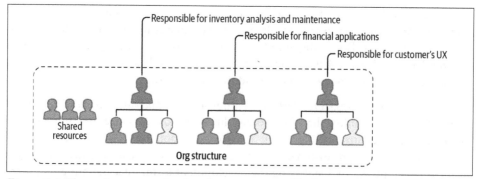

*Figure 8-1. Teams in an organization that are responsible for a particular business function of the application*

## Role-Based Access Control

Complex organizations need identity management solutions that distribute control and privileges without creating complexity. Organizations can choose from a number of strategies, such as role-based access control (RBAC), attribute-based access control (ABAC), and mandatory access control (MAC), which I introduced in Chapter 2.

In my opinion, RBAC provides an excellent framework for use with microservices, mainly due to its simplicity, small learning curve, and the presence of extensive tooling that is available in the AWS Identity and Access Management (IAM) services.

As discussed in Chapter 2, the process of using RBAC involves the creation of *roles* within an organization for each task that is performed by each identity—such as a user, application, or group—within that organization. Access to resources and services is then controlled and restricted to these roles based on the need and context in which this access is desired. Individuals and services are then permitted to *assume* these roles based on the tasks that they would like to perform. Thus, every activity that is performed by any individual (or service) within an organization involves first assuming a particular role and then using that role to perform the desired activity. This simplifies the access control process since security professionals simply have to apply the principle of least privilege (PoLP) separately to:

- The permissions that each role has
- The identities that are allowed to assume each role

In this chapter, I will make use of RBAC quite extensively to simplify the process of access control in large and complex organizations.

## Privilege Elevation

Throughout the book, I have stressed the importance of the PoLP. The most powerful defense against security attacks is to have fine-grained controls around access and to have a strict application of PoLP.

However, in my experience as a software developer, I have always seen this principle being broken with one common excuse: *What if there is an emergency and we need to quickly fix the system? Not granting developers the ability to move fast and fix production issues may result in significant losses for the company! Better to give them more access than required—just in case.*

This is a very valid concern that gets in the way of good access management and the application of least privilege in most organizations. It's not unreasonable for administrators and managers to extend more privileges to developers than is necessary simply out of a fear of being unable to contain a once-in-a-lifetime issue that may require access that's not granted at the time. In this section, I will discuss two models managers can use to provide controlled permission elevation to developers without compromising the PoLP.

These models are:

*AWS Systems Manager (AWS SSM) Run Command*
A model used for situations where the potential threats are known and hence the remedial action requires predefined scripts

*Just-in-time privilege elevation using Break-the-Glass (BTG)*
A model used for situations where the threat is unknown and hence the remedial action cannot be scripted in advance

> In my experience, if your developers can trust the emergency privileges escalation procedures, they will be more likely to accept and adhere to the PoLP.

### AWS Systems Manager run command

Before I talk about how the AWS SSM run command enables you to achieve privilege elevation, I will go into a high-level overview of what this model tries to achieve. This model is used for situations where incidents have a clearly defined runbook of actions (a set of predefined steps that need to be performed to mitigate incidents). This assumes your development/operations team (DevOps team) maintains such a runbook.

In this model, developers are provided with tooling (in the form of executable scripts) that elevates their access but restricts it to only the activities they can perform using these scripts.

I will simplify this with the help of an example. Assume that your production environment runs microservices that are prone to deadlocks. In such situations, your DevOps runbook dictates that the simple fix is to restart your production servers. However, in most operating systems, restarting a server requires you to have superuser access, which requires elevated access privileges, thus restricting ordinary developers from mitigating the incident.

In this model, to enable your developers to quickly mitigate such an incident, they are provided access to a script that allows them to reboot the servers, instead of providing them with full-blown superuser rights. This limits the scope of what developers can do in an elevated permissions environment, thus protecting the system from bad internal actors.

On AWS, these scripts are called *SSM documents*. SSM documents are scripts written using a special syntax (*https://oreil.ly/jiuDm*); they can be applied to any instance that is managed by (*https://oreil.ly/xVUqg*) AWS SSM. Figure 8-2 shows an example where I created my own SSM document that runs a Unix shell script, which in turn reboots the operating system.

---

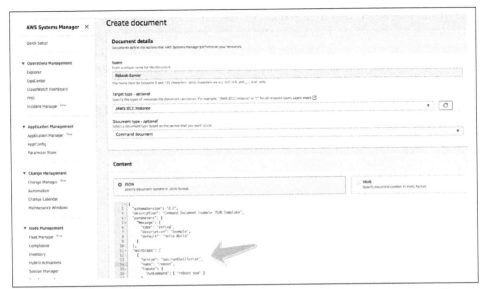

*Figure 8-2. A custom document can be created by going to the Documents tab on the AWS Systems Manager page*

AWS maintains an inventory of documents of their own that covers many typical actions which need to be taken for mitigating incidents. It is always recommended to use their managed document, whenever such a document is available.

The document from Figure 8-2, once created, lives within your account and can be used to run on multiple instances. It can also be shared across accounts, making this a scalable option for mitigating common incidents. However, the onus is on the DevOps team to maintain a set of such documents in order to remedy any incident.

AWS run command documents can be secured using AWS IAM policies that I discussed in Chapter 2. In most situations, a good idea is to create a separate role that is allowed to execute (send) these commands. Your developers can be allowed to assume this role whenever needed. You can apply PoLP there to limit those who can assume this role and the circumstances under which it can be assumed. Every attempt to assume this role can be logged on AWS CloudTrail for additional visibility and auditability.

I will use an example to illustrate the securitization process. Say you have a document you created that can reboot a production AWS Elastic Cloud Compute (EC2) instance. You can create a specific role, say "rebooter," that is allowed to run this command. Whenever there is a production incident, your developers can assume this role and reboot servers. You can take security a step further by using ABAC. In that, you can qualify the access that this "rebooter" role has to only those SSM documents and EC2 instances that have a specific AWS tag and a value attached to them, such as "rebootable." You can then tag your production instances with the tag. This way, the "rebooter" role will only be able to reboot instances that an administrator has marked as rebootable.

You can apply least privilege around the rebooter role in the form of ABAC by attaching the following IAM policy to it:

```
{
    "Sid": "VisualEditor1",
    "Effect": "Deny",
    "Action": "ssm:SendCommand",
    "Resource": "*",
    "Condition": {
        "StringNotLike": {
            "aws:ResourceTag/rebootable": "true"
        }
    }
}
```

This will ensure that the documents created will be executable only on instances that have an AWS tag—rebootable set to true.

Anytime a developer needs to reboot a production server (which has the AWS tag rebootable set to true), the developer can assume the rebooter role and run the command by going to the "Run command" tab on the AWS Systems Manager tab and selecting the document that you created in Figure 8-2. Figure 8-3 illustrates this flow.

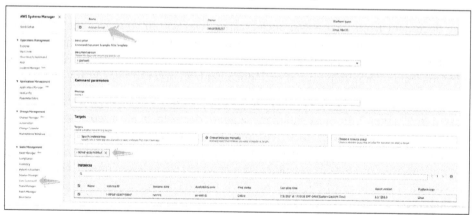

*Figure 8-3. You can run a document that you created by going to the "Run command" tab on the AWS Systems Manager page and selecting an instance that is managed by AWS SSM to send the command to*

## Break-the-Glass

While run command is a great option for incidents that have prescripted solutions, it may be useless against ad hoc incidents. In such situations, security professionals may have no choice but to elevate the access privileges of developers in order to mitigate the incident. One way to achieve privilege elevation is by having an alternate protocol for access control in place called *Break-the-Glass (BTG)*. This protocol deals with emergency access to cloud services or resources when an elevation of privilege is required for disaster mitigation. The term "break the glass" is derived from the action of breaking glass to pull a fire alarm. It describes a quick way for a person without permission to access certain resources, to be granted elevated access privileges during an emergency. This access should be temporary and should be revoked as soon as the critical issue has been mitigated or patched.

 Although I often talk about giving elevated (or at times superuser) access to users in the context of BTG protocols, that is not the only place where such a protocol is useful. Access granted can be lateral. As an example, you may wish to grant developer access to an external team member from a different team (working on a different functional domain) to services or resources within your context simply to assist in debugging production issues that may involve both of your teams. The same process has to be followed to grant this temporary access, as is described in the previous section where superuser access is granted to developers.

The BTG process should be made as quick and straightforward as possible in most functioning organizations, so that precious time is not wasted in bureaucracy in case of an emergency. During such an emergency, every action taken by a user who has elevated access should be documented using AWS's logging mechanisms, including CloudWatch and CloudTrail. Outside of an emergency, however, the organization is free to implement strict and very restrictive access control measures, thus improving the security posture of the organization. Each team within the organization should have quick procedures in place where this switch can happen.

 It is important to note that privilege elevation is indeed a compromise to the PoLP. Providing elevated access even during emergencies may open the application up for more security incidents from "trusted insiders," who may be able to game the system and obtain this elevated access. BTG should only be used as a last resort when other approaches are not feasible for incident mitigation.

Let me show you an example of how organizations can implement such a procedure on AWS while controlling access.

Figure 8-4 demonstrates how RBAC can be used to create a functional BTG protocol within organizations. Assume that you have a resource, Resource A, which is ordinarily not accessible to developers. However, you want to provide access to it in case of emergencies. This access has to be signed off by a senior stakeholder within the company.

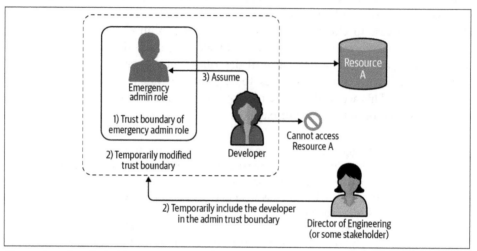

*Figure 8-4. A stakeholder can approve elevated access using trust boundaries to implement BTG protocols*

As seen in Figure 8-4, the steps involved may be described as such:

1. IAM architects come up with emergency situations where elevated access may be needed and groom the access policies of IAM roles that can be useful in mitigating such situations. These roles can continue to be in the organization with strict rules around them, which prevent users and developers within the company from assuming them during normal day-to-day operations.

2. Security professionals then devise protocols that can be used to confirm that an emergency has occurred. This may be as simple as deferring to the judgment of a senior manager within the company who can simply rule that the elevated access provided to developers for the time being is warranted and worth the risk.

3. When an emergency event occurs, developers are added to the trust boundary of the emergency administrator's role. The developers can assume the emergency admin role and access resources and perform actions that they would have been restricted from performing otherwise.

Some points worth noting in Figure 8-4:

- "Emergency admin role" can access Resource A. But under normal circumstances this role cannot be assumed by anyone in the company.
- The Director of Engineering can control who can assume this "Emergency admin role." However, they cannot assume the role themselves.
- The Developer can assume the role and thus access the resource, but only after the Director of Engineering allows them to.

## Permission Boundaries

A permissions boundary is a way in which administrators can assign permissions to other identities by specifying the maximum privileges they can receive. Unlike an IAM policy, it does not grant any new privileges to the recipient. Instead, it specifies the maximum permission that the recipient can have.

As a result, the effective permission after the application of a permission boundary to an IAM identity is always a subset of its IAM policy permissions, as seen in Figure 8-5.

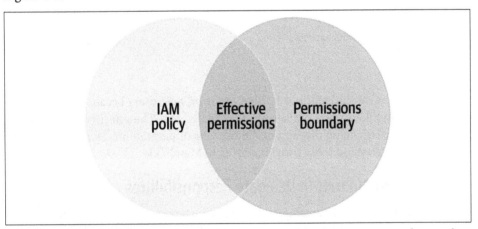

*Figure 8-5. Permission boundaries do not themselves add any permission to the users' accounts, but rather limit the extent to which you can delegate permissions*

For example, let's say that you have a team that should work only with AWS Simple Storage Service (S3) or AWS Lambda.

You would then set up the following permission boundary IAM policy condition:

```
{
    "Version": "2012-10-17",
    "Statement": [
        {
            "Effect": "Allow",
            "Action": [
              "s3:*",
              "lambda:*".... <permission to services that this team needs>
            ],
            "Resource": "*"
        },
    ]
}
```

Any identity that is assigned this permissions policy will, at the most, be able to use AWS S3 and AWS Lambda resources on AWS. This means that if you created a user "Gaurav" with this boundary policy, and if you attached an IAM policy that allows user creation, as defined thus:

```
{
  "Version": "2012-10-17",
  "Statement": {
    "Effect": "Allow",
    "Action": "iam:CreateUser",
    "Resource": "*"
  }
}
```

the user "Gaurav" would still not be able to create new users because the boundary policy does not allow iam:CreateUser in its statement. The effective permission of the user will end up being the least of the two sets of permissions (those provided by the boundary policy and those provided by its IAM policy).

## Permission Boundaries to Delegate Responsibilities

In small organizations, managing teams and cloud resources may be fairly simple. You may have a cloud administrator (or a centralized team of administrators) who is responsible for enforcing the security policy of the organization. The cloud administrator is responsible for carefully evaluating permissions of all users in all teams in the organization and implementing the PoLP across all of these users. They are also responsible for running and maintaining cloud resources across all teams. However, as the organization grows, such a centralized team may become harder to scale. Being able to have a centralized team control an entire company and its identities can pose a challenge.

This may mean delegating some cloud-administration tasks to leaders or developers within teams, rather than to centralized administrators. However, this team-level delegation must be qualified so that each team can only be given the privileges it needs to do its job (as outlined in the PoLP). This can be achieved by using permission boundaries.

Obviously, you can also assign permission boundaries to the members of a team based on the services they use. So if a team uses AWS Lambda, you can add a permission boundary that allows access only to AWS Lambda. However, the one tricky aspect is to allow these teams to manage identities of the team members.

To illustrate, let us consider a team (Team X) that uses AWS Lambda. You also want Team X's manager, Bob, to create or delete users from the team. So you can create a permission boundary (PBX) for all users of this team that only allows them access to AWS Lambda and the ability to create new users.

The boundary policy PBX can look something like this:

```
{
    "Version": "2012-10-17",
    "Statement": [
        {
            "Sid": "BasicPermissions",
            "Effect": "Allow",
            "Action": [
                "iam:*", <ability to add new users to the team>
                "lambda:*".... <permission to services that this team needs>
            ],
            "Resource": "*"
        },
    ]
}
```

Now, let's assume you have a secret database that stores sensitive information in your account, and let's assume that Team X does not need to access this data. As long as all the users from Team X are assigned the permission boundary PBX, administrators can be assured that access to the sensitive data can be restricted for Team X. However, since Bob from Team X is allowed to create new users, nothing stops Bob from creating a new user (Alice) who does not have such a restrictive policy assigned to her. Alice now has access to the secret database, which she should not. Figure 8-6 illustrates this example.

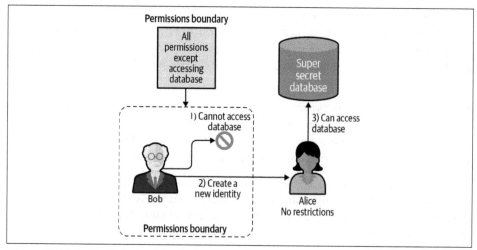

*Figure 8-6. Ideally, Bob should only be allowed to create an account that has permissions that are more restrictive than his own permissions*

To prevent such a permission escalation, instead of the original boundary policy, you can use a slight tweak to the boundary policy as suggested by AWS (*https://oreil.ly/fIUsC*).

Consider a permissions boundary called PBY that allows Bob access to AWS Lambda and to create users. You can add an extra condition to PBY that says, "You can only create new users that have PBY attached to them."

This can be achieved by adding a condition to the `iam:*` permission:

```
{
            "Sid": "CreateOrChangeOnlyWithBoundary",
            "Effect": "Allow",
            "Action": [
                "iam:CreateUser",
                "iam:DeleteUserPolicy",
                "iam:AttachUserPolicy",
                "iam:DetachUserPolicy",
                "iam:PutUserPermissionsBoundary",
                "iam:PutUserPolicy"
            ],
            "Resource": "*",
            "Condition": {"StringEquals":
                {"iam:PermissionsBoundary":
                    "arn:aws:iam::123456789012:policy/PBY"}}
    },
```

`CreateOrChangeOnlyWithBoundary` ensures that a new user can be created only if the permissions boundary `arn:aws:iam::123456789012:policy/PBY` is added to the newly created user and not otherwise.

This means that if Bob creates user Alice, then Alice will still have PBY as a boundary and still will not be able to access the database. In addition, if Alice had the permission to create users, then the new users will still have such a boundary added to them, thus making it impossible to breach privileges by creating new users. You should also restrict these users from being able to change or delete PBY. Such a policy would look like this:

```
{
        "Sid": "NoBoundaryPolicyEdit",
        "Effect": "Deny",
        "Action": [
            "iam:CreatePolicyVersion",
            "iam:DeletePolicy",
            "iam:DeletePolicyVersion",
            "iam:SetDefaultPolicyVersion",
    "iam:DeleteUserPermissionsBoundary"
        ],
        "Resource": [
            "*"
        ]
    }
```

Figure 8-7 illustrates the effect of adding these policies and permissions boundaries to delegate responsibilities. As seen, the resulting IAM structure ensures complete control without the risk of unintended privilege escalation.

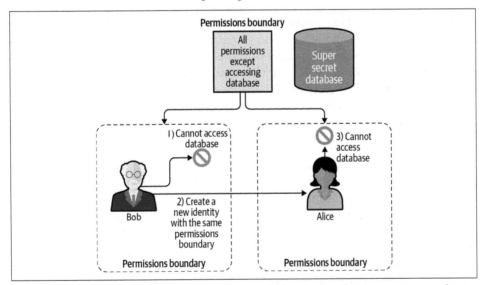

*Figure 8-7. A permissions boundary can be tweaked to ensure that any new user who is created is required to have the same permissions boundary attached to them*

To sum up, SID `BasicPermissions` ensures that any user within the account will have access only to the AWS Lambda that the team uses or to create new users for the team. SID `NoBoundaryPolicyEdit` will ensure that members of this team cannot change the basic permissions they have and thus cannot escalate their access privileges. And finally, `CreateOrChangeOnlyWithBoundary` will ensure that any new user who is created by a member of this team will continue to have the same restrictions that were put in place on the genesis user.

By now, I have made the case for having independent teams that are granted sufficient autonomy in managing their own identities and resources. With permissions boundaries, organizations can safely begin delegating administrative tasks to their teams. It is by far the best approach to scalability if your team is aligned around functionality, as with microservices.

# AWS Accounts Structure for Large Organizations

In discussing org charts and team structures in large companies, I want to underscore the fact that in large firms, individual teams prefer their own autonomy when it comes to performing their duties. On the other hand, stakeholders and upper management may be keen on applying checks and balances to the power held by each team. In most companies that I have seen, this results in a tug-of-war, making it difficult to apply PoLP.

In this section, I would like to talk about how this tug-of-war unfolds itself while setting up AWS accounts and other cloud infrastructure. At the outset, you want individual teams to innovate and quickly ship code to production, thus adding value to the company. These teams are also best equipped to maintain this infrastructure since they work closely with it every day. Therefore, it makes sense to empower each team with as much control as possible over their cloud infrastructure. But at the same time, you want to protect the company's resources from all the internal threats, such as disgruntled employees, inexperienced engineers, or possible intruders.

In my experience, most companies start their cloud journey by setting up one single AWS account to provision all of their cloud resources and infrastructure. Initially, such a setup may seem easy and simple since you only have to worry about a single account. You can hire cloud administrators who only have to think of a single account and apply PoLP to all the identities in this account. Upon terminating employees, you do not have to delete their accounts from multiple places. However, if you end up putting a lot of unrelated teams in the same account, you will increasingly observe that it becomes more and more difficult to scale such a cloud organization, especially when it comes to domain-driven organizations.

To begin with, you will immediately experience the fact that applying PoLP in such a large account with unconnected identities is a nightmare. Cost separation and auditing also become problematic due to the inability to divide the infrastructure cleanly. Overall, complexity around the management of identities and resources just exponentially becomes harder.

But apart from just pure management complexity, there are some very significant security implications, the primary issue being that of blast radius. If the root user or any administrator or power user of this account gets compromised, the entire account with all of your infrastructure is now at risk of being compromised.

Also, for compliance purposes, if all the resources end up in the same account, compliance auditors may consider all the resources to be within the scope of the audit. This may exponentially increase the complexity of an audit and thus make regulatory compliance a nightmare.

Hence, AWS recommends (*https://www.youtube.com/watch?v=tzJmE_Jlas0*) the use of a multiaccount structure where each business development team has its own account. While there is no specific guideline on how many teams each organization should have, decomposing an entire organization into individual accounts per business domain is a pattern that provides sufficient autonomy and isolation for a microservice environment.

Since domain-driven teams are likely to align their application domains with the organizational structure within the company, having an account per bounded context will make sure that teams working on each business domain have sufficient autonomy.

However, merely delegating all administrative responsibilities to the teams may not be feasible, and companies may prefer to have control and governance over the functioning of their accounts. This is where *AWS Organizations* comes in handy. In this section, I will highlight the basics of creating team-level accounts and then dive deeper into AWS Organizations.

A multiaccount structure is what provides domain-driven teams with the autonomy they need to innovate and quickly add value without going through a centralized bureaucratic process. AWS Organizations, on the other hand, serves as a governing body that permits administrators and senior management to add controls over the powers that individual teams have within their account. This way, AWS Organizations along with a multiaccount structure can provide an environment of controlled autonomy to organizations with domain-driven teams.

## AWS Accounts and Teams

In AWS, a sufficient level of autonomy can be granted to different teams by providing each team with a separate AWS account. This will ensure that the management of identities, resources, and security policies can be cleanly separated without interfering with one another. For the purposes of monitoring, security, and consolidated billing,

AWS Organizations allows administrators to group these separate and autonomous accounts, thus maintaining governance and control over highly functional autonomous teams.

For security professionals, there are many reasons why it makes sense to split teams and give them individual AWS accounts, as mentioned in the AWS documentation (*https://oreil.ly/EvkMm*). I will highlight a few of them here:

*Security controls*
Each account can be configured to have its own security policies so that granular control can be exerted on teams in a very customized way. This can also help in proving regulatory compliance.

*Isolation of attacks*
Potential risks and security threats can be contained within an account without affecting others.

*Autonomy and agility*
Having multiple accounts means the teams cannot interfere with one another, as they might when using the same account.

*Governance*
It is easier for administrators to manage and govern over smaller sets of resources than it is to pool all of the resources together into one giant account.

*Delegation*
Since there are multiple small accounts, administrators can delegate the process of managing and administering context-level accounts to different teams instead of one team being responsible for the entire architecture.

 It is not uncommon for large corporations to have hundreds of AWS accounts, each responsible for a business arm or initiative.

Going back to Chapter 1, if you wanted to implement a decentralized application with a team-account structure that is responsible for maintaining individual parts of the application, the team structure could look something like what is illustrated in Figure 8-8.

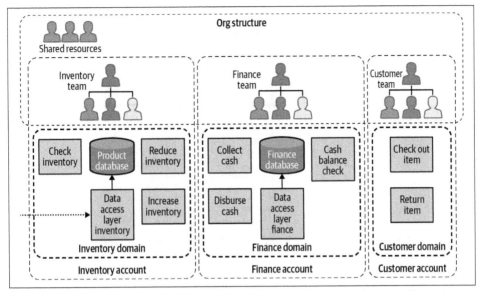

*Figure 8-8. Each team can have its own AWS account that holds all the resources that the team needs to maintain the functionality of the application*

Assigning separate accounts to every team allows for the autonomy that teams desire in large organizations. However, simply asking every team to have their own account may not be enough since companies have checks and balances. They may want to implement controls that protect them from internal threats such as disgruntled employees, rogue teams, and so forth. These controls are provided by AWS Organizations, which I will talk about in the next section.

## AWS Organizations

Now that I have established why it's important for organizations to have independent accounts for each bounded context, I'll discuss how complex businesses can support the creation of such independent accounts without compromising control or governance by using AWS Organizations.

Companies typically have an organizational structure that already includes some measure of control and governance. Roughly speaking, in many large companies, there are divisions aligned to their business domains, and each division may hold departments that are aligned to specific functions within the divisions. Figure 8-9 represents a sample organization with multiple products (or services) and departments.

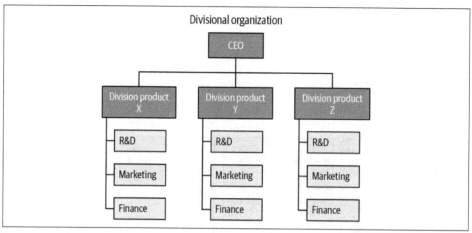

*Figure 8-9. A typical organization with multiple products that may reflect individual bounded contexts*

This section aims to ensure that the independent account structure (built based on the business functionality your application provides), discussed in "AWS Accounts and Teams" on page 285, follows the same hierarchy as the team and org structure of the company. This makes governance easier and more manageable for cloud administrators.

I recognize that the AWS account structure does not have to follow the exact same structure as your organization, but since a mirroring of org structure is unavoidable in many complex applications (as evidenced through the research around Conway's law), I am going to assume that your internal org structure is similar to your business functionality.

AWS Organizations is a great tool for creating governance models for accounts that scale well in large organizations. AWS Organizations is the way to introduce a top-level umbrella account, called a *management account,* that can help create a hierarchy of AWS accounts within your organization. With AWS Organizations, you can add existing accounts to this organization or create another AWS account for each department or division in this organization. The accounts that are added subsequently to the organization are called *member accounts.* Thus, you can set up a hierarchy of member accounts that is governed by a centralized management account at the organization level.

Figure 8-10 shows how AWS Organizations can be enabled in the AWS Management Console for the "Management account" and "New member accounts." Using AWS Organizations, companies can create a hierarchical governance structure for all of their accounts.

Figure 8-10. AWS Organizations can be created and new accounts can be added to a management account from within the AWS Management Console

Once created, the management account can be a top-level entity and the body responsible for ensuring the access, rights, and privileges of all of the individual accounts. The organization can then decide how much autonomy each account under its umbrella has and can ensure that least privilege is observed while granting autonomy to high-functioning teams. As seen in Figure 8-11, you can create new accounts or add existing accounts to the organization in the AWS Management Console.

Figure 8-11. New accounts can be created or existing accounts can be added in the AWS Management Console

> Whenever a new account is created under the organization, the resulting account automatically has a role `OrganizationAccountAc cessRole` that is automatically created in the member accounts. Any administrator or superuser from the top-level organization account can then assume this role and make changes in the member account, thus having the ability to administer members and maintain governance. If you register an existing account under the organization, however, such a role has to be manually created.

AWS Organizations can also help in setting up a consolidated billing solution for large companies. You can consolidate billing and payment for multiple AWS accounts with the consolidated billing feature in AWS Organizations. The top-level account in AWS Organizations can thus pay for all of its member accounts. Therefore, the accountants within your company can obtain access to the organization's account, while not requiring granular access to individual departments or domains within the company, thus preserving least privilege.

# Organizational Units and Service Control Policies

After having set up an AWS Organization and registered your accounts under this organization, you can see how the various bounded contexts within your organization can have sufficient autonomy while still not compromising on security. However, in large companies, the number of accounts can still get out of hand and may be difficult to manage. AWS accounts have the same need for a hierarchical structure as departments within companies, in order to establish proper control. To achieve such a structure, AWS provides us with two important tools.

### Organizational units

Each AWS account can belong to an organizational unit (OU). An OU is a way of classifying entities within an organization into one common group. With OUs, administrators have the flexibility of placing each member account either directly in the root or under one of the OUs in the hierarchy. If you have used directory services such as Active Directory or Lightweight Directory Access Protocol (LDAP), the term *organizational unit* may not be new to you. Very much in a similar way, in order to reduce the complexity within AWS Organizations, AWS provides administrators with OUs that can be administered as a single unit and can be used to generate a hierarchical structure similar to most org charts. This greatly simplifies account management.

Nesting is possible with OUs, which means each OU can belong to another OU. This allows administrators to create treelike hierarchies of OUs that better reflect a company's departmental hierarchy. By using OUs, AWS Organizations administrators can create hierarchies of AWS accounts that better reflect the organizations to which these AWS accounts belong.

### Service control policies

Service control policies (SCPs) are the other tool that organizations have for exercising control over individual AWS accounts or OUs. You can use SCPs to control the permissions for all accounts and OUs in your organization. SCPs alone are not sufficient to grant permissions to the accounts in your organization. Instead, an SCP defines the limits of permissions that can be granted in each account or OU. The user's effective permissions are the intersection of what is allowed by the SCP and what is permitted by the IAM.

### Representation of departmental hierarchy using OUs and SCPs

Using OUs, each company can create a hierarchical structure within an AWS organization. Once such a structure is created, it is easier to sharpen controls to incorporate the entitlements within the organization into the access control policies that you may set up. Figure 8-12 shows a sample organizational hierarchy represented in the form of an AWS Organizations setup using OUs and SCPs.

---

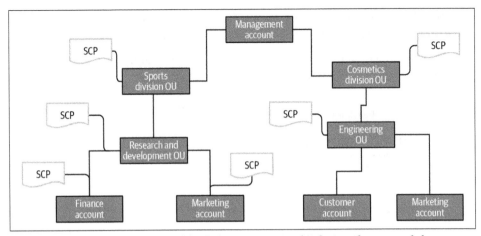

*Figure 8-12. At each level in the hierarchy, an SCP can be designed to control the access that accounts in that hierarchy get*

### Examples of control using SCP

Now, I will walk you through a couple of SCP recipes that can be employed by organizations to create a secure yet decentralized organization. AWS maintains a list (*https://oreil.ly/cniZ3*) of many suggested policies that can be used by administrators to create a very secure multiaccount setup in organizations.

The common theme in all of these SCPs is the use of the condition clause in IAM policy statements that I discussed in Chapter 2. You can use such a clause to deny actions to various teams through an SCP.

A few examples of such use cases are:

- Ensuring that the teams tag the resources they create properly
- Allowing the creation of only specific types of resources on AWS
- Disallowing the users from disabling AWS CloudTrail or CloudWatch logging or monitoring
- Preventing users from sharing resources externally using AWS Resource Access Manager (RAM)

**Example 1: Ensuring proper resource tagging.**  AWS tags make it very easy to categorize resources, for example, by purpose, owner, and environment. They also help in improving visibility over costs and budgets. Hence, it is important to ensure that every resource is tagged appropriately. However, if the control to create resources is decentralized, it may be difficult for administrators to enforce such a strict tagging policy. AWS SCPs can be employed in such a situation to make sure that every team uses the right tags while creating resources. This will also help in monitoring the activity of each team since each resource will be tagged appropriately.

The following policy shows how you can ensure that you cannot run instances in the account if the request does not include a MarketingTeam tag:

```
{
    "Sid": "DenyRunInstanceWithNoProjectTag",
    "Effect": "Deny",
    "Action": "ec2:RunInstances",
    "Resource": [
      "arn:aws:ec2:*:*:instance/*",
      "arn:aws:ec2:*:*:volume/*"
    ],
    "Condition": {
      "Null": {
        "aws:RequestTag/MarketingTeam": "true"
      }
    }
}
```

**Example 2: Ensuring that only a certain type of instance can be run by users of an account.**
Another common scenario is where an organization would like to delegate control of resources to child accounts. However, you want to restrict them from creating any expensive resources. So you would like to allow team members to only create EC2 instances that are of instance type t2.micro. This can be achieved using IAM policies such as the following:

```
{
  "Sid": "RequireMicroInstanceType",
  "Effect": "Deny",
  "Action": "ec2:RunInstances",
  "Resource": "arn:aws:ec2:*:*:instance/*",
  "Condition": {
    "StringNotEquals":{
      "ec2:InstanceType":"t2.micro"
    }
  }
}
```

This statement will ensure that the child account is not able to create any EC2 instance that is not a t2.micro.

## Purpose-Built Accounts

Another good way to utilize AWS Organizations especially for microservice architectures is to create *purpose-built accounts*. A purpose-built account is an account that is assigned a very specific task in an organization. Typically, this is a cross-cutting task (a task that affects multiple domains) within the application's architecture, and hence is difficult to classify in one account. Logging, monitoring, data archiving, encryption, and data tokenization are some examples of typical tasks that many applications perform that generally tend to extend beyond typical domains.

Purpose-built accounts enable organizations to carefully and successfully carve out critical *cross-cutting functionality* (functionality that touches multiple domains) into a separate account. This way, you can apply least privilege to this account and restrict access to very few users while the rest of the application can continue to run. I have already given a couple of examples of purpose-built accounts in Chapter 3 when I talked about having a separate account that hosts customer master keys (CMKs) for different domains.

Figure 8-13 illustrates a typical organization that has dedicated accounts for the purposes of IAM, CMKs, and maintaining logs. Any user from a different account who wants to access logs, for example, can be allowed to assume a role in this account, controlled by using trust boundaries.

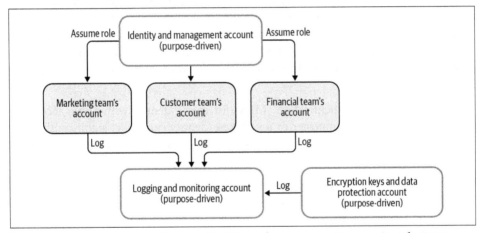

*Figure 8-13. Logging, encryption, and IAM are three cross-cutting services that may benefit from having a purpose-built account in certain organizations*

Purpose-built accounts simplify the process of granting privilege and access to critically sensitive functions by not bundling these activities with the rest of the domain logic.

# AWS Tools for Organizations

Having explained the concept of AWS Organizations and a multiaccount structure, I will now describe some of the tools that AWS provides that can be leveraged to make a multiaccount structure more powerful.

# AWS Organizations Best Practices

Securing an individual account is at times quite different from securing an entire organization. In an individual account, you can have clearly defined users. However, in an organization, you have to account for the possibility of employees transitioning in and out of the organization. Therefore, having a plan to ensure that the company continues to function in spite of changing employee bases is important. AWS Organizations allows for a superuser group to oversee each team and keep things in order. Hence, it is even more crucial to secure the "management account" by preventing unauthorized access and privilege escalation.

AWS provides some ways of securing the management account (*https://oreil.ly/qb9cp*). The most important task in ensuring the security of the management account is to have strong identity protection around it.

Security professionals should assume that the management account is a highly visible target, and hence will be more attractive to attackers. Some common ways in which attackers may gain entry may involve the use of password-reset procedures in order to reset the passwords of privileged users. Hence, the process to recover or reset access to the root user credentials should have checks and balances in place to ensure that a single user is not able to compromise the root access to the management account.

Enabling multifactor authentication (MFA) for every identity within this account is critically important. An imposter or a hijacked identity can inflict significantly more harm to the entire organization if this identity belongs to the management account than any of the other OUs.

Finally, it is even more important than any other account to follow the PoLP in granting access to this account. Each and every access should be carefully scrutinized and justified. Furthermore, each activity should be monitored on this account and every use case should be documented for compliance and scrutiny.

# AWS Resource Access Manager

Once you have separate accounts for separate bounded contexts, you naturally want to find a way in which the resources in these accounts can be made to work with one another.

For example, let's say that you have a virtual private cloud (VPC) inside a particular context and would like to set up rails for communication with other contexts. Chapter 5 already talked about the existing tools that architects have to set up such communication channels between contexts. These include VPC peering or VPC endpoints. In this chapter, however, I will introduce a slightly different approach to sharing: AWS Resource Access Manager (RAM).

While most microservice architectures don't share resources across contexts, there are some very specific situations where it's OK and even necessary to relax such a rule. Purpose-driven accounts are one such example, where some of the resources (for example, VPC) need to be shared with other accounts. AWS RAM is the answer to such unique situations where resource access needs to be shared while maintaining control and autonomy. I will share an example of such a pattern soon.

AWS RAM allows accounts to share certain resources (*https://oreil.ly/XZrzU*) within their accounts with other external accounts. This way, in multiaccount structures, contexts are not strictly bound by account-level structures and can still continue to have communication and shared resources.

Now, resources can be shared with:

- Any specific AWS account
- Within an OU
- Within the entire AWS Organization

Once shared, the resources can be accessed by the external accounts natively, as if these resources were part of their own accounts.

Sharing resources is slightly different from allowing cross-account access that I have talked about in the other accounts. With AWS RAM, even though the sharing account owns, controls, and maintains the shared resources, these shared resources can be accessed as if they are a part of the destination account.

Figure 8-14 shows a set of accounts sharing resources using AWS RAM.

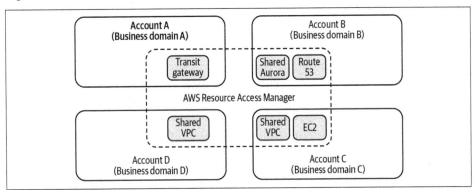

*Figure 8-14. Different accounts within AWS can share services using AWS RAM*

# Shared Services Using AWS RAM

This section discusses one common use case that I have seen where AWS RAM fits well with a microservice architecture. I have already mentioned that AWS VPCs are a common resource that benefits from AWS RAM. VPC, being an infrastructure component of a cloud design, does not have to face the "shared-nothing" rule (*https://oreil.ly/3Qphn*) that most microservice architectures dictate.

Figure 8-15 shows a typical multicontext architecture that has been split into a multi-account setup on AWS. For example, you might have a monitoring service that gathers metrics and logs from all the independent microservices to be centralized for administrators and auditors. In such a scenario, logs would be located centrally in VPC, but applications located on the independent microservice accounts would still need to send the logs to the logging service. This is where AWS RAM simplifies the design.

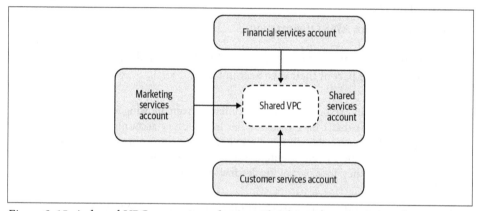

*Figure 8-15. A shared VPC account can be created to host instances from other accounts*

Using AWS RAM, you can have a shared services account that exposes a logging service. This logging service can be inside its own VPC, which can be offered as a share across the AWS Organization. Given that it is a shared VPC, the other accounts within this organization can natively apply routing rules and start sending logging data and metrics to this shared VPC as if it were a part of their own accounts and infrastructure. However, in spite of the illusion of having a native logging infrastructure, the separate account will be maintained and owned by the shared services team, thus maintaining control over the shared infrastructure.

> Logging, monitoring, DNS and certificate management services, encryption key management services, and tokenization services are some of the examples of cross-cutting shared services that may benefit from being carved out of existing domain accounts and shared using AWS RAM.

# AWS Single Sign-On

Recall from Chapter 2 that I talked about the concept of *identity federation*, which involves setting up an identity provider (IdP) that can be used to delegate the process of authentication in case you have multiple sets of identities in an organization. I would now like to provide you with an alternative to the original identity federation option in the form of AWS Single Sign-On (SSO).

> AWS SSO can be used in two cases. You could either log into a third-party service using AWS SSO or ask AWS to trust a third party's SSO. In other words, AWS SSO can act as the provider of identities for other cloud services that may require SSO-based login or access. Or it can act as the consumer of a third-party identity service, thus trusting a third-party IdP for its own identity federation.

AWS realized that this use case of trusting a third-party trusted provider is far too common in most organizations, and hence provided users with AWS SSO to simplify the setup of SSO for organizations. AWS SSO makes it easy for users to log in to multiple accounts and applications in a single place. AWS SSO enables a centralized administrator to control AWS Organizations access for all your accounts in a single place. Your AWS SSO account configures and maintains all permissions for your individual accounts automatically, without requiring any additional work on your part. AWS SSO can be enabled in the AWS Management Console, as seen in Figure 8-16.

*Figure 8-16. AWS SSO can be used by adding identity sources and managing SSO access to your AWS accounts*

Once set up, AWS SSO can then manage the user's permissions across your organization centrally without requiring duplication of identity and access-related activities. User termination is also simplified with the help of AWS SSO, thus keeping your cloud resources safe from disgruntled employees.

AWS SSO is designed to integrate with AWS Organizations. So if you have a multiac-count setup with multiple OUs, you do not have to configure multiple account access and can rely on AWS SSO providing the right permissions to the users of your organization.

 SSO is one of those circumstances where improving the security of the design yields the same result as improving its convenience. The use of SSO for identity management in almost every organization leads to more secure and systematic management while still offer-ing convenience to employees. I recommend you take full advan-tage of this service.

## Enforcing Multifactor Authentication in Accounts

Any organization would be failing in its duty to safeguard identities if they do not emphasize the importance of MFA to its users. Most security policies rely heavily on the ability of end users to be able to use MFA for authentication. There is a lot of liter-ature online highlighting the importance of MFA, so I won't get into the benefits here. A few examples can be found at OneLogin (*https://oreil.ly/0FslK*), Expert Insights (*https://oreil.ly/IaoQG*), and NIST (*https://oreil.ly/zWlea*).

As an administrator, you want to ensure that principals who have access to a particu-lar resource have passed the additional check using MFA. You can add the condition `"aws:MultiFactorAuthPresent": "true"` to an IAM policy to ensure that access is granted only to users that have gone through MFA:

```
{
  "Version": "2012-10-17",
  "Statement": {
    "Effect": "Allow",
    "Principal": {"AWS": "ACCOUNT-B-ID"},
    "Action": "sts:AssumeRole",
    "Condition": {"Bool": {"aws:MultiFactorAuthPresent": "true"}}
  }
}
```

This condition evaluates to true if `MultiFactorAuth` is present on the account of the user who is trying to access this resource. This way, you can ensure the security of your resources by making sure that individual identities have used MFA to log in to AWS.

MFA becomes tricky when using a multiaccount setup. MFA always has to be enabled in the trusted account that the user first authenticates against. Furthermore, it is this trusted account's responsibility to guarantee the credibility of the MFA. Since any identity with permission to create virtual MFA devices can construct an MFA and claim to satisfy the MFA requirement, you should ensure that the trusted account's owner follows security best practices.

It is almost always a good idea to enforce MFA on all the accounts within the organization.

# Simplifying a Complex Domain-Driven Organization Using RBAC, SSO, and AWS Organizations

I have shown you the tools that AWS administrators can use to tame organizational complexity, so now I will go over how these tools come together to simplify identity management and cloud architecture without sacrificing convenience. In this section, I will outline the steps that security designers can take to set up such a cloud-based system.

Let's assume that your application is an ecommerce website that offers various services to end users. I will also assume that you have a DDD for most components of your application, allowing you to set up a STOSA-type application. Hence, you can split your application into bounded contexts that align with the functional domains. As a result of what I have explained in this chapter, you are able to align your engineering teams with the business domain of the application.

You can use AWS Organizations to set up an organization for your entire application and then set up a multiaccount structure.

Each bounded context in your company can have its own AWS account. This will allow individual teams to be highly autonomous. These accounts can have multiple identities within themselves that will be defined using roles. Roles will be used as placeholders to design permissions and privileges for employees and services.

Apart from the accounts that represent individual bounded contexts, you can have a few purpose-built accounts that are used for certain shared and cross-cutting services. Thus, you can have an account for storing all of the log files and for monitoring purposes.

You can also have an account that is dedicated to identity management. This is the account that will hold all of the identities of your application. Each employee within your organization can first authenticate against this account. Upon authenticating, the employees can then assume roles within other accounts by exchanging their credentials from the identity management account using AWS Security Token Service (STS). I have already talked about the process of assuming roles in Chapter 2 and hence I will not go into its details here.

The authentication process can be further simplified by using AWS SSO in order to federate identities to third-party IdPs such as Microsoft Active Directory (*https:// oreil.ly/0GXUW*), Okta (*https://okta.com*), JumpCloud (*https://jumpcloud.com*), and so forth. This way, the IT service administrators can control the access and lifecycle of individual users by keeping their external identities up to date.

Figure 8-17 shows how you can use AWS Organizations and RBAC to simplify the management of access in large corporations.

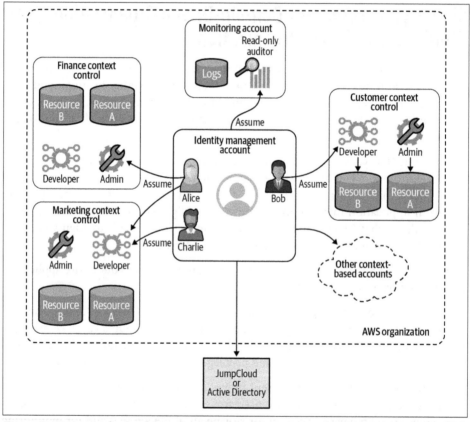

*Figure 8-17. A sample cloud-based application that uses a multiaccount setup and uses RBAC and identity federation to simplify the process of setting up identities*

The best part about such a setup is the simplicity and granularity that it adds to each individual account without compromising on security or functionality. It is significantly easier to scale new teams by simply delegating the responsibility of administration, identity management, and security to responsible teams instead of trying to set up a centralized security administration team.

Each team can control its own bounded context and, as a result, its own AWS account. SCPs can be used to control the permissions that each of these AWS accounts get in order to perform their jobs. As an example, from Figure 8-17, the team that is responsible for the marketing bounded context will be responsible for administering the "Marketing context account." This team will create roles within this account that will have the relevant permissions required for the smooth functioning of their day-to-day operations. The marketing team can apply the PoLP to each of its roles within its own account and only allow its team members to assume these roles using trust boundaries. If a new developer joins this team, the team leads can simply add this user to the trust boundary of the developer role. Thus, the teams have complete control of the identity management.

On the other hand, the company can use the Identity Management Account to manage the identities in the organization. Each employee that has onboarded into the organization can have an identity in this account. This account can further use AWS SSO to federate identities to an external IdP such as Active Directory, Okta, or JumpCloud.

The users from this Identity Management Account can then assume roles within their team's accounts and perform their day-to-day activities as members of their respective teams while still being employees of the company, thus maintaining their identity in a centralized account and location.

Whenever an employee resigns or a company decides to terminate an employee, the company administrator can simply delete the identity of the terminated employee from the Identity Management Account and this employee will then lose access to all of the other accounts within the organization. This way, the organization does not need to replicate identity management across multiple teams and can have an efficient onboarding/off-boarding process.

# Summary

In this chapter, I made a case for autonomy in the presence of strong security measures. Users can be granted this autonomy regardless of whether they utilize a strong RBAC mechanism in a single account structure or they actively create new accounts. I have also introduced you to tools that administrators can use to ensure that the autonomy granted to individual teams does not sacrifice the governance or the security of the organization. It is my strong belief that a highly functional company invests in making their employees productive through continuous investment into operational efficiencies, which ultimately result in the addition of value. This investment can only come through a combined effort where security professionals work with developers and other employees to provide security assurance to managers. A good operational environment also ensures that if a security incident takes place, the right set of people is empowered to take quick action to mitigate any impact or fallout. Chapter 9 will discuss these steps in detail and talk about how an organization can plan for and be prepared to respond to security incidents.

# Monitoring and Incident Response

Until now, I have talked about how to design a microservice system that has controls in place to prevent malicious users from gaining unauthorized access to resources. This chapter takes a slightly different approach. Consider what would happen if, despite your best efforts at segmenting, controlling access, and applying network security measures, an attacker has somehow managed to exploit a vulnerability in your organization and gain unauthorized access.

Every company has to deal with security breaches at some point. Incidents do not necessarily indicate how secure a company's security posture is or how they conduct their business. A humorous quotation made by John Chambers at the World Economic Forum (*https://oreil.ly/eWMak*) that I generally like to use whenever I talk about information security is, "There are two types of companies: those who have been hacked, and those who don't yet know they have been hacked." It is their level of preparedness for an incident that distinguishes a good company from a bad one.

In this chapter, I will be going through various types of *detective controls* that administrators have on AWS resources. It is the goal of detective controls to make security incidents more visible and reduce the time required for their detection or response. AWS provides every user with the ability to monitor all the activities that happen on the cloud. This includes the ability to log every action, specify metrics, and alert for any suspicious behavior. I will then introduce you to tools that can help you with certain detective controls that help in identifying the impact and scope of any suspicious activity. I will be following the incident response framework created by the National Institute of Standards and Technology (NIST) in order to respond to security incidents.

While my focus will be on the security aspect of monitoring and protection against known intruder patterns, some techniques mentioned in this chapter will also help in adding more monitoring across the board for better reliability and resilience.

# NIST Incident Response Framework

The ISO/IEC 20000 standards as part of their "Security Best Practices" define an incident as "a single or a series of unwanted or unexpected information security events that have a significant probability of compromising business operations and threatening information security." IT service management professionals are typically required to follow a response strategy in the event of an incident as part of most operational compliance standards. In this chapter, I will discuss such incidents and how they are handled when they occur in the security domain.

An incident may be caused by a variety of reasons, including but not limited to hardware failures, power outages, malicious intent, theft, terrorism, and more. Recall from Chapter 1 that a *security incident* usually occurs due to an unauthorized actor known as a *malicious actor*. It is imperative that a time-sensitive process is implemented following an act of malicious intent so that the organization can avoid serious financial or reputational losses.

Although every security incident is likely to be different and there may not be a one-size-fits-all approach, certain common threads can be found in many security incidents. In the event of a security incident, you can use these common threads to form a framework of procedures and policies in order to guide critical decisions. In this section, I will discuss such a framework (*https://oreil.ly/Mrt2q*) that has been created by the NIST, a part of the US Department of Commerce, based on extensive research and analysis of cybersecurity incidents that have occurred across many organizations.

The NIST incident response framework is published as part of the *Computer Security Incident Handling Guide (https://oreil.ly/4wirI)*, available for reading on the NIST website. This chapter will explore how various AWS services can be leveraged to apply NIST's incident response plan.

NIST Incident Response Plan—IR-4 as prescribed by the NIST can be roughly summarized in these six steps:

*Step 1: Design and Preparation*
> This is where the security team works with architects to prepare the organization for security incidents. It means putting measures in place that contain malicious actors' potential to cause damage or putting monitoring and logging in place to help better detect security events.

*Step 2: Detection and Analysis*
> Often, detecting and assessing the impact of incidents correctly is the most challenging aspect of incident response. In this step, the team gathers information to conclusively identify and corroborate the presence of a security incident.

*Step 3: Containment and Isolation*

Containment is important before an incident overwhelms resources or increases damage. Keeping an incident contained minimizes the risk of escalating losses by preventing the possibility that the incident is still under way. In this step, the security team implements various controls to contain the attack so that the malicious actor cannot compromise the system further.

*Step 4: Forensic Analysis*

Once the incident has been contained and business continuity has been achieved, security engineers may be able to perform a root cause analysis of the incident. Although the primary reason for gathering evidence during an incident is to resolve the incident, it may also be needed for legal proceedings.

*Step 5: Eradication*

Once the root cause of the security incident has been identified, security architects can take steps to prevent future such incidents from occurring. This might include fixing security loopholes or adding additional measures to keep attackers out and restore business continuity.

*Step 6: Postincident Activities*

Having addressed all existing security loopholes and analyzed the incident properly, businesses can regain normality and can gradually de-escalate security protocols. Possibly, this will involve reverting changes made during Steps 3 through 5. This step may also involve conducting a postmortem meeting and documenting the steps taken to resolve the incident.

Generally, security responses may involve an iterative process of resolution. Even after following all of these steps, there is a possibility that the malicious actor may still be able to infiltrate the system. This would mean repeating all of the steps until the security of the system is strong enough to prevent another attack from this malicious actor.

# Step 1: Design and Preparation

The design and preparation step is the first step of the NIST incident response plan and probably the most crucial part of the incident response framework. This phase dictates that every organization should be proactive in setting up controls to preemptively block security incidents from becoming catastrophic events.

## Architecture for incident control and isolation of blast radius

A well-architected system is probably the best defense against a potential attack. Even if such a system is compromised, a well-designed system has controls in place that ensure that access to one compromised resource of the system does not compromise the entire system, but instead contain the unauthorized access to the very specific region. To use security-related terminology, the blast radius of a security incident is isolated to a specific module. Systems implement architectural techniques such as the principle of least privilege (PoLP), need to know, microsegmentation, zero trust, request-response strategies, and strong multifactor authentication (MFA) for all of its users.

As an example, consider a microservice system that has implemented good segmentation at the network, application, and transport layers. Figure 9-1 shows a typical microservice application with multiple bounded contexts. There are four bounded contexts in this example: Marketing, Analytics, Finance, and User profile (which displays the personal information of each customer). Now assume that one of the microservices inside the User profile service context is compromised by an attacker.

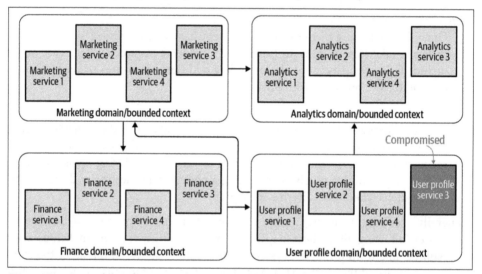

*Figure 9-1. One of the services within a particular bounded context that represents a business domain is affected.*

As soon as such an attack is detected, security professionals can jump on the incident by taking remedial measures to isolate the affected bounded context (User profile services) and all the services within that context.

While the services inside the affected bounded context will be isolated, and hence taken down for a short duration of time, the rest of the application can possibly still continue to function. How much of your business will be affected will of course depend on the criticality of the service in question.

Figure 9-2 shows how security professionals can quickly isolate the infected part of the network.

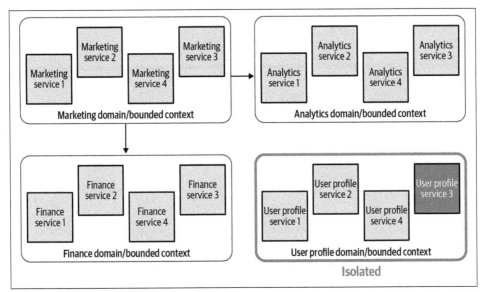

*Figure 9-2. When one domain is infected, security professionals can quickly isolate the domain while the rest of the application can continue to function.*

This ability to isolate based on functionality is possible only because of the ability of microservices to be grouped into bounded contexts based on the business domain. With proper alignment of business domains with microservices, the security professionals can immediately communicate the effects of the outage to the stakeholders and possibly the end users of the application.

Since microservice contexts are aligned with business domains, the effect of the degradation of one particular service may generally be contained within its business domain. Figure 9-3 shows how service status dashboards can show an isolated incident on the status page.

Throughout this book, I have covered all of the different ways in which a well-architected system can block unauthorized access at various levels of the network and application layers. Hence, I will not go into the details of these in this chapter. However, it is worth knowing that the probability of attacks can be significantly reduced through the adoption of such design philosophies. Although incident response teams are generally not responsible for securing resources, they can be advocates of sound security practices.

*Figure 9-3. Due to a cleanly segmented design, it may be possible to contain the effects of a security incident within one business unit while the rest of the application can continue to function without disruption. The business can also set up a status page that can provide customers with updates on the status of the outage.*

### Activity logging

One of the common places to find unauthorized activity is inside activity logs. Once a malicious user gains unauthorized access to your cloud infrastructure, they may attempt to use your resources to perform other unauthorized activities. This may include spinning up new resources or possibly changing identity and access management (IAM) permissions on other users and allowing wider access to other cloud resources.

AWS CloudTrail is a service that allows you to monitor all API requests and activities of all users. Enabling CloudTrail on all of your accounts will enable you to monitor for any suspicious activities when it comes to resources. You can also find out what resources were used, when events occurred, and other details to track and assess your account's activity.

**AWS CloudTrail events.** *CloudTrail events* are the main data object that CloudTrail wishes to log. These events are the record of an activity in an AWS account. These events can be created as a result of any command issued by the user, either through the AWS Console, the AWS Command Line Interface (CLI), or the AWS SDK.

On CloudTrail, all events can be divided roughly into three distinct types:

*Management events (aka control plane events)*
Management events provide information about the management tasks that you perform on your account's resources. These may include changing the security policies of AWS resources, creating new AWS resources, creating new Cloud-Trails, or attaching new IAM policies on existing resources. Monitoring these events can help administrators identify some of the most impactful events that could happen on AWS accounts. Management events are generated and logged free of cost, although storage of these logs may incur storage fees.

*Data events (aka data plane events)*
The data events for a resource provide information about the operations performed on or within a resource. These may include performing operations on existing AWS resources for purposes that they were provisioned for, such as invoking an AWS Lambda function or adding or deleting files within AWS Simple Storage Service (S3) buckets. Data events are often high-volume activities and hence logging for these is not enabled by default.

*Insights events*
These events usually capture unusual activity that may happen on each account. Insights events are usually secondary events that are generated by aggregating individual management events. CloudTrail Insights continually monitors management events and uses mathematical models to estimate each management event's creation rate. This leads to identifying behavior outside of normal patterns, translating them into insights events.

**CloudTrail logging.** One way of accessing the CloudTrail events is by storing them in log files. These files can contain multiple events in a JavaScript Object Notation (JSON) format logged together.

On CloudTrail, this set of events that constitutes the state of your application is called a *trail*. You can enable this trail to log per region, per account, or per AWS Organization. An AWS Organization-wide trail is called an *organization trail*.

In order to maintain durability and high availability, all CloudTrail logfiles can be logged into an AWS S3 bucket that you specify. After a trail is created, CloudTrail automatically begins logging API calls to your S3 bucket. Stopping logging on the trail is as easy as turning it off or deleting it.

Figure 9-4 shows how you can create a CloudTrail trail using the AWS Management Console, then going to the CloudTrail page and enabling the logging of management events within the trail.

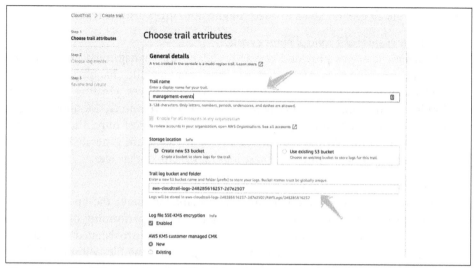

*Figure 9-4. CloudTrail can be enabled to log management events by specifying a trail name and an AWS S3 bucket to store the logs.*

While creating the trail, you also get the choice of choosing which types of events you want to log in the bucket. Figure 9-5 illustrates the process of choosing the events.

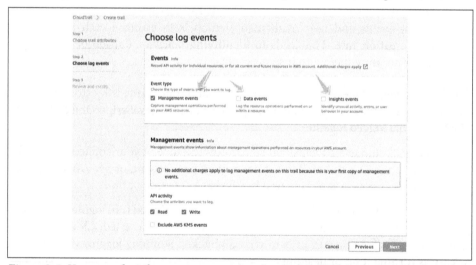

*Figure 9-5. You can select the events you wish to log in the AWS Management Console.*

**VPC flow logs.** A virtual private cloud (VPC) flow log allows you to capture information about traffic going to and from a network interface in your VPC. It can be created for either a VPC, a subnet, or a network interface.

A compromised cloud resource may perform unusual network activity. VPC flow logs can be used when analyzing such activity that may have taken place at the network layer. In a microsegmented network (a network that is partitioned based on business domains), aggregated flow logs may indicate patterns of communication. You can use these patterns to establish a baseline that describes the network communication that exists within your application. At the time of a security incident, you may observe that there is a deviation in terms of structure or the volume from the baseline patterns that you are used to. Thus, by using aggregated statistics around flow logs, you may be able to identify security-related breaches that other metrics or indicators in your microsegmented application may not be able to point to.

On the other hand, in my experience it is very possible for well-meaning security professionals to cause security incidents. Sometimes a security professional may implement a blunt security control at the network level to prevent a particular communication pattern that they feel is unusual. However, unknown to them, such an act may in fact interfere in day-to-day operations. VPC logs will, in such a situation, be useful in identifying the offending control and sharpening it to incorporate the nuance associated with the underlying communication, thus helping to mitigate the issue as soon as it is identified.

Flow logs are logged outside of the network's path, so they don't affect network throughput or latency.

**Application logging using AWS CloudWatch.** AWS also provides you with a fully managed log aggregation service in the form of CloudWatch logs, as part of AWS CloudWatch (*https://aws.amazon.com/cloudwatch*). CloudWatch logs provide you with a safe place to aggregate, store, and retrieve application logs. Unlike CloudTrail, which logs API activity on the infrastructure as a whole, AWS CloudWatch provides cloud applications with a centralized log display service that can collect and display application-level logs of your microservices that run on AWS Elastic Cloud Compute (EC2), AWS Lambda, or any other AWS resource.

It is important to realize the difference between AWS CloudWatch and AWS CloudTrail. While CloudTrail logs API calls and calls that change the infrastructure, AWS CloudWatch is where logs related to applications running on this infrastructure end up. In my experience, it is very common for clients to get confused between the two.

### Composable monitoring

Apart from logs, a different way of monitoring activity is through the use of metrics. These metrics are preaggregated data points that indicate the state of your infrastructure. These may include CPU utilization for compute services, storage utilization for storage services, or many other such statistics. In contrast to monoliths, microservices include multiple servers running in multiple locations, which generate a variety of metrics associated with each microservice. As a result, unlike monoliths where monitoring the health of one application can identify the health of the entire system, microservices require aggregation of multiple data points across the system.

A common term you may hear in most organizations is a *single pane of glass*. Many marketplace observability solutions offer the promise of being able to observe all the metrics that your organization needs and display them to your stakeholders in one place. Over the years, I have become a huge cynic of such an approach to monitoring. A one-size-fits-all approach to monitoring just does not seem to work well, in my opinion. In an environment such as a microservice environment where flexibility and autonomy are valued, different tools are better at capturing different aspects of a runtime microservice. Hence, in my opinion, it is best to use the right tool for collecting the right sets of metrics based on the task that the microservice performs. For example, one tool may be better at capturing metrics for Java-based microservices while another tool might be better for Python. Just because you want stakeholders to be able to view the metrics in the same place does not mean the microservice developers should have to compromise on the type of tools they use to capture the data.

A strategy known as *composable monitoring* is utilized for aggregating such metrics across various microservices and storing them in a single place. Composable monitoring prescribes the use of multiple specialized tools, which are then coupled loosely together, forming a monitoring platform. For those interested in specialized knowledge on monitoring, *Practical Monitoring* by Mike Julian (O'Reilly) (*https://oreil.ly/Ao8St*) goes into the details of how you can set up a composable monitoring strategy on your microservice organization.

Knowing the importance of composable monitoring, AWS decided to provide us with a fully managed service in the form of AWS CloudWatch in order to aggregate, compose, and visualize all your application metrics in one place.

**CloudWatch namespace.**   Since the monitoring in a cloud microservice environment involves composing and aggregating metrics from various sources into one location, managing the monitoring solution may get out of hand if you have a large number of metrics. Thus, to improve the manageability of metrics, it is important to introduce some structure to the metrics you may capture.

A *namespace* encapsulates a group of metrics. Namespaces provide administrators with the ability to separate statistics out in a clean and manageable way so that statistics from different namespaces will not be accidentally aggregated into a single statistic.

 Every data point must be published to CloudWatch with a namespace. There is no default namespace.

**Monitoring data using CloudWatch.** There are four key elements to monitoring data in CloudWatch:

*Datapoint*
Each individual reading of data that needs to be tracked is a *datapoint*.

*Metrics*
A *metric* is the informational vector you want to track. A metric is a series of datapoints published to CloudWatch. Each metric gives you time-based information about your infrastructure.

*Dimension*
Within a metric, it is possible to have multiple datapoints tracking different *dimensions* of information.

*Resolution*
For every metric, the sampling of datapoints can be adjusted based on the choice of the administrator. This is known as the *resolution* for the metric.

It's easiest to explain how CloudWatch monitors your infrastructure with an example. Let us assume you run a number of EC2 instances across multiple regions. These instances can also be tagged to run different types of services. In such a situation, you want to track the CPU utilization and the memory utilization of these instances:

*Datapoint*
If the CPU utilization is what is needed to be tracked for our example cluster, the reading of the CPU utilization at each second is the datapoint for this reading.

*Metrics*
You can have two metrics, CPU utilization and memory utilization, which represent a time-series set of datapoints across all of the instances.

*Dimension*
You can categorize metrics related to CPU usage based on the geographic region or based on which service it runs. Each metric can have up to 10 dimensions and can track datapoints independently across each dimension.

*Resolution*

You can decide how frequently you want to sample your instance's CPU utilization. A metric that is sampled each minute is known as a *standard resolution metric*; a metric that is logged every second is known as a *high resolution metric*. I will revisit this further in this chapter.

## Synthetic monitoring

A third way of monitoring an application is through the use of a technique called *synthetic monitoring*. In synthetic monitoring, behavioral scripts are created to mimic an action or path a customer or an end user might take on a site or a system. It is often used to monitor paths that are frequently used by users and critical business processes. Amazon CloudWatch Synthetics lets you monitor your endpoints and APIs using configurable scripts that are triggered based on a predefined schedule. Canaries are scripts (*https://oreil.ly/jS8bJ*) written in Node.js or Python. AWS creates AWS Lambda functions within your account to run and execute these scripts.

Canaries can be created in the Synthetics tab on the AWS CloudWatch page within the AWS console, as seen in Figure 9-6.

*Figure 9-6. Canaries are generally used as passive monitoring tools for ensuring the smooth functioning of an application.*

## Other AWS monitoring and security services

Now that I have introduced you to the monitoring tools, let me discuss a few other services that AWS offers that can help you secure your application. It is important to remember that there is no single best solution for monitoring, and you may have to utilize all the services that AWS has to offer in order to minimize the probability of an incident.

**AWS Systems Manager.** You can use AWS Systems Manager (AWS SSM, due to its legacy name—Simple Systems Manager) to view and control your infrastructure on AWS. Using the SSM console, you can evaluate operational information from multiple AWS services and perform automated tasks across your AWS resources. To use AWS SSM as an incident response tool, cloud administrators should install AWS SSM Agent on each instance in their cloud infrastructure. The AWS SSM Agent makes it possible for SSM to update, manage, and configure EC2 instances, on-premises servers, and virtual machines (VMs). The SSM Agent is preinstalled on EC2 instances that host images such as Amazon Linux, Amazon Linux 2, Ubuntu Server 16.04, and others.

**Amazon Macie.** Using machine learning and pattern-matching technology, Amazon Macie (*https://aws.amazon.com/macie*) is a fully managed data security service that helps security professionals in discovering, monitoring, and protecting your sensitive data stored in AWS. Macie's automated discovery service helps identify sensitive data, such as personally identifiable information and financial data, in Amazon S3. It will monitor and evaluate each AWS S3 bucket that contains sensitive data in real time for security and access control.

With the explosion in popularity of data collection, it is common for organizations to have a lot of data stored across various data storage mediums. Taking this to a new level is the use of microservices, which prefer not to have a shared storage layer, thus resulting in a lot of storage infrastructure.

However, not all data is created equal. All types of data need to be protected against malicious attacks, but the most sensitive data, such as personal identifying information of customers, medical records, financial records, and the like, require special attention. From a security perspective, it is important for security engineers to identify and categorize all systems that could potentially be storing sensitive data; this way, such data can be hardened against security threats.

Domain-driven design (DDD) places responsibilities for data storage on each bounded context. Therefore, in practice there may be hundreds of such contexts with thousands of datastores. A certain team might be storing data that is sensitive in an unprotected datastore without the security team knowing about it. Amazon Macie allows administrators to identify the resources that should be protected due to the fact that they contain sensitive data.

# Step 2: Detection and Analysis

You will develop an architecture that is fairly secure and heavily monitored if you have followed some or all of the recommendations in Step 1. However, even the most secure environments are vulnerable to breaches. Hence, you may want to employ systems that can filter out the signals of a security breach from the rest of the noise. In this section, I will outline some of the AWS services (such as AWS EventBridge (*https://aws.amazon.com/eventbridge*)) that can help you in identifying such indicators. Security professionals can detect breaches early with the help of these services before they cause any significant damage.

In this phase, the job is not to find the root cause of the breach but rather to clearly identify:

- What kind of an attack is taking place?
- Which resources or services have been compromised?
- How are the resources compromised? Has someone gained elevated access to your infrastructure? Or is someone using your resources to launch attacks on an external system?
- What is the bare minimum step that security professionals can take so that the rest of the application can continue to function while the incident can be investigated?


## Precursors to an incident

In most cases, a threat may not have any detectable or identifiable precursors. However, in the rare event when a precursor (an indicator of a legitimate, forthcoming security breach) is detected, there is a possibility to prevent the incident by adjusting your security posture to save a target from attack. At a minimum, the organization can monitor activity more closely that involves the target. Precursors to an incident may include but are not limited to:

- Common vulnerability scanners alerting on the presence of common vulnerabilities inside the code
- VPC flow logs showing the use of port scanners
- A sudden increase in denied authentication requests
- A sudden change in the traffic patterns of incoming traffic for a web application

For certain sensitive applications, the presence of such a precursor may be enough to trigger the entire incident response plan, without waiting for the actual incident to occur. Unfortunately, not all indicators or precursors are 100% accurate, reducing the likelihood of detection and analysis. As an example, user-provided indications such as a complaint of a server being unavailable may often be false. As a consequence, a great number of security precursors act as very noisy indicators of security events.

 In spite of the fact that alerting is prone to false positives, complacency may be the biggest threat to well-designed secure systems. Modern information systems remain vulnerable to cyberattacks, and ignoring important alerts as false positives could have disastrous results. Information systems have detective controls for a reason, and every datapoint that triggers an alarm should be thoroughly investigated. It is possible that the outcome of this evaluation will be that the alert needs to be tweaked to incorporate the nuance involved in detecting deviations from the norm.

## AWS EventBridge

AWS provides users with the ability to interact with almost all the events that take place on their accounts. These events are streamed into a centralized fully managed service called *AWS EventBridge*. In a secure system, the baseline behavior of a cloud system that is normal can be identified proactively. When this event stream deviates significantly from baseline behavior, security architects can place alerts.

In this section, I will talk about how the AWS EventBridge can be used to better identify security breaches. I will start by introducing some of the components of AWS EventBridge.

**EventBridge event bus.**  Each account has an *event bus* where events from every AWS service within the account can be streamed. Security architects can then attach various filters around these events to identify any anomalous behavior on their account and take corrective action accordingly.

**EventBridge rules.**  Once you have the event bus configured to centrally stream all of the events in the account, you want to be able to distinguish between malicious and normal events. AWS EventBridge allows you to specify rules that will be evaluated against each event that is streamed to the event bus. If a rule matches the event data (and its associated metadata), you can specify any automatic action to take. Actions may include alerting the right people to a security incident or perhaps addressing the issue itself automatically. Specifically, a rule can invoke any other AWS service to take further action, such as the AWS Simple Notification Service (SNS) or AWS Lambda.

Figure 9-7 shows how you can specify a rule using an event pattern that is evaluated against the events that are observed on AWS EventBridge. AWS provides extreme flexibility in specifying a pattern for events. Most AWS services send events to AWS EventBridge. Events contain metadata along with the event that includes data such as the name of the service, type of event, time of occurrence, AWS region, and more. Patterns can be specified to include or filter based on any of these values.

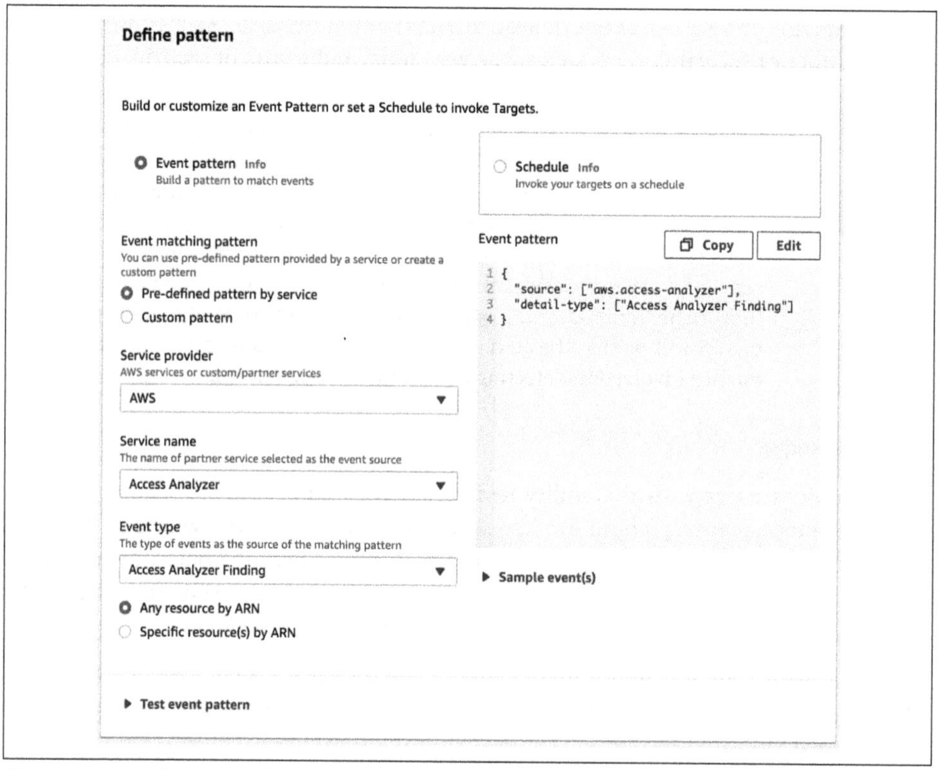

**Define pattern**

Build or customize an Event Pattern or set a Schedule to invoke Targets.

○ **Event pattern** Info
Build a pattern to match events

○ **Schedule** Info
Invoke your targets on a schedule

**Event matching pattern**
You can use pre-defined pattern provided by a service or create a custom pattern

● Pre-defined pattern by service
○ Custom pattern

**Service provider**
AWS services or custom/partner services

```
AWS                                ▼
```

**Service name**
The name of partner service selected as the event source

```
Access Analyzer                    ▼
```

**Event type**
The type of events as the source of the matching pattern

```
Access Analyzer Finding            ▼
```

● Any resource by ARN
○ Specific resource(s) by ARN

▶ Test event pattern

**Event pattern**          [ Copy ]  [ Edit ]

```
1 {
2   "source": ["aws.access-analyzer"],
3   "detail-type": ["Access Analyzer Finding"]
4 }
```

▶ Sample event(s)

*Figure 9-7. In this example, I am defining a rule for anytime there is a finding as reported by AWS Access Analyzer.*

**EventBridge targets.**   Upon matching a rule to an event on the event bus, you can specify a target AWS service that AWS can automatically call for you. The target can be another AWS service you would like to invoke automatically or perhaps an HTTP API endpoint. AWS is extremely flexible in allowing you to configure event targets. The targets are called asynchronously outside of your application's critical path; therefore, you don't need to worry about performance implications. Figure 9-8 shows how you can define a target in the AWS Management Console.

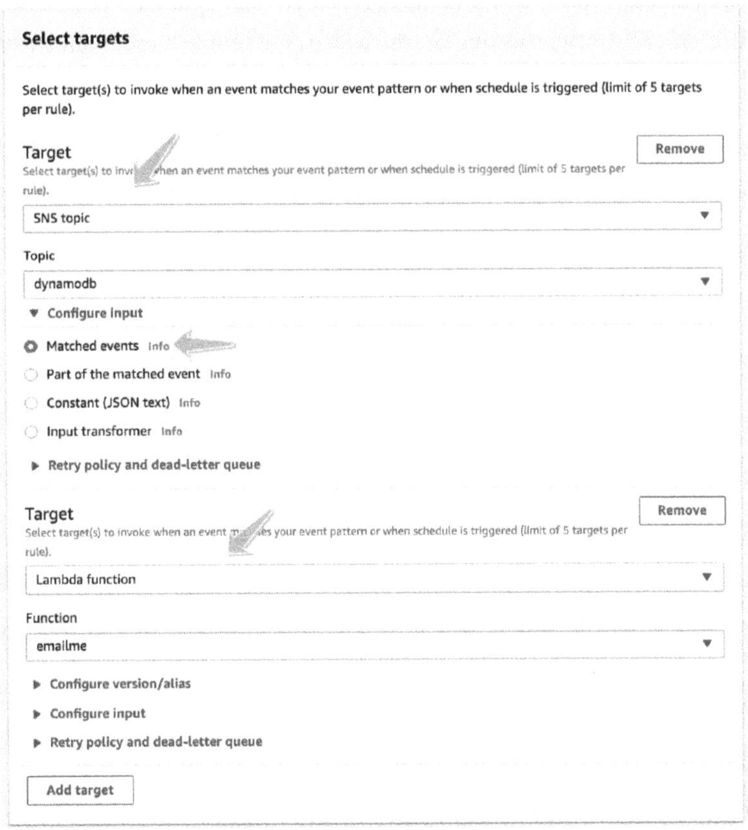

**Select targets**

Select target(s) to invoke when an event matches your event pattern or when schedule is triggered (limit of 5 targets per rule).

**Target**                                                    [ Remove ]
Select target(s) to invoke when an event matches your event pattern or when schedule is triggered (limit of 5 targets per rule).

| SNS topic                                                ▼ |

**Topic**

| dynamodb                                                 ▼ |

▼ Configure input

◉ Matched events  Info

○ Part of the matched event  Info

○ Constant (JSON text)  Info

○ Input transformer  Info

▶ Retry policy and dead-letter queue

**Target**                                                    [ Remove ]
Select target(s) to invoke when an event matches your event pattern or when schedule is triggered (limit of 5 targets per rule).

| Lambda function                                          ▼ |

**Function**

| emailme                                                  ▼ |

▶ Configure version/alias

▶ Configure input

▶ Retry policy and dead-letter queue

[ Add target ]

*Figure 9-8. AWS SNS for alerting and AWS Lambda for automatically attempting to remediate incidents are two popular targets for EventBridge events.*

The input to the target services can be tweaked to match the expectations of the target service. AWS EventBridge also allows integrations with other third-party alerting and monitoring services such as Zendesk, Splunk, Datadog, and others. More information can be found from AWS (*https://oreil.ly/wRlZx*).

# Step 3: Containment and Isolation

After identifying (and perhaps verifying) that there has been a security incident within your application, you can proceed to the next step in the NIST framework to contain the incident. It is important to contain an incident to ensure the amount of damage caused is minimized and limited to only a very small subset of your services. A well-architected secure system is your best defense during an attack, and the modularity that microservices affords you will enable you to contain the incident.

As an example, consider a Kubernetes-based microservice; your monitoring alerted you on a certain Service C running on the Kubernetes Node 3 that seems to have been compromised, as shown in Figure 9-9.

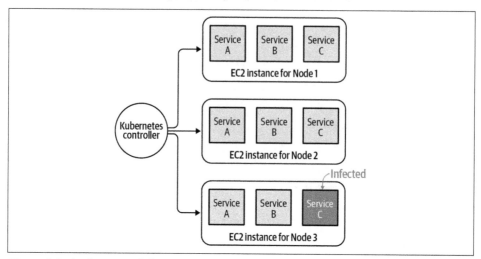

*Figure 9-9. At the time of alerting, you are made aware that a certain service running on a certain node may have been compromised.*

If you have identified a security breach and narrowed down your analysis to a microservice, your security incident will fit into one of these two categories:

- Our infrastructure that is running the microservice may have been compromised. This may include the underlying EC2 instances that run your Kubernetes nodes or possibly any other service that your microservice connects to or a malware application being installed on self-hosted instances.

- There may be an application layer bug or a loophole that allows an unauthorized user to gain elevated access.

Your response to such an event may be different based on which of the following two possibilities has resulted in a security incident.

### Possibility 1: Compromised infrastructure

The problem of compromised infrastructure happens when the microservices are deployed in environments where the customer bears the responsibility of securing the infrastructure as part of the AWS Shared Responsibility Model (SRM).

In our example, it is possible for malware to be deployed on an EC2 instance that hosts Kubernetes nodes in a Kubernetes setup. An attacker may also gain access to your cloud infrastructure using a known exploit on a self-hosted service.

If the EC2 instance on which a microservice runs is compromised, taking down the service may not contain the threat effectively. The vulnerability will continue to exist in your infrastructure as long as the EC2 instance is running. In such situations, the main objective is to isolate the underlying cloud resource and not just the microservice that you identified to be the problem.

 In cases where AWS assumes the responsibility of securing the infrastructure, you can expect AWS to be proactive in fixing incidents without any indication of a security breach to the end user. Hence, you do not have to be worried about the infrastructure that runs AWS Lambda, Amazon Elastic Kubernetes Service (EKS), or AWS Elastic Container Service (ECS) containers if they are running in the Fargate Mode. In such situations, the only aspect that you should be concerned about would be a compromised code at the application layer.

The AWS incident response framework (*https://oreil.ly/tsuXP*) recommends starting from the network layer by blocking and completely isolating any affected hardware in order to perform further analysis on it. In its guide, AWS prescribes a step-by-step process for performing this isolation task in a responsible way so that you and your team can then perform analysis on the affected pieces of infrastructure:

1. Take a snapshot. Capture the metadata from any of your affected cloud infrastructure. This means somehow registering the state of the infrastructure at the time of the attack to ensure that any forensic activity will not result in losing precious information about the infrastructure. If your application runs on EC2 instances, this will mean taking a snapshot of the AWS Elastic Block Store (EBS) volume that backs this instance. If you have AWS Relational Database Service (RDS) instances that were compromised, it will mean taking a snapshot of the database.

2. Freeze the instance. Once the initial state of the application has been registered in the snapshot, you may want to disable any automated processes that may interfere with the state of the infrastructure. So if you have any autotermination enabled on instances or any other policy that alters the state of the instance, it might be best to make sure the forensic analysis is not affected by such rules.

3. Isolate. After Steps 1 and 2, you are ready to isolate the instance. Recall from Chapter 5 that network access control lists (NACLs) are best suited for specifying policies that deny access to network resources at a subnet layer. They are applied at a subnet level, so you may want to move your affected resource into its own subnet and isolate and contain any access to this resource using NACLs (and possibly security groups as a supplemental layer of protection). The NACLs should make sure that any access apart from forensic analysis will be explicitly denied in

the access policy of this subnet. This isolation will ensure that only the security engineers will have access to or from the infected resource, and the rest of your application can continue to function as expected.

4. Mitigate. Once isolated, you should also remove the resource from any autoscaling or load-balancing groups that it may be a part of. You should also deregister this instance from any load-balancing groups that it may be a part of.

5. Maintain records. Finally, for recordkeeping it is important to set a predetermined AWS tag on such resources to indicate that these resources are kept isolated for the purposes of digital forensics and may be destroyed after the analysis is complete.

Figure 9-10 shows the result of a successful containment of an incident when the underlying infrastructure was compromised.

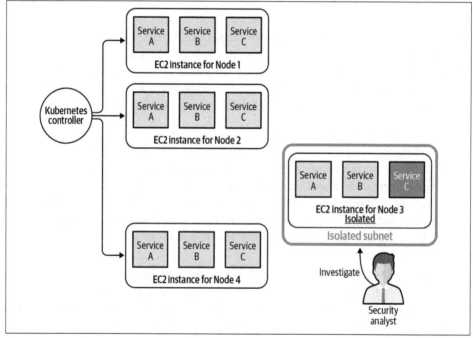

*Figure 9-10. After containment and isolation, the original infrastructure, as described in Figure 9-9, will have a similar structure with a new node being spun up to replace the infected node.*

## Possibility 2: Compromised application

In the event that there is an application layer bug or a loophole that allowed an unauthorized user to gain elevated access, isolating the underlying compute instances may be a waste of time. This is mainly because restarting the same application on another piece of infrastructure will result in resurfacing the breach on another resource.

When only the infrastructure is compromised, your best business continuity plan may involve spinning up all services on new cloud infrastructure. However, the original breach will simply be replicated if a new service is spun up on new resources with compromised application logic. As a consequence, businesses must be prepared to encounter downtime of critical services while the root cause is resolved. A microsegmented system is significantly easier to contain attacks on since microsegmentation helps you isolate segments within your application at the infrastructure level.

In addition, because it is the application logic that was affected, even services that are hosted on a fully managed AWS environment such as AWS Lambda or Amazon ECS/EKS Fargate will likely continue to face the same problems.

In such a situation, the remaining microservices would typically continue to run on the existing infrastructure. The affected service is moved into a separate, isolated environment where security analysts can carefully assess its security vulnerabilities in a controlled environment. Figure 9-11 highlights this process.

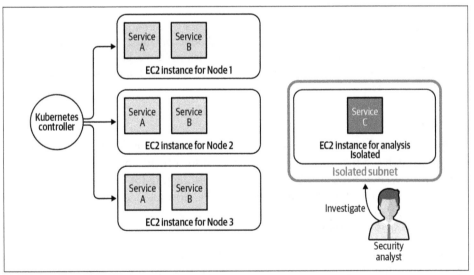

*Figure 9-11. Upon isolating the infected service and the instance that it runs on in a subnet using NACLs, the security professionals can perform forensic analysis in a safe and isolated environment while the rest of the application can continue to run on regular instances.*

Identity and Access Management (IAM) is another choice that security professionals have for containing applications that might have been compromised. A great place to start is to reduce access privileges for roles that your application is using to access other AWS resources. This will help in ensuring that the compromised microservice does not bring down the entire architecture.

# Step 4: Forensic Analysis

After an incident has been contained successfully, security professionals should turn their attention to determining the cause of the incident. In order to do that, security engineers need to examine the state of the application at the time of the incident and search for clues and evidence on what caused the security breach. The evidence gathered during forensic analysis may be circumstantial in many cases instead of definitive; it needs analysts experienced in this field to evaluate its legitimacy.

Some incidents are easy to detect, such as a defaced web page or a demand for a ransom. However, in many cases, incidents may be very subtle and may require precision monitoring for identifying. It is not uncommon for incidents to go undetected anywhere from hours to months before some rule or event in Step 2 is able to detect it. At the forensic analysis stage, it is considered standard practice to analyze logs from before the earliest observation of the incident, as well as to analyze logs from before the actual report of the incident.

 Since this activity may be long and time-consuming, it is critical to ensure that the incident has indeed been contained. At times, security professionals will need to go back to Step 3 because containment procedures performed in Step 3 the first time may not have been sufficient.

## AWS Athena

In the process of forensic analysis, security professionals may require parsing and sifting through log files to find evidence related to security incidents. I have already highlighted various ways in which you can enable logging for different types of AWS activities (CloudTrail logs, CloudWatch logs, VPC flow logs). AWS Athena is a multipurpose tool that security professionals may want to use in going through these files if they are stored on AWS S3.

AWS Athena is an interactive query service that makes it easy to analyze data directly in AWS S3 using standard SQL. In AWS Athena, you can specify the format of your logs, and AWS Athena allows security professionals to perform complex analysis directly on log files as if it were part of a queryable database. Sample scripts (*https://oreil.ly/3nElE*) from AWS for Athena setup for all logging datasets are available from Amazon.

## Live-box forensics

For organizations that are confident of their containment measures from Step 3, probably the best way of analyzing the incident may be to keep the affected resource running and analyze the live environment under which the incident took place. This analysis is called *live-box forensic analysis* since it is performed on the same resources that were affected.

This means, if an EC2 instance was affected, security professionals can log into the box and take memory dumps to analyze for patterns of malicious code. Live-box forensics may be the most efficient form of analysis since it involves the preservation of most of the original evidence. It also allows security professionals to run common exploit scanners on the live environment where the breach occurred with a lower risk of having to deal with dead evidence. Live-box technique (*https://oreil.ly/HkSMO*) preserves and harvests vital evidence from an instance's memory, cache, and other runtime processes.

## Dead-box forensics

Although live-box forensics is great for performing analysis, security analysts may not always feel comfortable allowing an infected machine to run regardless of how isolated it may be. Furthermore, in Step 2 security professionals may have taken steps while isolating the machine that may have already tampered with the existing evidence. As a result, an alternative method of digital forensics may also be used by security analysts to perform their root cause analysis.

This method uses any snapshots that were created during Step 3, just before containment, to re-create the machine and an environment that may be identical to what it was, when the attack actually took place. This method of analyzing based on a re-created environment (out of snapshots and events) is called *dead-box forensic analysis*.

Dead-box forensics allows for an extended and detailed investigation process to be performed in parallel on the same resource. It also allows for security professionals to revert back to the original state of the instance after performing each analysis since it relies on a re-created instance.

Multiple analysts can re-create the environment under which a resource was compromised by re-creating the resource from the snapshot image, allowing for parallel analysis. Having said that, the loss of the vital in-memory information may result in the dead-box forensics becoming useless against attacks that rely only on in-memory attack vectors.

### Tools for performing digital forensic analysis

In this section, I will introduce you to some tools that security professionals use to perform forensic analysis on AWS.

**Run Command.**  I have already talked about *AWS SSM Run Command* in Chapter 8 and how it can help in allowing ordinary users to execute predefined scripts (called *SSM documents*) that require elevated access privileges. AWS Run Command can be used in the process of forensic analysis.

Assuming you have isolated your compromised EC2 instance by following the steps outlined in Step 2, you will then want to perform analysis on the instance. Using Run Command, it is possible for you to securely execute commands on EC2 instances inside a closed perimeter without enabling any network connections to the outside world. Any live-box or dead-box forensics that needs to be performed can be performed remotely by issuing commands through the AWS console while SSM Agent assumes the responsibility of connecting to the machine inside this closed perimeter and executing the commands on your behalf.

**EventBridge event replay.**  With EventBridge, you can create an archive of events so that later you can reprocess them by starting a replay of events that allows your security professionals to go back to a particular state of the application in the past. Event replays combined with a microservice event store can help in further replicating the scenario under which particular security events may have taken place, thus allowing for easier and more efficient debugging and forensic analysis.

**Marketplace solutions.**  Apart from all of the analysis that you can perform on your infrastructure, AWS also partners with other third-party solution providers that can assist you in the process of digital forensics. These tools involve the use of machine learning for log analysis and better common vulnerability detection and analysis. A list of marketplace solutions (*https://aws.amazon.com/mp/scenarios/security/forensics*) can be found on Amazon.

## Step 5: Eradication

Generally, in most large organizations the eradication step happens in parallel to Step 3 where analysts are working on the digital forensics. The aim of this phase is to remove the root cause of the security breach and ensure that any loophole that was created is no longer available for the attacker. It is also part of this step to include additional security measures to ensure better security compliance for future breaches that may be similar to the incident but not the same as the one in question.

## Cleanup

A good rule of thumb is to assume that anything an attacker may have come in contact with could have been compromised. Some common activities that cloud administrators can perform as part of this step include, but are not limited to:

- Re-encrypt all the sensitive data and snapshots using a new customer master key (CMK)
- Force users to change their passwords and enforce a stronger password policy across the organization
- Tag data and resources that may have been compromised and set up added monitoring on these resources

## Security posturing

The root cause of the attack might be due to a leaked security key, a weak password, a weak encryption cipher, or just plain brute force. However, activities that occurred after the attack also have to be taken into consideration when performing the eradication step. Security professionals generally take this as an opportunity to improve the security posture of the organization to better prevent similar attacks from occurring. These include:

- Enforce MFA for all principals who are trying to access the compromised resources (if not all the resources)
- Enable new firewall rules that block any access patterns that may be unnecessary and could have been exploited by the attacker
- Review access control across the organization and narrow access to roles that may be too wide and that may have allowed attackers to gain unauthorized access

# Step 6: Postincident Activities

Once Steps 1–5 are completed, security professionals begin the process of closing the incident and resuming normal activities on the infrastructure.

## Recovery

Although many microservices may be resource agnostic, cloud administrators may still want to reuse some of the infrastructure that may have been altered or modified in the incident-response process. If you were running a Kubernetes node on EC2 and suspected a malware infected it, you would isolate it as part of Step 2. After successful eradication of the malware, you may want to reuse the instance. Resource recovery is the step where you would start reverting back to the original state in a very careful and controlled manner.

This does not have to apply only to resources. Taking down your application may have been necessary if the application logic of any microservice was thought to have been compromised in Step 2. There may be a patch available from your development team to address this previously exploited vulnerability. Once this vulnerability has been patched, you may use this step to resume the service that was shut down in Step 2.

Recovery may involve such actions as restoring systems from clean snapshots, rebuilding systems from scratch, replacing compromised files with clean versions, and so forth. Constant monitoring during this phase is crucial to identifying any issues in the recovery process.

### Simulate and iterate

Recovery is, however, a dangerous process. The vulnerability that existed in the first place may not always be fully patched. In the real world, it is very common for security professionals to believe that a loophole that existed originally has been patched and business can resume, only to find out that that is not the case. Hence, it is important for security professionals to prepare for the possibility of going back to Step 2 and repeating the entire process. In its whitepaper (*https://oreil.ly/jj3lr*), AWS recommends users simulate various security incidents and continuously iterate upon the security measures that may have been put into place before closing the incident.

# Securing the Security Infrastructure

The incident response framework is a great starting point for cloud security professionals. However, it has a fatal flaw in that it relies on logging, metrics, and other services for it to successfully mitigate the impact of incidents. Empirically, however, it has been observed (*https://oreil.ly/QBHr0*) that once hackers gain access into a system, they may attempt to disable auditing and delete any trail they may have left behind. These acts of obfuscating their footprints are called *anti-forensics*. Anti-forensics may result in rendering the incident response framework useless and allowing the malicious actor to go undetected. Hence, as security administrators, it is important to design around these limitations.

I will discuss some best practices for securing your security infrastructure that will make it less likely that your incident response system will get compromised.

## Securing a CloudTrail

Until now, I have talked about the importance of using AWS CloudTrail for the purpose of incident management. The logging infrastructure, however, is generally the first target after a malicious actor gains unauthorized entry into the system. It is, therefore, necessary that CloudTrail logs are encrypted and securely stored. In this section, I will go over some of the ways in which you can ensure the security and the integrity of your CloudTrails.

### Encrypting a trail

Although CloudTrail uses AWS S3 for storing logs, just like any other AWS S3 bucket, the logs can be encrypted using AWS-managed encryption. AWS CloudTrail logs are ultimately AWS S3 objects, so the process of enabling and tweaking encryption is the same as it would be for any other AWS S3 object.

> The default method of encryption is to use AWS managed server-side encryption for S3 (AWS S3-SSE). However, you get more control over the encryption process by specifying the AWS Key Management Service (KMS) key that you would like to use to secure the bucket (using AWS SSE-KMS), as I have described in Chapter 4.

Apart from securing the infrastructure, encrypting logs also helps in maintaining compliance. Despite the fact that it is almost never acceptable for sensitive data to be kept inside logs, the fact that these logs are encrypted makes it less concerning if an application unintentionally logs more data than it is supposed to and keeps companies from violating compliance under such situations.

### Log validation

From a security perspective, a principle to remember is that of nonrepudiation. Having a log trail that cannot be tampered with is an excellent way to prove compliance. AWS provides administrators with the ability to demonstrate the integrity of Cloud-Trail logs through a digital signature mechanism known as *log validation*.

Log validation can be enabled on individual trails through the AWS Console while enabling the trail, as seen in Figure 9-12.

*Figure 9-12. Log validation can be enabled through the AWS Management Console.*

Through log validation, AWS will start hashing and digitally signing the trails on behalf of the account. So if regulators needed proof of log trail authenticity, AWS CloudTrail can provide administrators with the confidence they need.

## Purpose-Built Accounts

I have already talked about purpose-built accounts in Chapter 8. Logging and monitoring is one place where purpose-built accounts can help in preventing attackers from gaining access to logfiles.

Instead of storing CloudTrail or VPC flow logs within the same account, a purpose-built logging account works as such:

1. A new and independent AWS account is created, either under the same AWS Organization or at times as a separate account altogether.

2. New AWS S3 buckets are created for this independent account for each of the domain or bounded contexts that exist in the current AWS account that runs your microservices.

3. The bucket policy (AWS resource policy for S3 buckets) is then used to grant CloudTrail access to put objects into this bucket. No entity from the current account is allowed to delete or read any of the objects from this bucket.

4. Independent roles are created within this account for analysts who wish to read these logs. These roles are also not allowed to put or delete any files.

Figure 9-13 shows a typical purpose-built account that is used for storing cloudtrail and VPC flow logs, which can be accesed securely by auditors or analysts.

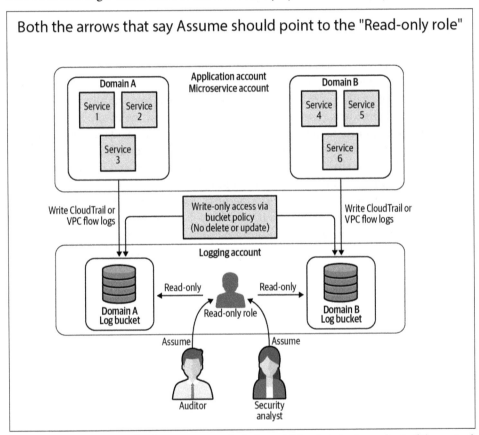

*Figure 9-13. A purpose-built account can help keep S3 buckets independent of the rest of your infrastructure.*

Using purpose-built accounts allows your logging infrastructure to stay independent of the rest of your application. The logfiles are kept safe from malicious users even if the original account is compromised since principals from the original account can only write new files to the destination bucket.

It is also possible to create new roles within the security account if the security team decides to outsource the analysis of logs to a third-party consultant. They will merely have to create roles within the security account for providing granular access to the logfiles.

In case of compliance audits, auditors can also be granted granular read-only access to these AWS S3 buckets through roles that are restricted to reading logfiles. This way, the permissions, security, and access control logic surrounding the logs can be kept separate and isolated from the rest of the application.

## Summary

Incident response is probably one of the most important aspects of a security professional's job. However, in my opinion, it is also one of the most overlooked aspects. Microservices and DDD afford the security team a great opportunity for setting up monitoring and incident response strategies at the forefront of their design. It is important for architects to grab these opportunities and put incident prevention and incident response strategies in place. In this chapter, I discussed a few well-known frameworks that formalize the process of incident prevention and incident response. The primary framework that I used as my guiding star is the incident response framework proposed in the NIST *Computer Security Incident Handling Guide*. I talked about the various services that make it easy for you to implement the steps as highlighted in the NIST's incident response framework. And finally, I talked about how you can set up controls to protect the incident response infrastructure from attacks.

# Terraform Cloud in Five Minutes

A cloud infrastructure requires a provisioning and maintenance regime in the same way as your application code. Clicking through AWS Console screens is an easy way to get started, but it won't scale in larger organizations. This is where tools like Cloud Formation, AWS CDK, and Terraform come in handy. Terraform is an open source "infrastructure as code" tool written in Go by HashiCorp that relies on a simple descriptive language to define all your cloud resources. Terraform specializes in creating entire server instances on AWS for you while making a detailed map of all the infrastructure that you have running on AWS. Thus, it's a highly effective tool for managing your AWS inventory at scale.

Terraform is also extremely modular and lets you reuse your infrastructure-provisioning code efficiently. So if you need to re-create your infrastructure for an additional team or environment, Terraform's modular design protects you from code repetition. This is especially useful when dealing with microservices since it is common to have independently running replicable architecture for each end user use case.

Many books on Terraform do a great job explaining it in depth. I personally enjoyed reading *Terraform: Up and Running* by Yevgeniy Brikman (O'Reilly). HashiCorp also provides great documentation on its website (*https://oreil.ly/oMZOe*) if you want to learn more. Here, I go over the basics to teach you what you need to get started and use the source code that is provided with the rest of the book.

For the purposes of this appendix, I have created a sample GitHub repository (*https://oreil.ly/VAzWS*) that you can fork and use to test your own code.

# Setup

The easiest and probably quickest way to use Terraform is to sign up for Terraform Cloud (*https://www.terraform.io*), a fully managed cloud offering. You can sign up for a free account, as shown in Figure A-1.

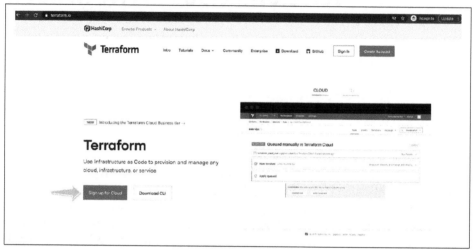

*Figure A-1. Signing up for Terraform Cloud*

## Creating Your Workspace

Within each cloud account, you can create workspaces that mirror an infrastructure setup you would like to deploy to the cloud environment. Each workspace corresponds to a Git repository where you can stage and save your Terraform scripts. You can choose the version control workflow while creating your workspace, as shown in Figure A-2.

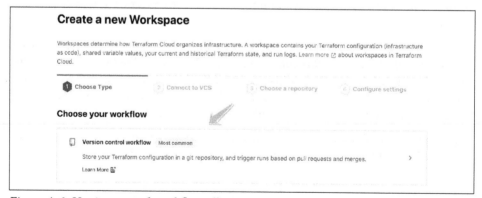

*Figure A-2. Version control workflow allows you to connect your version control system of choice with Terraform Cloud by following the instructions in this setup wizard*

Version control workflow is the easiest way of connecting your GitHub repository to Terraform Cloud. This way, you can have a Git-versioned infrastructure setup in your GitHub repository that you automatically deploy to the cloud provider whenever you make any changes. Figure A-3 highlights how you can enable these triggers.

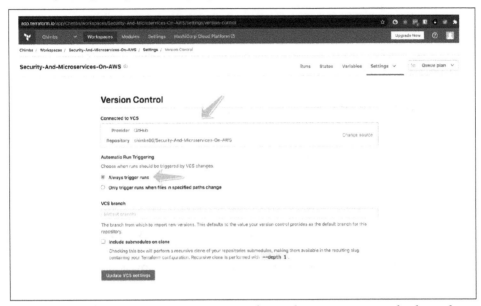

*Figure A-3. Adding a new VCS integration and providing a trigger to apply plans whenever you make changes in your infrastructure code*

As you can see, Terraform Cloud can deploy your infrastructure changes as soon as you push them to your repository based on the triggers you provide, making your infrastructure setup and deployment seamless.

## Adding AWS Access and Secret Key

Within your new workspace, visit the Variables page. Terraform Cloud supports both Terraform variables and environment variables. We'll use both types in this tutorial. Scroll down to the Environment Variables section and create two variables:

- `AWS_ACCESS_KEY_ID`
- `AWS_SECRET_ACCESS_KEY`

Check the Sensitive checkbox for both variables and click the "Save variable" button to save each one. Once you are done, the environment variables section should look as shown in Figure A-4.

*Figure A-4. These predetermined environment variables are what Terraform will use to authenticate with your AWS account*

# Terraform Process

In this section, I will walk you through some of the building blocks of the Terraform process that allow you to convert your Terraform-managed code into cloud resources on AWS.

## Providers

Terraform uses the *provider* to integrate with various cloud systems. A provider takes Terraform syntax and translates it into API calls for the cloud system you are using (in this case, AWS). Once this is done, the provider can provision various resources for you.

Terraform has built-in provider support for major cloud providers. You can use AWS in our case:

```
provider "aws" {
  version = "2.33.0"
  region = "us-east-1"
}
```

This code asks Terraform to create a provider that can connect to the AWS provider in the us-east-1 region.

## State

Terraform state maintains an up-to-date map of the resources that were created in your AWS account as a result of Terraform usage and updates it based on any change to the code. This allows you to make code changes in the config to add or delete resources on the cloud.

## Plans

The Terraform plan phase builds an execution plan that compares the desired state of your AWS account with its current state. If Terraform does not detect any changes to resources or root module output values, the Terraform plan will evaluate that no change is required. A list of resources that require creation or destruction on the cloud is then created, and finally, basic validation on your code syntax is performed.

## Apply

Terraform's apply phase takes the changes generated by a Terraform plan and applies them to your provider (in this case, the AWS account) to reach the desired state based on your configuration.

# Writing Your Terraform Infrastructure as Code

As we have reviewed the basic building blocks of Terraform, let us now look at how your Terraform modules are implemented.

## Root Module and Folder Structure

When running Terraform plan or Terraform apply in your working directory, the *.tf* files together form the root module. Any resources that you declare in these files will be added to your desired state during the plan phase and created on your cloud when you apply this plan.

The root module can also call other modules, thus enabling code reuse.

## Input Variables

You can declare input variables in your *.tf* files using the following syntax:

```
variable "table_name" {
  type = string
}
```

These variables can be passed to the main module through the same interface where you passed environment variables, as shown in Figure A-5. Secrets and other sensitive variables are good candidates to be passed as Terraform variables.

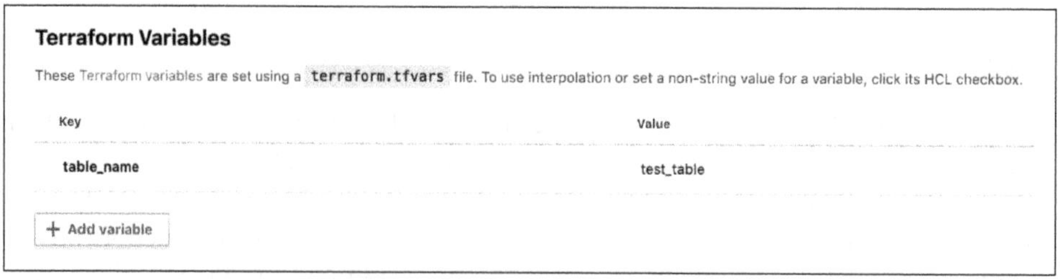

**Terraform Variables**

These Terraform variables are set using a `terraform.tfvars` file. To use interpolation or set a non-string value for a variable, click its HCL checkbox.

| Key | Value |
| --- | --- |
| table_name | test_table |

+ Add variable

*Figure A-5. Passing variables to the main module*

Reference these variables using this syntax:

```
var.<variable_name>
  table_name = var.table_name
```

You can also declare local variables (called *local values*) in order to promote code reuse. They can be included in any of your *.tf* files by adding the following code:

```
locals {
  table_name = "test_table"
}
```

Reference these values using the following syntax:

```
local.<value_name>
table_name = local.table_name
```

## Resources

Each resource in your module defines one or more infrastructural items, such as AWS Elastic Cloud Compute (EC2) instances, DynamoDB tables, or any other storage services on AWS. The goal of your module will be to create these resources on the AWS cloud and track their state through your Terraform configuration files:

```
resource "aws_dynamodb_table" "test_table" {
  name = "test_table"
  read_capacity  = 1
  write_capacity = 1
  hash_key       = "UUID"
  attribute {
    name = "UUID"
    type = "S"
  }
}
```

## Running and Applying Your Plan

The final step is to run and apply your plan so your resources can be created. Click the "Queue plan" button, as shown in Figure A-6.

*Figure A-6. You can queue your plan with any description of your run*

Depending on your configuration, Terraform Cloud may ask for your confirmation before applying a plan, as shown in Figure A-7. In this phase, it is important for administrators to look at the output of the plan phase to make sure no surprises are in store when Terraform moves from its current state to the desired state.

*Figure A-7. Click Confirm & Apply once you have validated the plan output from the plan phase*

If all goes well, you should see your plan being applied successfully on your AWS Cloud account, and you'll see a successful application, as shown in Figure A-8.

*Figure A-8. Plan was successfully applied to your AWS account*

Once applied, you should be able to see your resources being created on your AWS account.

# Example of a SAML Identity Provider for AWS

In most corporations, upon getting hired, employees typically register with a preferred system of choice, such as Active Directory for their corporate accounts. These companies require their employees to maintain strong security practices around securing their corporate accounts. In Chapter 8, I argued for the need to have individual AWS accounts per team with strong authentication. This means that the large corporations have to maintain multiple sets of identities: one for their corporate accounts within their identity management system of choice, and on top of this, identities within the multiple team-level AWS accounts. This brings about a significant rise in the complexity of management. This also makes it harder for companies to onboard, maintain, or terminate employee identities across all of these accounts.

To avoid such a scenario, security professionals recommend the use of federated identities (see Chapter 2). A *federated identity* is a portable identity that allows users to be authenticated across multiple systems without having to prove their identity multiple times.

## A Hands-On Example of a Federated Identity Setup

AWS allows you to use any compatible identity provider (IdP) to manage the authentication aspect of identity management. Some popular IdPs include Okta (*https:// www.okta.com*), OneLogin (*https://www.onelogin.com*), Ping Identity (*https:// www.pingidentity.com*), JumpCloud (*https://jumpcloud.com*), and others. Identity federation on AWS can happen using one of two identity federation standards: OpenID Connect (OIDC) or Security Assertion Markup Language (SAML). This appendix discusses how to implement federated identity management using an external IdP that I am personally familiar with, JumpCloud and AWS Identity and Access Management (IAM).

In doing so, we will look at using user attributes to control identities and then using role-based access control (RBAC), as discussed in Chapter 2. In a nutshell, the roles that each identity within JumpCloud can assume will be determined by the custom attributes that your JumpCloud administrator will add to these identities. More access can be granted by adding more custom attributes, and access can eventually be revoked by removing these attributes. All of these actions are performed using SAML.

Before you start setting up your AWS account, I will assume that you have set up a SAML IdP of your choice. This IdP will have all of the identities you wish to allow to authenticate against your AWS account. In case of my example, I will be using JumpCloud as my IdP of choice. However, you are free to use any SAML providers of your choice.

As a reminder from Chapter 2, the flow for identity verification will work something like what is outlined in Figure B-1.

 If you want to simplify the process of single sign-on (SSO) using entitlements or group memberships, AWS SSO (introduced in Chapter 8) abstracts away and simplifies the process significantly. Because I am focusing on the attribute-based identities, I will be using AWS IAM for setting up federated identities for the purposes of this book.

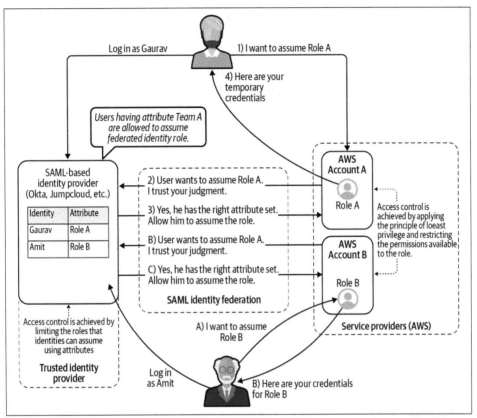

*Figure B-1. A sample identity federation authentication flow using a SAML-based authentication provider, as discussed in Chapter 2.*

This implementation will accomplish the following setup (explained in the next sections):

1. Configure the IdP to be able to provide authentication and identity services for your AWS account.

2. Export the SAML metadata from your IdP in order to upload it to your AWS account. This metadata includes cryptographic keys and certificates, and it is part of the SAML process that establishes a baseline of trust and interoperability between AWS and the IdP.

3. Configure your AWS account to trust the identity verification provided to you by your IdP. This can be achieved by adding the IdP as a trusted IdP to your AWS account and uploading the metadata exported in Step 3.

4. Now that you have configured your AWS account to trust your SAML-based IdP (in my case, JumpCloud), you want to create roles within your AWS account that

your corporate identities can assume. These roles can then be assigned IAM policies and secured using the principle of least privilege (PoLP; see Chapter 2).

5. You may have multiple roles on AWS, and you may wish to control how the identities on your IdP map to the roles on AWS. In the case of JumpCloud, you must add these attributes as custom attributes to your identities. This step may depend on the IdP you use. As you are using RBAC within AWS, the custom attributes will determine the roles that your identities are permitted to assume.

## Step 1: Configure Your IdP

The first step toward setting up a federated identity-based authentication system is to configure your IdP to provide SAML-based authentication services to AWS. You may want to use your IdP to provide SSO services to items other than AWS, such as for your emails, partner accounts, and so on. On JumpCloud, this involves adding AWS as an SSO service to the JumpCloud account, as seen in Figure B-2.

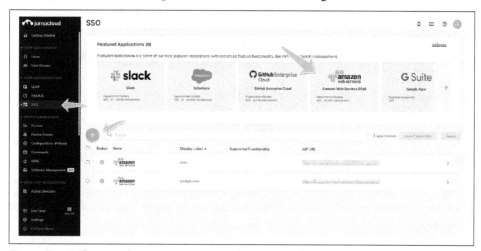

*Figure B-2. When you log in to your JumpCloud account, add Amazon Web Services as an SSO application.*

After following the steps highlighted in Figure B-2, you will be able to create an application within your SSO. This step includes creating a page where AWS can redirect end users to a page (called a *landing page*) to authenticate against your IdP to prove their identity. You will be configuring AWS to trust the result of the authentication process that takes place on this landing page. In my case, I used the URL *https:// sso.jumpcloud.com/saml2/login-url*. You can then fill out all relevant information and finish the wizard. At that point, your IdP account (JumpCloud) is willing to provide identity services to your service provider (AWS) that you just added.

## Step 2: Export Metadata to Be Imported into AWS Account

Now that you have configured your IdP to accept incoming requests, you want to make sure that your AWS account trusts the identity services that are provided by your IdP. SAML prescribes the standardized steps that identity and service providers can use to establish this trust.

The first step in creating a trusted identity connection is to exchange certain metadata between the service provider (AWS) and the IdP (in my case, JumpCloud). This metadata includes information such as the authentication endpoints, cryptographic keys, and so forth.

In Figure B-3, I am exporting the metadata from my JumpCloud account so that I can import it into my AWS account in the next step.

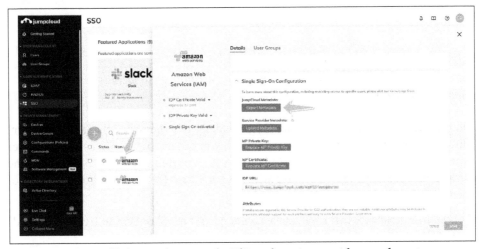

*Figure B-3. To establish trust between the IdP and service provider, you have to exchange SAML metadata. On JumpCloud, this involves exporting the metadata from JumpCloud in order to be imported onto AWS.*

## Step 3: Add Your SAML IdP as a Trusted IdP

As discussed in Chapter 2, on the AWS side, you have to create an IdP that allows you to import the SAML metadata from Step 3 into AWS, as shown in Figure B-4. This IdP inside AWS acts as a proxy for your external IdP (in my case, JumpCloud).

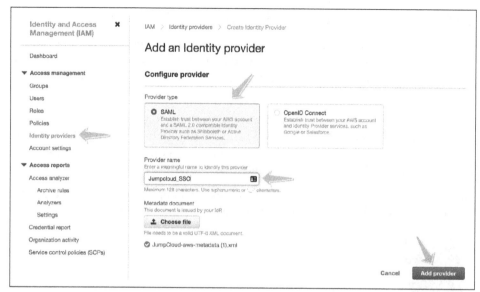

*Figure B-4. In the AWS Console, using your root account, go to Identity and Access Management (IAM).*

On the IAM page, click on the "Identity providers" tab, then click the "Add provider" button. Since JumpCloud is a SAML provider, you can choose SAML as the "Provider type" and upload the *metadata.xml* file that you exported in Step 2. Go through the wizard, and when you're done, you will see your new IdP appearing in your list of identity providers.

This step completes SAML's metadata exchange and enables AWS to trust your third-party IdP.

## Step 4: Create a Role That Your Federated Users Can Assume to Interact with Your AWS Account

Now that you have your trusted IdP set up on your AWS side, you want to allow external identities to get granular permission to your AWS resources. You do this by allowing authenticated users to assume roles within your service provider (AWS) account, and then using RBAC for controlling access. To do that, you first need to create the role that you want these external identities to assume, as shown in Figure B-5.

*Figure B-5. First make sure that your parameters, such as your SSO service location, match what you entered in Figure B-3. Once done, you will need to create a new role that you want your federated identity users to assume when they authenticate against your IdP. You also need to note down the Amazon Resource Name (ARN) of the newly created IdP (you will need it later).*

Once these external identities have been authenticated against your IdP, their presence within your account will be in the form of an AWS role that you are creating. The onus is now on you to restrict this role using the PoLP discussed in Chapter 2.

The role-creation process and access control around roles are done through the AWS IAM console by going through the role-creation wizard, as seen in Figure B-6.

I assume you have already come up with the perfect AWS policy for this role. However, in order to have the right controls in place, it is important to use the PoLP to frame the security policies for this role. I have already discussed in detail the process to come up with the permissions for roles (see Chapter 2), and hence I will not go into the details here.

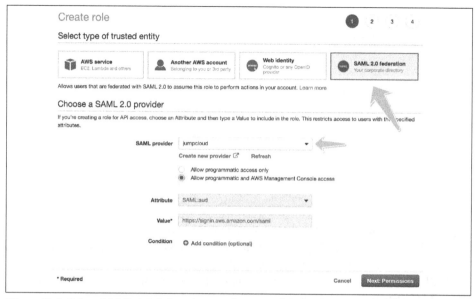

*Figure B-6. Select SAML 2.0 federation as the type of trusted entity and the IdP that you created in Figure B-5 as your SAML Provider.*

The access that your federated corporate users get through identity federation to resources will be determined by the access privileges that are assigned to this role, as seen in Figure B-7. In most large organizations, it is common to have multiple such roles per corporate user. Corporate users are then required to assume the correct role for the task they are currently performing.

*Figure B-7. To secure the role, it is important to restrict the access privileges that your role has by applying the PoLP.*

Upon finishing the wizard, note the ARN of the role you just created, since this role will specify the access you have to your cloud infrastructure through the identity federation process.

## Step 5: Control Access to Multiple Roles Using Custom Attributes Within the IdP

Since you are using attributes-based identities, in the final step, you will need to copy back the ARN of your role into your IdP account so that it knows the role that the users will be attempting to authenticate for. (The role in JumpCloud is represented as <arn of your role, arn of your identity provider>) and added, as seen in Figure B-8.

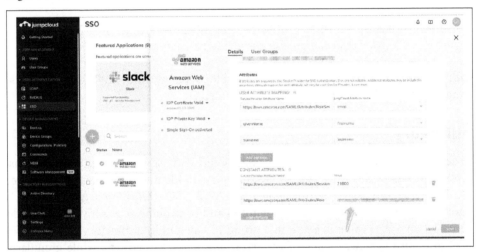

*Figure B-8. Enter the ARN combination as an attribute in the SSO application you created in JumpCloud.*

You can control access to your cloud resources on AWS through the use of IAM permission policies, as highlighted in Step 4. Every user who wants to access cloud resources has to assume the roles that you created for specific purposes. However, you may not want everyone in the organization to have the ability to assume all the AWS roles you created. In technical terms, you may want to restrict the federation of identities on your IdP. In attributes-based IdPs, this can be achieved by using custom attributes that specify within the identity the roles that each user is allowed to assume. This way, a user is only allowed to assume certain roles that are described by the custom attributes, which are a part of their identity. Your identity administrator can set these attributes by applying the PoLP on all the identity accounts. Figure B-9 shows an example of custom attributes being set to specify the roles that a JumpCloud user can assume in my account.

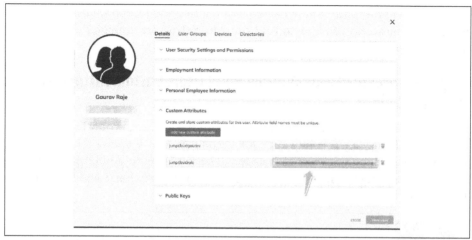

*Figure B-9. The ARN information also has to be entered as a custom attribute.*

Once this process is completed, you will be able to log into your AWS account by visiting your SSO URL that you bookmarked in Step 1.

# Summary

Federated identities are great for managing identities at scale for large organizations. AWS IAM-based IdPs work best when working with identity management using user attributes, as discussed in this appendix. AWS SSO (*https://oreil.ly/NWFKN*) is another way of providing federated identities and controlling access if you want to do so based on a user's membership in a group in a centralized directory service. AWS SSO also abstracts away some of the setup that I had to perform, while granularly granting access through custom attributes. For this appendix, I decided to stick with custom attributes since I believe they help in understanding identity federation more conceptually.

# Hands-On Encryption with AWS KMS

Chapter 3 talked about the importance of encryption for all the data that is stored on AWS. You can use AWS Key Management Service (KMS) to simplify the process of data encryption and to manage the encryption keys that are used to encrypt your data. In this appendix, I will give you a practical overview of the process and show you how you can encrypt your sensitive data on AWS using envelope encryption. As a reminder, envelope encryption is the process where you encrypt large amounts of data with an encryption key (called the *data key*) and then use AWS KMS to encrypt this data key using a key controlled by AWS Customer Master Key (CMK).

In order to work with this example, you will need the following applications installed on your computer:

- AWS Command Line Interface (*https://oreil.ly/SrihY*) (CLI)
- OpenSSL toolkit (*https://oreil.ly/LJ1Ow*)

Once you have your CMK ready, let's start using it to encrypt plaintext. In order to work with binary data, you need to encode your data with Base64. Base64 is a group of binary-to-text encoding schemes that represent binary data in an ASCII string format. Typically, Base64-encoding schemes are used when digital data needs to be encoded using algorithms that predominantly deal with text. In this way, the data will remain intact during the encryption and decryption process.

# Basic Encryption Using the CMK

To transmit a message, follow these steps:

1. Create CMK on AWS. This will be the key that will be used to encrypt your data.

2. Encode your message with Base64 (*https://oreil.ly/oyTPr*). This common step in most encryption procedures ensures that binary data can be transported over channels without modification.

3. Encrypt your message using the CMK by calling the `aws kms encrypt` command.

As a reminder, the CMK is used to mainly encrypt your data key using envelope encryption. Figure C-1 shows how you can create a CMK using the AWS Management Console.

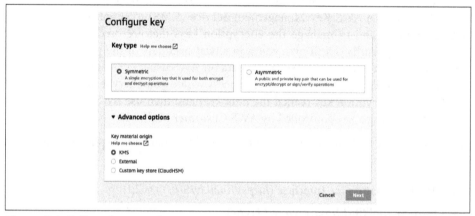

*Figure C-1. Follow the wizard to generate the key and grant relevant access to users*

Next, Base64-encode your data:

```
$ echo <plain text message> | base64
```

Finally, encrypt using the CMK:

```
$ aws kms encrypt --plaintext $(echo <plain text message> | base64) --key-id
  alias/worklaptop
```

# Basic Decryption Using the CMK

The decryption process is similar to the encryption process. You simply call the AWS KMS service with the ciphertext-blob that you wish to decrypt:

```
$ aws kms decrypt --ciphertext-blob
"AQECAHjbw6xdyJKSCUiwAFsMp6vMYbXV2mHSY9cg2qHmkIZ2gwAAAGswaQYJKoZIhvcNAQcGoFwwWg
IBADBVBgkqhkiG9w0BBwEwHgYJYIZIAWUDBAEuMBEEDFPI6F3UdqaYj6iBMwIBEIAoCz2LrUes+
3SM70iFjgqAkxQoQYB/I617gN5zK4h/1aAp/ciweS8+5g=="
```

# Envelope Encryption Using the CMK

As discussed in Chapter 3, basic encryption is great for payloads of small sizes. However, AWS KMS sets a limit of 4 KB on any data that can be encrypted using basic encryption. Hence, for the vast majority of your encryption needs, you would be using envelope encryption. As a reminder, envelope encryption is a three-step process:

1. Create a master key. This master key can be used to encrypt or decrypt smaller payloads of data, which include data keys.

2. Create data keys to encrypt or decrypt your actual plaintext data.

3. Encrypt your data using the data key and encrypt your data key using the CMK. The encrypted data key can be stored alongside the ciphertext data, while the plaintext data key can be deleted.

The only way to decrypt the ciphertext is by first decrypting the data key, which is not available to anyone except the third party that wants to decrypt it.

Creating a master key is identical to the first step in basic encryption given earlier. You can create a CMK either using the AWS CLI or within the AWS console.

For generating data keys, AWS lets you make a single call to generate a data key. AWS will return the plaintext data key as well as the encrypted data key back to you. In this way, everything you need in the next step is made available to you:

```
$ aws kms generate-data-key --key-id alias/demo --key-spec AES_256
{
    "CiphertextBlob":
    "AQEDAHjbw6xdyJKSCUiwAFsMp6vMYbXV2mHSY9cg2qHmkIZ2gwAAAH4wfAYJKoZIhvc
NAQcGoG8wbQIBADBoBgkqhkiG9w0BBwEwHgYJYIZIAWUDBAEuMBEEDD2ZhMHl8hgr2DP
AawIBEIA7Z14WGErIjA/T+qZi7cVsXIHeySa8FYSuox07nyHs7JO6g39jBo1XSWsVjSu
YL8paWRgqbFKcUQX482w=",
    "Plaintext": "IyBK1p9nMFCFtwDT/PbFf3DjM/nRlUcw37MTb/+KYgs=",
    "KeyId": "arn:aws:kms:us-east-1:248285616257:key/27d9aa85-f403-483e-
9239-da01d5be4842"
}
```

You will be using the plaintext data key in the next step to encrypt the plaintext data. Remember, when AWS returns the key to you, it is Base64 encoded. In case your encryption algorithm expects a Base64-decoded plaintext data key, Base64 decodes this key before storing it:

```
$ echo teQj2q4G6CdDbLr+uoENkCef9y/ila6P6+rp9UbInmc= | base64
  --decode > plain-text-data-key.txt
```

You will also be storing the encrypted data key next to the ciphertext data. So it is best to save it in this step:

```
$ echo
  "AQEDAHjbw6xdyJKSCUiwAFsMp6vMYbXV2mHSY9cg2qHmkIZ2gwAAAH4wfAYJKoZIhvc
  NAQcGoG8wbQIBADBoBgkqhkiG9w0BBwEwHgYJYIZIAWUDBAEuMBEEDD2ZhMHl8hgr2DP
  AawIBEIA7Z14WGErIjA/T+qZi7cVsXIHeySa8FYSuox07nyHs7J06g39jBo1XSWsVjSu
  YL8paWRgqbFKcUQX482w=" > cipher-text-data-key.txt
```

In the final step, you can use the plaintext data key from the previous Step 2 and use the AES-256 (*https://oreil.ly/878Ev*) algorithm to encrypt your data. If you use OpenSSL to encrypt, you can encrypt your plaintext and store it in a file called *enc.txt*:

```
$ openssl enc -e -aes256 -in <plain text file> -out cipher-text-data-blob.txt
  -k plain-text-data-key.txt
```

> Once you are done with the encryption, you should delete your plaintext data key to make sure that the only way to decrypt this data (in the absence of the *plain-text-data-key.txt*) will be by first decrypting the *cipher-text-key.txt*:
>
> ```
> $ rm ./plain-text-data-key.txt && rm ./<plain text file>
> ```

# Decrypting an Envelope Encrypted Message

The decryption process is similar to the encryption process:

1. Since the only place that has the key is your disk in an encrypted form, first you need to get the plaintext version of the data key.

2. Use the plaintext version of this key to decrypt *cipher-text-data-blob.txt*.

The plaintext data key can be obtained by decrypting *cipher-text-key.txt* using AWS KMS:

```
$ aws kms decrypt --ciphertext-blob $(cat ./cipher-text-data-key.txt)
{
    "KeyId":
    "arn:aws:kms:us-east-1:248285616257:key/27d9aa85-f403-483e-9239
      -da01d5be4842,
    "Plaintext": "IyBK1p9nMFCFtwDT/PbFf3DjM/nRlUcw37MTb/+KYgs=",
```

```
        "EncryptionAlgorithm": "SYMMETRIC_DEFAULT"
}
```

As you might have guessed, the plaintext data key returned in this step is Base64 encoded, and if your decryption algorithm requires a Base64-decoded key, you may have to Base64-decode this key:

```
$ echo teQj2q4G6CdDbLr+uoENkCef9y/ila6P6+rp9UbInmc= | base64
  --decode > plain-text-data-key.txt
```

Now you'll use the plaintext data key to decrypt *cipher-text-data-blob.txt*. You have your ciphertext as well as the plaintext form of the key that is required to decrypt this text. So you can decrypt it using the OpenSSL toolkit, which you used to encrypt this text in the first place:

```
$ openssl enc -d -aes256 -in cipher-text-data-blob.txt -k ./plain-text-data-key.txt
<plain text data>
```

# A Hands-On Example of Applying the Principle of Least Privilege

In this appendix, I will try to show you a hands-on example of how security professionals can apply the principle of least privilege (PoLP) to create Identity and Access Management (IAM) policies on AWS. Chapter 2 talked about PoLP at length, but as a reminder, the purpose of PoLP is to ensure that each principal (an AWS user or AWS role) within an organization gets only the bare minimum access privileges they need in order to perform their job and nothing more. Access is controlled on AWS using IAM policies. Each IAM policy in an account should serve a specific purpose and exist independently of the principal to which it is attached.

Let us consider a typical organization that has many departments. For the sake of this example, I want to allow employees of the finance department to gain access to objects in a certain Amazon Simple Storage Service (Amazon S3) bucket within the organization's account. As a responsible security administrator, I want to make sure that I apply the PoLP while defining access policies for the principals (users or roles) within my organization.

Hence, in order to secure access, I will enforce the following conditions:

- The principal who this policy is attached to should have the AWS tag *department* set to *finance*. In other words, I want to make sure that the principal (the user or role who attempts to gain access to these objects) belongs to the finance department.

- Multifactor authentication (MFA) should be enabled on the account of the principal before they can gain access to any kind of data. This will prevent imposters from fooling the authentication system and stealing financial details.

- Objects must be accessed only over a "secure transport" (HTTPS connection).

# Step 1: Create an AWS IAM Policy for Your Task

For the purpose of this appendix, I will be creating an access policy using the AWS visual editor, which can be launched by going to the Identity and Access Management page and clicking "Create policy," as seen in Figure D-1.

*Figure D-1. The first step toward creating a policy is to open the visual editor in the Policies tab on the Identity and Access Management (IAM) page.*

Once you are in the visual editor for creating the IAM policy, you can start defining your IAM policy. Upon framing the policy, you can attach it to a principal in the account. This will grant them (the principal) qualified access to AWS resources. Recall from Chapter 2 that an IAM policy is a collection of statements that allow or deny access to resources. So the next step is to start defining each of the individual statements within the policy.

# Step 2: Define the Service, Actions, and Effect Parameters of an IAM Policy

You can then define your policy statements one by one in the wizard by selecting the service you wish to specify (allow or deny) access to (in this case, AWS S3) and then selecting the action you wish to specify access to. You may also import existing policy statements from AWS-managed policies, as elaborated further. This step is illustrated in Figure D-2.

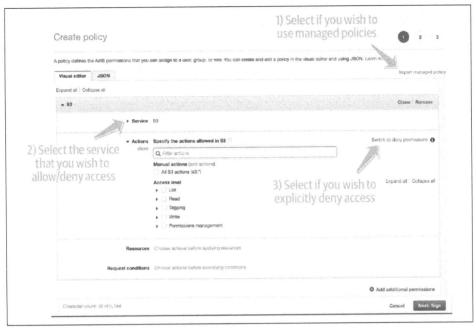

*Figure D-2. You could select whether to import policy statements from an AWS-managed policy (1) and then customize as necessary. Or you could specify your statements by selecting the service and action that you wish to control access to (2) and then selecting whether you wish to grant or deny access (3).*

If you already have an AWS-managed policy that fits your application use case, you can automatically import the policy statements from that AWS-managed policy and work off the boilerplate, as seen in Figure D-3.

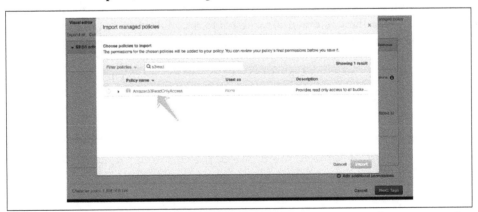

*Figure D-3. If you import an AWS-managed policy, AWS will import the common policy statements for you so you can sharpen the security controls around a baseline policy.*

# Step 3: Define the Resource

Though it is tempting to provide access to all resources that match the service you define in Step 2, based on PoLP, it is best to qualify access only to the resources that you want to grant access to. This can be done by explicitly specifying the resource in the "Resources" section of the wizard, as shown in Figure D-4.

*Figure D-4. Adding a resource ensures that least privilege is applied to all the statements in your policy.*

# Step 4: Request Conditions

One of the most powerful tools that AWS provides you with is the ability to add conditions to your access control policies. By applying these conditions, you are ensuring that you can take the context of a request into account when deciding whether to grant (or deny) access. These conditions are specified on the policy in Figure D-5.

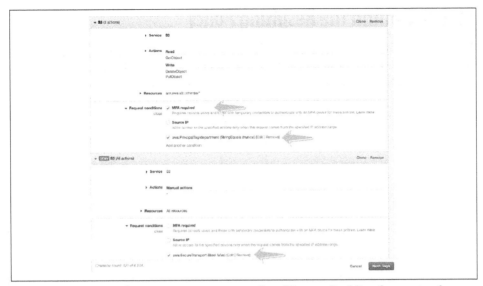

*Figure D-5. IAM conditions are a strong way of enabling or disabling fine-grained access to your resources. In this case, I am forcing the principal to have MFA, have a tag {department: finance}, and use a secure transport while accessing this resource.*

As you can see in Figure D-5, you can conditionally allow or block access in two ways:

- Specify your condition within the statement that allows access to the resource.
- Create another statement that denies access to any request that does not satisfy the condition.

 Because statements that explicitly deny access tend to trump statements that allow access, in my personal experience, it is best to add multiple statements with a "deny" clause in order to evaluate conditional logic.

There are many powerful conditions that are available in AWS to make it possible to sharpen the access control mechanisms for just about every use case you can imagine. A list of all the conditions can be found in an AWS article on context keys (*https://oreil.ly/UK1hJ*).

# Step 5: Confirm the Resulting Policy

You can confirm the resulting policy that you created using Steps 1–4 by going into the JSON tab of the policy and checking the statements within the policy. Figure D-6 shows the JSON summary of all the statements that we have created until now.

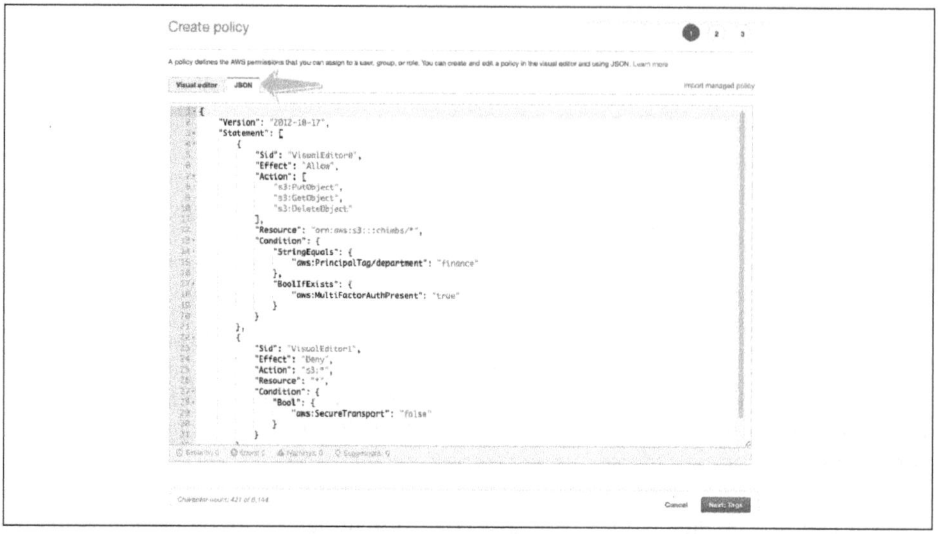

*Figure D-6. You can always switch to the JSON tab to check the result of the AWS Visual IAM Policy editor.*

# Step 6: Save the Policy

Once you have confirmed that your policy statements match your expectations, you can save your policy within your AWS account as a customer-managed policy, as shown in Figure D-7.

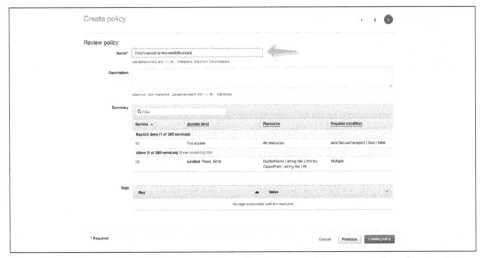

Figure D-7. As mentioned in Chapter 2, a policy is a standalone control and can exist independently of a principal.

Be sure to use descriptive names to save your policies. In large organizations, a planned reuse of IAM policies can help in maintaining scalability.

# Step 7: Attach the Policy to a Principal

Each time a new employee joins your finance department, you can attach this policy to the employee to grant them access to the S3 bucket. Figure D-8 shows an example of an IAM policy getting attached to a user named "gaurav."

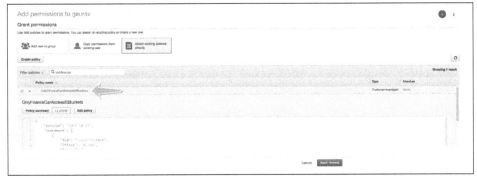

Figure D-8. You can attach policies to users or roles by entering the Identity and Access Management page, then the "Add permissions" wizard on your desired user in the Users tab (or going into the "Attach policies" wizard on your desired role in the Roles tab).

# Summary

This appendix showed you how you can use the AWS visual IAM policy editor to create strong and focused AWS policies that provide granular and precise control against unauthorized access. Your IAM policy can contain multiple statements that ensure that PoLP is applied while granting access to your resources. To further fine-tune access control, you can use IAM policy conditions to ensure compliance with various security policy requirements within your organization.

You can use statements and conditions to make sure of the following:

- Only the right set of principals are granted access to the resources.
- The access is granted only under the right circumstances by examining the context of the request.
- Access is explicitly denied when some required security conditions are not satisfied while requesting access.

# Index

# S

trust, 261
trust boundary, 11
trusted CA (trusted certificate authority), 228
trusted entity, 55
trusted signer, 214
truststore, 207
tuple, 88
24x7 AWS DDoS Response Team, 222
TypeScript, 124

## U

unit-of-deployment, 19
URLs, signed, 213-217
US National Classification Scheme, 113

## V

ViaService, 90
viewer request, 218
viewer response, 218
virtual gateway, 256
Virtual machine layer, 23
virtual node, 256
virtual router, 256
virtual service, 254, 256
VMs (virtual machines), 23
VPC (virtual private cloud)
    about, 154, 262, 294
    flow log, 310
    links, 196
    microsegmentation at Network layer, 155
    route tables and, 149

routing in, 155
VPC endpoint service, 158, 165-172, 173
VPC peering, 157, 158-162, 173
VPN (virtual private network), for remote
    employees, 11
vulnerability, 2
vulnerability matching, 220

## W

waterfall process, 239
web ACIs, in AWS WAF, 219
WebSocket API, 190
Wetherall, David, Computer Networks, 141
workspace, creating, 334
World Economic Forum, 303
WORM (write once read many), 123

## X

X-ENI (cross-account ENI), 183

## Y

YubiKey, 63

## Z

Zendesk, 319
zero trust architecture, security through, 11, 16
zero trust network, 77, 144, 182
zero trust security, 186
zone of trust, 44, 144

## About the Author

**Gaurav Raje** has worked as a software architect for over 10 years. He has extensive experience in building and scaling applications that host sensitive data and have high availability requirements. Gaurav has paid special attention to safeguarding every user's information with security best practices. He has also worked on the AWS Certified Database Specialty Exam as a subject matter expert by writing and moderating various questions that ended up in the official test. He is author of the SHA-224 package within the Jython programming language. Gaurav holds an MBA in finance from NYU Stern School of Business and an MS in computer science from Rochester Institute of Technology.

## Colophon

The animal on the cover of *Security and Microservice Architecture* is the Southern Cassowary (*Casuarius casuarius*), also known as a double-wattled Australian cassowary.

These large, robust birds have long, powerful legs for running and claws on their toes —up to 12 cm in length—for self-defense, but they are unable to fly. They can move almost silently, but when alarmed, are capable of running through dense brush at almost 50 km an hour, breaking vegetation as they escape. Their bodies are covered with dark brown or black feathers that look more like thick, coarse hair, and their heads are mostly bald and colored blue and red.

Cassowaries are frugivorous, feeding mostly on fruit that has fallen to the ground. Females lay bright green eggs two or three times a year, each nest incubated solely by the male parent. Male cassowaries raise the chicks until they become independent at around nine months of age.

Many of the animals on O'Reilly covers are endangered; all of them are important to the world.

The cover illustration is by Karen Montgomery, based on a black and white engraving from *Cassell's Natural History*. The cover fonts are Gilroy Semibold and Guardian Sans. The text font is Adobe Minion Pro; the heading font is Adobe Myriad Condensed; and the code font is Dalton Maag's Ubuntu Mono.

Milton Keynes UK
Ingram Content Group UK Ltd.
UKHW050428310824
447623UK00003B/8